The Contemporary British Novel

Edited by James Acheson and Sarah C. E. Ross

© in the edition, Edinburgh University Press, 2005
© in the individual contributions is retained by the authors

Edinburgh University Press Ltd
22 George Square, Edinburgh

Typeset in 10.5/13 Sabon
by Servis Filmsetting Ltd, Manchester, and
printed and bound in Great Britain by
MPG Books Ltd, Bodmin, Cornwall

A CIP record for this book is available from the British Library

ISBN 0 7486 1894 5 (hardback)
ISBN 0 7486 1895 3 (paperback)

The right of the contributors
to be identified as authors of this work
has been asserted in accordance with
the Copyright, Designs and Patents Act 1988.

Contents

Acknowledgements

We would like to thank, first and foremost, the contributors to this volume. Each wrote her or his essay specifically for this collection; interacting with their intellectual energy and enthusiasm has been the greatest pleasure of the project. We would also like to thank colleagues, students, friends and family, whose conversation, debate and support inform our thinking and the production of this work.

More specifically, James Acheson would like to thank Professors Porter Abbott and Lyn Innes for their encouragement when the collection was in the planning stages, Professor Bruce King for his help at every stage of its development, and Professor Brian McHale for his editorial advice as the collection neared completion. He is also grateful to his wife Carole for her many helpful suggestions.

Sarah Ross would like to thank her colleagues at Massey University – in particular, Dr Doreen D'Cruz, who read her essay in its early stages – and Alex Ramsey for her invaluable editorial assistance. She is also grateful, as always, to Sue and Campbell, Andru and Amelia for their ongoing support and patience.

Finally, we would like to thank our editor, Jackie Jones, for her encouragement and support.

Introduction

An increasingly complex contemporary world has given rise to increasingly complex contemporary novels – novels that students in schools, colleges, polytechnics and universities around the world often find daunting. The novels themselves, as well as the reviewers, scholars and others who discuss them, frequently invoke views of the world, ideologies and theories that can baffle; for those who write about contemporary fiction are not always clear what they mean by key terms like 'realism', 'postcolonialism', 'feminism' and 'postmodernism'. *The Contemporary British Novel* seeks to define (or identify the problems involved in defining) these terms not just for students, but for teachers and interested members of the reading public; and it reveals the extent to which the practice of twenty-two leading British novelists embodies, exemplifies, modifies or rejects the theories that these terms represent. In recognition of the fact that novels often embody combinations of realism, postcolonialism, feminism and postmodernism, and include other '-isms' as well, the collection is divided into four parts, each devoted to one of the four major '-isms', yet each admitting other '-isms' into the discussion of the novelists concerned.[1]

This collection of hitherto unpublished essays examines the work of some of the most major contemporary British novelists of the past twenty-odd years. The novelists selected for discussion here are some of the most widely taught at educational institutions in Great Britain and elsewhere in the English-speaking world, as well as being some of the most widely read by members of the reading public interested in 'serious' contemporary fiction. John Fowles is not represented, since the focus of this volume is on the novel since 1980, and he has published only one novel since then; William Boyd, Malcolm Bradbury, David Lodge, Christine Brooke-Rose, Timothy Mo and Fay Weldon, among others, have been excluded simply because there is a limit to the number of novelists who can be accommodated in a book of this length. While the collection might have included some contemporary American and/or Irish novelists, this would have led to even greater problems of selection, and could also have meant increasing the number of '-isms' dealt with in the essays.

Realism is the oldest of the major '-isms' to be discussed in the collection. Ian Watt notes in *The Rise of the Novel* that the term was first used in France in 1835, but that some of the earliest English novels – those by Defoe,

Richardson and Fielding, especially – anticipate in practice certain aspects of nineteenth-century French theory.[2] In particular, Defoe and the others seek to create the illusion that their characters are real people living in the real world. In contrast, however, to 'the novelists of the eighteenth and nineteenth centuries, [who] had a shared view of the nature of reality, those of the twentieth and twenty-first centuries', comments Fredrick Holmes in Chapter 1, 'are generally aware that what constitutes reality is a matter for speculation and debate'. To represent the complexities of contemporary life adequately, Kazuo Ishiguro, the subject of Holmes' chapter, blends realism with a combination of more modern '-isms' in his novels – surrealism, expressionism, fabulism and postmodernism.

In Chapter 2, Judith Seaboyer finds 'generic precursors' for Ian McEwan partly in 'the great reformist exponents of nineteenth-century sociopolitical realisms'. In some of his novels, she says, McEwan works and reworks themes familiar to readers of Victorian realism, updating them in the light of the extraordinary rate of change that has characterised life in the twentieth and twenty-first centuries. Darkly gothic, McEwan's novels are 'explorations of individuals and relationships within a claustrophobic private sphere . . . in which the private sphere is not only mirrored in that of the public but is a way of addressing broader social and political issues'. A good example is *The Innocent*, in which the death and dismemberment of a German ex-army sergeant becomes a metaphor for the brutality not only of the Third Reich, but of the Allies, too, exercised against civilian populations.

The main focus of Irvine Welsh's novels, says Alan Riach in Chapter 3, is 'people in conditions of social squalor and economic poverty'. This suggests that Welsh belongs to the tradition of Zola and the other French novelists of the nineteenth-century realist/naturalist school.[3] Yet Welsh's realism, like Ishiguro's, is subject to 'surreal realignments', so that his narrative focus is often more on the characters' dreams and nightmares than on the events of their everyday lives. 'None of [Welsh's] technical modes, narrative devices and contexts', comments Riach, 'adheres to conventional canons of realism.'

David Punter begins Chapter 4, on Angela Carter, with a definition of magic realism taken from *The Bloomsbury Guide to English Literature*. Magic realism, we are told there, is 'a term applied in literature primarily to . . . novelists . . . whose work combines a realistic manner with strong elements of the bizarre, supernatural and fantastic'. In 'The Bloody Chamber', for example, a castle becomes a ghostly character; and in 'Wolf-Alice' the narrative viewpoint is that of some wolves who adopt a little girl. In some of her other fictions, Punter comments, Carter's characters 'often seem as though they are characters from *somebody else's* story – not their own, nor even their apparent author's, but stories that come from a different, irreversible past, even if this past can be known only through a certain virtuality, a consciousness that has already in some sense been traumatised, and which is now moving in a dreamy afterlife in which the presence of a ghost at the breakfast table would be anything but surprising'. None of this is consistent with conventional realism.

In Chapter 5, Laurence Nicoll shows how James Kelman's interest in existentialism impacts on the basic realism of his novels. Nicoll begins by reminding us that existentialism is 'a notoriously elusive term', varying from philosopher to philosopher; however, he finds that central to existentialist thinking is 'a radical notion of freedom'. Kelman writes about poverty and squalor, much like Zola and the other realist/naturalist French novelists of the nineteenth century; yet for Zola 'realism amounts to the insistence that identity, character, is *necessarily determined* by society and historical circumstance', while for Kelman to portray his characters as deterministically regulated 'would mean abandoning the central existentialist notion of a freely chosen and freely choosing self'. Kelman thus presents his characters as exercising complete freedom of will. He also refuses to employ conventional omniscient narrators, for the omniscient narrator is an analogue to God, where, as an existentialist, Kelman denies God's existence. He concerns himself not with abstractions, but with the here and now of 'facticity', the 'finite and concrete aspects of human being'. Kelman's facticity (a term used by Kierkegaard, Heidegger and Sartre) gives his realism a distinctly existential character.

Daniel Lea argues in Chapter 6 that Martin Amis' *Money* and *London Fields* 'lie firmly within the conventions of nineteenth-century realism'. Indeed, they belong to the tradition of the 'condition-of-England' novel, a tradition beginning with such novels as Benjamin Disraeli's *Sybil* (1845) and Elizabeth Gaskell's *North and South* (1855). Like Disraeli and Mrs Gaskell, Amis comments on contemporary life, in *Money* satirising Thatcherism's tendency to reduce the individual to a commodity. Thatcherism has made of John Self, the novel's main character, 'an extension of the world in which [he] exists; not only does he indulge in a culture of junk, but that junk . . . renders him internally, as well externally corrupted'. *London Fields* places the blame for a lack of stable individual or national identity not on local British economic and social policy, but on global destabilisation. 'The players of *London Fields* do not have static selves from which they temporarily deviate', Lea comments, 'but consist of a fragmented collection of partial selves which alternate freely. The barriers between performed roles are no longer solid therefore, but allow an endless interpenetration.' The London Fields of the title constitute a dream image of England as it was in the distant past, before the complexities of late twentieth-century life began to intrude on individual and national stability.

Postcolonialism is a critical and theoretical term with an application wider than literature, also being used in relation to the critical analysis of history, politics.[4] Aijaz Ahmad identifies the first use of the term in political theory in the 1970s, to describe the state of nations that had thrown off European control in the wake of the Second World War.[5] Since then postcolonialism has come to refer to the critical analysis of modes of discourse more generally, about and in the former colonies of European imperial powers. Postcolonialism is about self-definition: the self-definition of individuals and cultures impacted by dominant cultures, those dominant cultures having constructed them during the imperial phase as 'other' and inferior. Postcolonialism seeks to deconstruct such binary conceptualisations and to recognise the impact of colonialism on colonial subjects and culture. By its nature, it is primarily concerned with colonial impact after the withdrawal of colonial powers; as Bart Moore-Gilbert and others comment: 'The "post" in postcolonial . . . hints at withdrawal, liberation and reunification'.[6]

While the emphasis of postcolonial studies has for the most part been on the modern day, postcolonialism also has far-ranging implications and applications, beginning as early as medieval and early modern studies (the Crusades, Renaissance Europe's engagement with the New World). Postcolonial theory is also invoked in reference to dispersed (diasporic) peoples such as Jews, or to minority struggles with a dominant culture, in the case of feminism or queer studies. In such ways, postcolonial literary criticism enjoys fruitful interactions with other literary-critical movements. The essays in this collection reflect such interactions.

Because this volume is a survey of British fiction since 1980, postcolonialism is addressed in the following essays as it is manifest in writing coming from *within* Britain. In Chapter 7, Bruce King focuses on two very different minority writers: Abdulrazak Gurnah, who immigrated to Britain from Zanzibar, and Hanif Kureishi, who grew up in Bromley, Kent, as the son of an Indian immigrant. King provocatively argues against 'postcolonialism' or 'postcolonial resistance' as adequate definitions for the distinct writings of these two men. He recognises Gurnah as part of an Arabised elite pushed from Zanzibar by a black African revolution, and Kureishi as a product of British suburbia, for whom racism is essentially a class issue, and whose interests lie less in postcolonialism than in the 1960s British counter-culture. King's essay both evokes a postcolonial critical approach and warns against the too easy use of literary-critical labels.

Hermione Lee, in Chapter 8, addresses the figure of the father in the work of perhaps Britain's most prominent postcolonial writer, Salman Rushdie. Lee argues that in Rushdie's fiction, fathers carry both personal and political significances, a 'weight' that sons carry and with which they struggle to come to terms. Rushdie's emphasis on dynasties, she argues, 'is not just personal; it has everything to do with the politics of the countries he is writing about and with postcoloniality'. In Chapter 9 Bart Moore-Gilbert examines the two novels to date of Zadie Smith, who rose to prominence in 2000 with the publication of *White Teeth*, alongside the bleaker work of Caryl Phillips. Moore-Gilbert relates postcolonial interests in the dispersal of indigenous peoples at the hands of imperial powers with the dispersal of the Jews over the last 2,000 years, exploring the figure of the Jew in the work of these two writers.

Chantal Zabus' chapter on the novels of Marina Warner, Chapter 10, serves as a link between the 'postcolonialism' and 'feminism' parts of this volume, exploring the highly productive interaction in Warner's work between these two '-isms'. As Zabus shows, postcolonialism and feminism both 'question the very concept of history and the way it foregrounds the point of view of the winners and the male sex'. Zabus explores the way in which Warner's fiction tells the stories of women and the colonised, bringing each out from under the yoke of colonialism and patriarchy, and giving voice to alternative versions of selfhood and history.

Feminism, like postcolonialism, is not just a literary theory or a literary-critical method, but a political movement, concerned with the role of women in essentially patriarchal societies, and with giving voice, opportunities and status to women and girls. Virginia Woolf is a vital precursor to modern feminist thinkers and writers, in her writings on the need for female independence, most notably in *A Room of One's Own* (1929). What is termed 'second-wave feminism', however, took off in the 1960s, with texts such as Betty Friedan's *The Feminine Mystique* (1963) and Kate Millett's *Sexual Politics* (1969), and feminist literary criticism developed through key texts such as Ellen Moers' *Literary Women* (1976) and Sandra Gilbert and Susan Gubar's *The Madwoman in the Attic* (1979). American and English feminist thought is complemented by the more highly theoretical French feminism, represented in the work of Julia Kristeva, Hélène Cixous and Luce Irigaray.[7]

Since the 1960s feminism has, arguably, exploded like no other movement, and now impacts on all areas of literary criticism and concepts of the 'literary canon';[8] the literature taught in schools and universities now includes writers such as Mary Sidney, Aemilia Lanyer, Aphra Behn and Christina Rossetti. Notably, in recent years the term 'post-feminist' has been evoked to suggest that feminism is itself passé, or overly reductive in its definition of female identity and concerns. Many of the essays in this collection engage implicitly with the idea of post-feminism, arguing that the female writers at issue are 'not *only* feminist' or are 'feminist in a unique kind of way'. Such care is indicative of the wide-ranging nature of current feminism, and each essay does continue to assert the value of 'feminist' as at least one useful way of regarding the writers at hand.

In Chapter 11, Sarah Ross approaches Pat Barker as 'at first' a feminist, exploring the interaction between Barker's early novels, which focus on underprivileged women and female communities, and her later novels, which tend to focus on more masculine spheres. Barker can also very usefully be termed a 'realist' writer, and Ross argues that Barker's feminism and her recent conscientious social realism are linked by a concern with the nature of evil.

Glenda Norquay and Dorothy McMillan, in Chapters 12 and 13, respectively, explore the work of two female Scottish writers, A. L. Kennedy and Janice Galloway, who are frequently compared but who practise two quite different kinds of feminism. McMillan identifies in Galloway's fiction a 'fighting-back female voice' that is brought to life through narrative and visual experimentation: the evocation of bricolage, or 'odd-jobbery', and the use of typographical tricks. Glenda Norquay describes A. L. Kennedy as resistant to categorisation as a feminist – or, for that matter, a Scottish – writer. Kennedy pays particularly close attention to individual subjectivity, to the subject's desire for completion through interaction with others; Norquay argues that she is able to do so only in relation to the previous 'achievements of feminism, postcolonialist thinking and earlier challenges to realism'.

Chapters 14 and 15, by Sarah Sceats and Katherine Tarbox, respectively, both focus on desire. Tarbox explores A. S. Byatt's Booker Prize-winning novel, *Possession*, as underpinned and driven by characters' desire for syzygy, a hermaphroditic state achieved by one who joins together reason (conventionally male) and passion (conventionally female). Tarbox explores the novel's pastiche-poetry, as well as its Victorian and modern plots, elucidating the rich connections that exist among all three in the central characters' desire to achieve syzygy. Sarah Sceats focuses on appetite, desire and belonging in the novels of Rose Tremain – in particular, on individuals' desire to achieve a significant sense of belonging. Sceats acknowledges that Tremain focuses on male protagonists as frequently as she does on female ones, but argues that her sensitivity to marginalised people, as well as her focus on the pursuit of self-fulfilment, is what constitutes her particular feminism.

In Chapter 16, the last in this part, Paulina Palmer explores a fruitful relationship between two '-isms' in the work of one writer: feminism and postmodernism. Palmer describes the connections that exist between lesbian and postmodern persepectives, and their manifestations in Jeanette Winterson's *The Passion* and *The Powerbook*. As Palmer indicates, Winterson uses strategies associated with postmodernism, such as an emphasis on performativity and intertextuality, to construct lesbian love stories that subvert the heterosexual conventions of the romance genre.

Postmodernism has been defined in a number of ways by a variety of commentators. As Daniel Bedggood points out in Chapter 17, however, Fredric Jameson and Jean-François Lyotard are often referred to where there is a need for a concise definition. For Jameson, says Bedggood, postmodernity is 'a condition brought about by the "radical break" in cultural forms and systems in the 1950s and 1960s, with the wane of political, social and philosophical models of modernity. Jameson suggests that the old certainties, aims and ideals of modernity are now insecure and debatable, and this is expressed in postmodern cultural forms as diverse as architecture, film, advertising and literature.' Lyotard similarly expresses his distrust of 'metanarrative' or 'grand narratives' – the theories of Marx or Hegel about the course of history, for example, or the modern concept of 'Progress'.[9]

In the novels of Graham Swift and Julian Barnes, Bedggood argues, we find a similar distrust of 'metanarratives' and 'old certainties'. In Swift's *Waterland*, the idea that there can be a single, definitive history of any given series of events gives way to the conclusion that there is always 'a rich diffusion of "histories" . . . without *one* becoming dominant'. Much the same point is made in *Flaubert's Parrot*, where Julian Barnes presents 'many possible orders of "containing" Gustave Flaubert in the historical record, in a manner that effectively exposes this contingency of selecting the "truth" and makes ridiculous claims to "priority" for any one order'. Also questioned in both authors' novels is the possibility of Progress: as the narrator of *Waterland*, Thomas Crick, puts it, 'we believe we are going forward, towards the oasis of Utopia. But how do we know – only some imaginary figure looking down from the sky (let's call him God) can know – that we are not moving in a great circle?'

David Leon Higdon begins Chapter 18 by noting that although Peter Ackroyd 'rejects being called either an historical novelist or a postmodernist', his novels exploit 'the full range of postmodern techniques, turning to anti-realism, grounding themselves in a range of structural play, steeping themselves in layers of intertextuality, foregrounding their fictionality, and fully exploiting historical discontinuities, pastiche and parody'. Ackroyd's presentation of alternative worlds in his fiction, comments Higdon, falls into line with 'Brian McHale's theory that postmodern writers dramatise the shift of dominant from problems of *knowing* to problems of *modes of being* – from an epistemological dominant to an *ontological one*'. In bringing the world of an eighteenth-century architect into juxtaposition with that of a twentieth-century detective in his novel *Hawksmoor*, Ackroyd finds his 'unique postmodern voice' and a template for his subsequent fiction, which similarly alternates between the twentieth century and various earlier periods.

Chapter 19, the final chapter in the collection, begins by identifying the stylistic elements of Iain Banks' postmodernism as 'the fusion – or confusion of high and popular culture; delight in the detail of new (or invented) technologies; the play of multiple and competing levels of ontology (human versus superhuman; author versus characters; art versus life); together with a great deal of black comedy that mocks the "traditional" values of Western culture'. Cairns Craig also finds in Banks' novels 'the play of different ontological levels within the novel, each level implying that another level, previously assumed to be "real", is no more than a fiction, reduces reality to a series of games, none of which can be assumed to have priority over any other'. Banks' language games, argues Craig, games involving 'the conflict between being a player and being played upon, and the difficulty of discovering the rules of the game in which one is playing, are the insistent themes of Banks's fiction'.

While it would have been desirable to include more contemporary British novelists in the volume, considerations of space made this impossible. Such considerations also made it impossible for us to supply a list of each author's novels at the end of each essay; instead, we have referred interested readers to bibliographies either in hard copy form or on the internet. In addition, we have asked each essayist to provide a list of some five or six secondary books and/or articles for those who wish to read at greater length about the '-isms' and the novelists represented in this volume.

James Acheson
Sarah C. E. Ross

NOTES

1 Basic definitions and discussion of each of the '-isms' covered in this volume can be found in M. H. Abrams, *A Glossary of Literary Terms*, 7th edn (Boston: Heinle & Heinle, 1999).
2 Ian Watt, *The Rise of the Novel* (1957; rpt. Harmondsworth: Penguin, 1968), p. 10. For a fuller introduction to French realism, see Damian Grant, *Realism in Literature* (London: Methuen, 1970).
3 For a helpful introduction to French realism/naturalism, see Lilian Furst and Peter Skrine, *Naturalism* (London: Methuen, 1971).
4 Two excellent introductions to postcolonialism are Bart Moore-Gilbert, Gareth Stanton and Willy Maley, eds, *Postcolonial Criticism* (London: Longman, 1997); and Bart Moore-Gilbert, *Postcolonial Theory: Contexts, Practices, Politics* (London: Verso, 1997).
5 Aijaz Ahmad, 'The Politics of Literary Postcoloniality', *Race and Class*, 36, 3 (1995), 1–20.
6 Moore-Gilbert et al., *Postcolonial Criticism*, p. 2.
7 For an introduction to French feminist theory, see Toril Moi, *Sexual/Textual Politics: Feminist Literary Theory* (London and New York: Routledge, 1985).
8 Excellent introductions to feminist literary criticism include *Feminist Literary Criticism*, ed. Mary Eagleton (London: Longman, 1991); and *Feminisms: an Anthology of Literary Theory and Criticism*, ed. Robyn R. Warhol and Diane Price Herndl (New Brunswick, NJ: Rutgers University Press, 1993).
9 Two very helpful introductions to postmodernism are Linda Hutcheon's *The Politics of Postmodernism* (London and New York: Routledge, 1989) – not to be confused with her *A Poetics of Postmodernism: History, Theory, Fiction* (London: Routledge, 1988), a more advanced study – and Brian McHale's *Postmodernist Fiction* (London: Methuen, 1987).

PART I

Realism and other -isms

1

Realism, Dreams and the Unconscious in the Novels of Kazuo Ishiguro

Frederick M. Holmes

A critical consensus has emerged about the themes, modes, narrative techniques and interrelationships of the five novels that Ishiguro has published to date. The first three – *A Pale View of Hills* (1982), *An Artist of the Floating World* (1986) and *The Remains of the Day* (1989) – have been celebrated for their historically grounded realism, achieved through the limpid, masterfully controlled prose styles of their first-person narrators, all of whom depend upon memory as they look back over their troubled lives and times. Realism in fiction is a vexed concept, but it can be defined as the attempt to use linguistic and narrative conventions to create a fictional illusion of social and psychological reality that seems plausible to ordinary readers. Writers of realist fiction, David Lodge comments, assume that 'there is a common phenomenal world that may be reliably described by the methods of empirical history'; however, he adds that 'to the later writers in the [realist] tradition what this world *means* is much more problematical'.[1] In other words, although the novelists of the eighteenth and nineteenth centuries had a shared view of the nature of reality, those of the twentieth and twenty-first centuries are generally aware that what constitutes reality is a matter for speculation and debate. Neither is contemporary realism usually premised on the belief that the language used to describe what Lodge calls the 'common phenomenal world' is a transparent medium that creates a perfect correspondence between its symbols and an objective reality external to it. On the contrary, most realists recognise that language does not so much mirror reality as use conventions to construct simulacra of what some readers can accept as reality.

While Ishiguro seeks to construct simulacra of this kind in his novels, thereby grounding them in realism, both he and the critics who have written about his fiction have also used the terms 'surrealism' and 'expressionism' to characterise certain aspects of it. These terms were originally coined to identify two different movements in twentieth-century literature and art. Originating in the 1920s under the influence of recent discoveries in psychology (Freud's *The Interpretation of Dreams* [1900] was especially influential), surrealism explored the creative possibilities afforded by dreams and other unconscious states. It was, in M. H. Abrams' words, 'a revolt against all restraints on free creativity, including logical reason, standard morality, social and artistic conventions and norms, and all control over the artistic process by forethought and intention'.[2] Ishiguro's preferred term for the non-realist features of his most recent novel, *When We Were Orphans* (2000), is expressionism, 'where everything is distorted to reflect the emotion of the artist who is looking at the world'.[3] Like surrealism, expressionism was an overturning of realism within many different art forms early in the twentieth century, and it presents, as Chris Baldick has stated, 'a world violently distorted under the pressure of intense personal moods, ideas, and emotions: image and language thus express feeling and imagination rather than represent external reality'.[4] Finally, the term fabulism (a variant is fabulation) identifies works of fiction that 'violate . . . standard novelistic expectations by drastic . . . experiments with subject matter, form, style, temporal sequence, and fusions of the everyday, the fantastic, the mythical, and the nightmarish' (Abrams, p. 196). This term, too, characterises important aspects of Ishiguro's fiction.

Ishiguro himself has said that his third novel, the Booker Prize-winning *The Remains of the Day*, was a kind of rewriting of *An Artist of the Floating World*, which in turn reworked the artistic methods and themes of his first novel, *A Pale View of Hills*.[5] The shift that Ishiguro made to an English setting and cast of characters in *The Remains of the Day* from the Japanese ones of the first two books did not prevent readers from seeing that the ageing narrators of all three novels are similarly subjective and unreliable.[6] The three novels are not examples of unalloyed realism, for the selective, frequently distorting, expressionistic memories of the widow Etsuko, the painter Masuji Ono and the butler Stevens all testify to their inability to come to terms psychologically with the historical trauma of the Second World War and their involvement in events immediately preceding and following it.[7] The very tight stylistic and emotional control which all three narrators exhibit conveys the paradoxical message that potentially uncontrollable, dangerous feelings always have to be kept at bay. Although Etsuko, Ono and Stevens interpret their interactions with others rather self-approvingly and want to judge their lives as having been successful, Brian Finney is right to say that 'all of [Ishiguro's] novels are haunted by a sense of Angst, regret, and sadness'.[8]

Ishiguro's fourth novel, *The Unconsoled* (1995), was universally received as a radical departure from his first three in its mode of unabashed surrealism and fantasy. The novel seems initially to be realistically anchored in the present-day cultural life of an unnamed European city to which the narrator, an English pianist named Ryder, has come to give a concert, but readers quickly discover that the narrative unfolds according to the chaotic logic of a dream. As various critics have noticed, space and time for Ryder and the numerous characters whom he encounters have an unpredictable elasticity, just as they do in dreams.[9] And those other characters are related to Ryder just as the figures in our dreams might well be related to us. As Ishiguro explains in an interview with Eleanor Wachtel, they are to some extent autonomous, but primarily they are 'versions of [Ryder] at various stages in his life; sometimes they are versions of key people in his life, such as his parents . . . sometimes they are . . . projections of what he fears he might become' (Wachtel, p. 31). In using the other characters in this way, Ishiguro has devised an unorthodox method of telling Ryder's entire life story.

If *The Unconsoled* obviously breaks sharply with Ishiguro's earlier novels, some critics have recognised that it also reveals continuities with them: all feature unreliable narrator-protagonists whose memories and perceptions cannot entirely be trusted and who seem afflicted by neuroses that originated in childhood.[10] Moreover, the first three novels can be seen upon closer inspection to contain in less conspicuous form non-realist elements like those that dominate *The Unconsoled*. For example, in *A Pale View of Hills* the relationship between Etsuko and Keiko, the daughter who committed suicide at some point after emigrating to England with her mother and her English stepfather, can be seen to parallel the neglectful, abusive relationship between Sachiko, the woman befriended by Etsuko in Nagasaki shortly after the end of the Second World War, and her little daughter, Mariko. As Barry Lewis has observed, Etsuko may be projecting her own guilt about making Keiko unhappy by taking her to a foreign country onto Sachiko, who is planning to leave Japan with Frank, her American lover. Lewis states that it is even possible that Etsuko's guilt has been displaced onto a fantasised rather than a remembered woman, but Brian Shaffer is more persuasive in arguing that readers are meant to see Sachiko as neither completely imagined by Etsuko nor separate from her.[11] Like the characters in Ryder's narrative, they occupy a middle ground.

Indeed, one could claim that the entire fictional worlds of Ishiguro's first three novels – and not just some of their characters – are located in a middle ground between an historically veridical realism and fabulism.[12] Ishiguro himself has said that his aim in creating the Japanese and English settings, characters and situations of those books was less to represent faithfully the social particulars of those nations in the 1930s, 1940s and 1950s than to create metaphors to express personal concerns.[13] Conversely, as he also states, certain novels that strive to be realistic might not make a deep impression upon readers. In keeping with this claim, Ishiguro holds that his non-realist methods allow for the depiction of themes which are of broader significance than those which would emerge from strict realism.[14] For example, Ishiguro has said that he intended to use the figure of the butler in *The Remains of the Day* as a metaphor for the subordinate position, in relation to power, of ordinary people in contemporary society, and he has also said that his intention was to create a mythical rather than an historically real picture of life in a manor house. The novel became a kind of parable in which he explored the personal and collective damage caused when people internalise a national ideal that entails the denial of their own emotional needs.[15]

Because he locates his fictional worlds between realism and fabulism, Ishiguro's work has been allied with postmodernism.[16] It is difficult to supply a brief definition of this complex cultural and artistic phenomenon that is not superficial and misleading, but Jean-François Lyotard is helpful in arguing that the postmodernist character of contemporary Western society is manifested principally in 'an incredulity towards metanarratives', the large-scale narratives (the theories of history put forward by Marx or Hegel, for example) that seek to explain the nature of physical and social reality.[17] Postmodern fiction displays this incredulity by exposing the explanatory structures and conventions that organise and mediate our experience of life as contingent social constructions, not as the natural, universal ground of reality. In this vein, Ishiguro's novels deny access to versions of historical reality that readers can accept as foundational or unambiguously true. None of his fictions supplies an authoritative alternative to the fallible perspectives of the narrators, and readers infer that all other possible points of view would be distorted by the subjective needs of the witnesses. What Ishiguro says of Christopher Banks, the narrator of *When We Were Orphans*, is true to some extent of all of his narrators: none is conventionally unreliable in the sense of allowing readers some means to 'measure the distance between [his or her] craziness and the proper world out there'. Rather, as Ishiguro says of Banks, 'a lot of the time the world actually adopts the craziness of his logic' (Richards, p. 4).

And yet, just to identify the logic as crazy implies some norm of sanity. John McLeod is perceptive in stressing the reluctance of Ishiguro's novels to wholeheartedly embrace and celebrate the postmodernist historiography that they all exhibit.[18] This ambivalence is particularly noticeable in *When We Were Orphans*, in which the expressionistic, dream-like method of *The Unconsoled* only gradually overruns the formal realism of a narrative set in London and Shanghai in the 1930s and cast in the high society detective genre popularised in the inter-war years. As Ishiguro says, the novel moves 'from occupying one kind of world to occupying another kind of world'.[19] His talk of proliferating and competing worlds in *When We Were Orphans* seems to accord exactly with Brian McHale's definition of postmodernist fiction as ontological in character. The novel invites the same questions that McHale says are typically generated by postmodernist texts: 'What is a world? . . . What kinds of world are there, how are they constituted, and how do they differ? . . . What happens when different kinds of world are placed in confrontation, or when boundaries between worlds are violated?'[20]

John Carey answers the last question with regard to *When We Were Orphans* by saying that a seemingly real, but actually false, world is supplanted by a truer one. Carey applauds this transformation, claiming that

'Ishiguro's abandonment of realism is not a defection from reality but the contrary. . . . [His] inextricable fusion of memory, imagination, and dream takes us down into the labyrinth of reality which realism has simplified'.[21] It is my contention, however, that the expressionistic ontology – the projection of Banks' hitherto repressed needs and fears – does not acquire a privileged status or cancel the realist one, which continues to exert a conflicting force, despite the absence in the novel of some objective view point that would authenticate it. Rather, these different and incommensurable ontologies coexist uneasily, and, if Ishiguro shows us that we have a propensity to construct reality subjectively, he also shows us that historical forces and events external to us are not so easily made to fit the contours of our psyches.

The progressively expressionistic quality of Christopher Banks' narration emerges, at least in part, from an exaggeration of the unrealistic features of the genre that Ishiguro resurrected in *When We Were Orphans*. British detective novels written in the inter-war years (the genre's 'golden age') usually maintain a surface realism, but their plots and characters have elements that violate ordinary readers' beliefs about the nature of everyday life. The detective genre is fundamentally escapist in locating the action in communities that are essentially morally innocent. Evil is contained within the figures of murderers, who are exposed and apprehended by master detectives. As Ishiguro says, 'all it takes is for [such a] detective to come from outside and unmask the murderer and everything goes back to being rosy again'.[22] Readers of works of this kind easily suspend disbelief when it comes to the protagonists' implausibly acute powers of deduction, and, in making Banks a celebrated detective in a line of such figures stretching back to Sherlock Holmes, Ishiguro creates the expectation that Banks' deeds will have heroic potential. But when Banks returns in 1937 to Shanghai, where he spent his boyhood, to solve the mystery of his parents' disappearance, readers are taken aback by his belief that his parents are still alive in the hands of the kidnappers so many years after the occurrence of the crime. We also wonder, along with Brian Finney,[23] why he waited so long to return to Shanghai after becoming a detective, if he believed all along that his parents still needed to be rescued. What is even more staggering is that Banks confidently expects that in freeing them he will single-handedly avert the geopolitical disasters threatening at the time: the triumph of fascism and imminence of global war. It is one thing for readers to accept that Banks is a great detective; it is quite another to credit his claim that he is the potential saviour of the world, especially in the absence of any apparent connection between the crime involving his parents and political issues that transcend the local context of Shanghai.

But other characters in the novel *do* blindly take Banks at his own messianic valuation, or at least they seem to him to do so. This is what Ishiguro is referring to in the previously quoted remark that 'a lot of the time the world actually adopts the craziness of [Banks'] logic'. Upon his arrival at a social gathering of the English elite in Shanghai's International Settlement, the crowd parts for him like the Red Sea before Moses. 'Do you have any idea at all how relieved we all feel now that you are finally with us?' one of the guests asks Banks, who takes the veneration in his stride.[24] They seem to expect that he will not only solve the case but also somehow put an end to the Sino-Japanese War, which has begun to threaten the comfortable existence of this unofficial colony of English foreigners.

Many other textual details could be cited as evidence that Banks' narrative after his return to Shanghai is skewed by his psychological needs and that other characters collude in this distortion. Brian Finney identifies two such details, the last of which he calls 'a clear instance of wish fulfilment on Banks's part' (Finney, p. 6). The first one is the absurd interest of an official from the Municipal Council in meticulously planning the welcoming ceremony for his parents even before Banks has had a chance to establish for certain that they are still alive, and the second is the equally implausible willingness of the Chinese family occupying the house that he lived in as a child to return it to his parents once they have been rescued, despite the fact that the English couple were never its owners. Another example is the highly improbable readiness of the Chinese lieutenant, beleaguered as he is by a Japanese assault, to leave his post in order to escort Banks to the house where he believes his parents are being held. In the midst of war's devastation, that house (or at least the part of it that he can see) is miraculously undamaged, 'an apparition from another more civilised world' (p. 267). It represents a nostalgic refuge in his mind that he has carried intact since his childhood. The fact that the back part of the house has been destroyed by the shelling perhaps symbolises the illusory character of this mental haven.

The status of the war between the Chinese and the Japanese in relation to the tension between the realistic and expressionistic aspects of Banks' narration is interestingly paradoxical. On the one hand, as critics have said, the chaotic destruction and human suffering that he witnesses while searching in the war zone for his parents can be read as an expressionistic projection onto the external world of his painful and increasingly disorderly mental processes.[25] Because it is the very nature of war to violate the social norms of quotidian existence, descriptions of it can easily seem fantastic rather than realistic. But, on the other hand, wars really do occur, and writers of fiction have frequently attempted to recreate their first-hand experience of them realistically. For example, J. G. Ballard drew impressively on his boyhood experiences in Shanghai between 1930 and 1945 in writing *Empire of the Sun*. But Ishiguro is too young to have experienced the Japanese conquest of China and the occupation of Shanghai, a city in which he has never lived. He has said that all of the historical detail that went into *When We Were Orphans* was garnered from books (one of which might have been *Empire of the Sun*, although he does not mention particular titles).[26] Ishiguro seems much less interested in the historical realism of his discursive account of the war years in Shanghai than he does in its potential to serve as an objective correlative for the operations of his protagonist's psyche.

The rather odd title of the novel is one of several clues that Banks' unreliable perceptions had their origins in the trauma that left him an orphan as a child. Ishiguro has been at pains in interviews to state that he intended his protagonist's orphaned condition to be a metaphor for the much more common experience of emerging from the protected world of childhood into the harsh existential realities of adulthood.[27] In this sense, all who are lucky enough to have enjoyed secure childhoods inevitably become orphans. Banks' increasingly surrealistic narration is a neurotic result of his desperate need to heal the emotional wound inflicted by his parents' disappearance and to regain the Edenic innocence that he had known as a boy. Finney believes that Banks' career as a detective has been an 'unconscious adult compensation for the impotence of his childhood games of detection' (Finney, p. 14), in which he and his Japanese friend, Akira Yamashita, had enacted the discovery and rescue of his parents. His career choice is, then, escapist and regressive, like the literary genre glorifying that career which Ishiguro is parodying in his novel.[28] The novelist has commented in print on the futility of Banks' attempt 'to repair something from the past when it's actually far too late' (Shaffer, 'Interview', p. 3), and on the logical disconnection between the destruction of his family and the international crisis that he hopes to resolve by finding his parents and bringing their kidnappers to justice.[29]

Ishiguro has pointed out the similarity between Banks and *The Unconsoled*'s Ryder, whose career ambitions are also a quixotic attempt to undo the irreparable emotional damage that he suffered as a child. Both characters have sacrificed whatever personal happiness they might have enjoyed in order to satisfy the exacting demands of their professional life. Like Banks, Ryder believes that performing his duties successfully will both restore his family to unity and have a beneficial effect on the community at large, even though there is no rational link between his psychological problems and the cultural malaise being suffered by the town that he is visiting. In contrast, the narrators of Ishiguro's three earlier novels have much more reasonable, if somewhat exaggerated, ideas about how they can contribute to the overall good of society.[30] *The Unconsoled*'s townsfolk, who share Ryder's megalomaniacal delusion, look to him for cultural salvation and accept all of his pronouncements on modern music as having absolute authority.

If the other characters of *The Unconsoled* are, in effect, figures in Ryder's dream, then it is clear why they seem oblivious to the weirdness of the experiences that they share with him. But *When We Were Orphans* reinstates realism, or at least it seems to do so. Why, then, do characters in that novel, such as those mentioned above, seem to validate and participate in Banks' increasingly expressionistic formulation of events? Why, as in *The Unconsoled*, do some of the characters seem to be reflections of the protagonist, or of others close to him? Maya Jaggi, who notices this phenomenon, cites the example of the relationship between Sarah Hemmings and Sir Cecil Medhurst, which projects the failed marriage of Banks' parents.[31] Broken emotionally in old age, Medhurst, who set out in advance of Banks to conquer the source of the world's evil in Shanghai, can be seen to embody Banks' unacknowledged fear of what he might himself become should his idealism prove ineffectual. Ishiguro offers a way to square this sort of mirroring with the expectations of realism when he argues that, in our waking lives as well as in our dreams, we mould others in forms dictated by our own psychological drives: 'Our view of other people is often shaped by our need to work certain things out about ourselves. We tend to appropriate other people–more than we perhaps care to admit. We perhaps don't see them for what they are; they become useful tools'.[32]

But it still needs to be explained why many of the characters in *When We Were Orphans* seem to acquiesce so readily in Banks' constructions of both them and himself. For do we not, in life, resist the attempts of others to make our identities conform to the preconceived images that they have about us? Can we be made so easily to share the delusions of others? Or might we be weaker in this regard than we like to believe, especially under certain circumstances? Brian Finney identifies one of those circumstances when he asks rhetorically, 'don't people in imminent danger of a collapse of their civilisation regularly project their needs and fantasies onto potential saviours, however unsuitable?' (Finney, p. 12). Finney is right to stress that the novel's expressionism is not just personal and private but collective and political. Subscribing to Banks' representation of events enables the foreign imperialists to infantilise themselves and so repress guilt over their exploitation of the Chinese, whom they have enslaved to opium and impoverished.[33] Ironically, Banks mercilessly judges them for the harm which they have done even as he appropriates them for inclusion into the narrative vehicle designed to recreate the guilt-free world of his childhood: 'What has quietly shocked me, from the moment of my arrival [in Shanghai], is the refusal of everyone here to acknowledge their drastic culpability' (p. 162). The clear implication is that the International Settlement of his boyhood was never the morally innocent place that he nostalgically longs to re-enter as an adult. Since it was built on corruption, it could not have been, as he must recognise in order to utter his criticism of his fellow countrymen.

This example of irony can be read as an illustration of how Banks' distorted perceptions and interpretations come under increasing pressure from what I previously referred to as the realist ontology of *When We Were Orphans*. He is forced at certain points to encounter phenomena which are incongruous with the expressionistic narrative that he is driven from within to create. This pressure is shown in Ishiguro's depiction of Banks' reunion as an adult with his childhood friend Akira, whom, he tells us, he is almost positive that he saw on the street in Shanghai very soon after returning to that city in 1937. What gives readers pause is Banks' admission that he did not at that time hail Akira, despite his strong desire to renew their friendship. The strangeness of Banks' response here is a faint signal that the reappearance of Akira figures in the expressionistic logic governing Banks' narrative, and the way in which the two finally do meet, both confirms our suspicion and frustrates Banks' attempt to make reality conform to his vision of things. What I mean is that he tries but fails to recast the man whom he takes to be Akira in the role that his friend had enacted in their play as children: that of co-detective and partner in Banks' fight against the evil criminals who had taken his parents from him. As critics have observed, it is by no means certain that this soldier really is Akira; he seems at first not to know Banks at all, and he might be feigning to be Akira in order to save his own life.[34] Whatever the truth of his actual identity might be, it is thematically significant that 'Akira' reappears as a soldier in the Japanese Army, which is launching an assault on Shanghai. Rather than helping Banks transform the International Settlement into the haven that had protected them as boys, Akira has become part of the force menacing its very existence. As a child, he had tried to resist returning to Japan to live, since during an earlier sojourn there he had been ostracised on account of his foreign ways, but he cannot prevent being swept up in the historical reality of Japanese militarism, just as Banks cannot avoid his complicity in the destructiveness of British imperialism.

The climax of this section of the narrative supplies an unequivocal refutation of Banks' belief that his mother and father are still being held by the kidnappers. Instead of his parents, the house contains something much more plausible under such circumstances: the dead bodies of a Chinese family victimised by the war and a pair of survivors, a little girl and her dog. After Banks has been returned to the International Settlement by the Japanese, empirically verifiable facts are disclosed that expose how delusive his ambition has been to restore his family to wholeness and heal the emotional wound that he suffered as a child. He discovers that his father had not been abducted because he opposed the opium trade by which the company that employed him profited. Far from being a hero, he abandoned his family to live with his mistress before dying of typhoid. His mother, Banks ultimately learns, now lives in an institution for the mentally ill, having been freed years before from the warlord who kidnapped her. When Banks goes to see her, she is too deranged to recognise him as her son. Moreover, much like Pip in Dickens' *Great Expectations* (whose narration also blends realistic depictions with expressionistic distortions), he learns that the inheritance which enabled him to be educated as a gentleman had its source in crime; he is told that the detested warlord, Wang Ku, made an agreement with his mother to support him financially. Banks, then, is inextricably enmeshed in the very evil that he is impotent to defeat.

Ishiguro has said that he provided more unambiguous clarity in the *dénouement* of *When We Were Orphans* than is usually the case in his novels because the detective genre in which it is written carries with it the expectation that mysteries will be solved.[35] His pastiche of this genre ensures that his detective will suffer disillusionment and defeat. He becomes, as Ishiguro himself implies, a ridiculous figure with a simplistic, childish understanding of the nature of good and evil: 'He had this magnifying glass, and he would investigate high society crimes. By the end [he is] doing the same thing in war zones trying to find out who the murderer is' (Wong, p. 324). The realist ontology that undermines his expressionistic construction of life and renders him ludicrous is, in the final analysis, simply another rendition of the familiar masterplot of twentieth-century history as dislocation, horror and apocalypse. It is summed up in Fredric Jameson's formulation that 'history is what hurts . . . what refuses desire and sets inexorable limits to individual as well as collective praxis, which its "ruses" turn into grisly and ironic reversals of their overt intention'.[36] The disturbed emotions that animate Banks' script are both symptomatic of this larger hurt and ironically powerless to heal it.

This essay began with the observation that although the novelists of the eighteenth and nineteenth centuries had a shared view of the nature of reality, those of the twentieth and twenty-first centuries are generally aware that what constitutes reality is a matter for speculation and debate. *When We Were Orphans*, Ishiguro's most complex novel to date, embodies within it elements of realism, expressionism, surrealism and postmodernism, its complexity suggesting that 'reality' in the twentieth century is a more elaborate concept than in previous centuries. This concern with making the form of his novels correspond to the complexity of contemporary life is also apparent in the novel preceding *When We Were Orphans*, *The Unconsoled* and, less obviously, in his first three novels, *A Pale View of Hills*, *An Artist of the Floating World* and *The Remains of the Day*. Though critics have said that his first three novels are grounded in historical realism, Ishiguro brings several '-isms' together in each, to show that conventional realism is best used in conjunction with other, more recent '-isms' to mirror the complexity of the contemporary world.

FOR FURTHER READING

For a hard copy list of Kazuo Ishiguro's work up to 2001, see *Contemporary Novelists*, ed. David Madden et al., 7th edn (New York: St James Press, 2001). For a more up-to-date list on the internet, see the British Council website: <http://www.contemporarywriters.com/authors/>.

Adleman, Gary, 'Doubles on the Rocks: Ishiguro's *The Unconsoled*', *Critique*, 42, 2 (2001), 166–79.
Appiah, Anthony, 'Liberalism, Individuality, and Identity', *Critical Inquiry*, 27 (2001), 305–32.

Davis, Rocio G., 'Imaginary Homelands Revisited in the Novels of Kazuo Ishiguro', *Miscelanea*, 15 (1994), 139–54.

Lang, James M., 'Public Memory, Private History: Kazuo Ishiguro's *The Remains of the Day*', *Clio*, 29, 2 (2000), 143–65.

Robbins, Bruce, 'Very Busy Just Now: Globalisation and Harriedness in Ishiguro's *The Unconsoled*', *Comparative Literature*, 53 (2001), 426–41.

Wong, Cynthia F., *Kazuo Ishiguro* (Tavistock: Northcote House in Association with the British Council, 2000).

NOTES

1 David Lodge, *The Modes of Modern Writing: Metaphor, Metonymy, and the Typology of Modern Literature* (London: Edward Arnold, 1977), p. 47.

2 M. H. Abrams, *A Glossary of Literary Terms*, 7th edn (Fort Worth: Harcourt Brace, 1999), p. 310.

3 Linda Richards, 'January Interview: Kazuo Ishiguro', *January Magazine* (January 2000, 10 July 2003), 2. <http://www.januarymagazine.com/profiles/ishiguro.html>.

4 Chris Baldick, *The Concise Oxford Dictionary of Literary Terms* (Oxford: Oxford University Press, 1990), p. 78.

5 Cynthia F. Wong, 'Like Idealism is to the Intellect: an Interview with Kazuo Ishiguro', *Clio*, 30 (2001), 309–25, 325.

6 See Brian W. Shaffer, *Understanding Kazuo Ishiguro*, Understanding Contemporary British Literature Series (Columbia: University of South Carolina Press, 1998), p. 7.

7 See Eleanor Wachtel, *More Writers and Company* (Toronto: Knopf Canada, 1996), p. 24.

8 Brian Finney, 'Figuring the Real: Ishiguro's *When We Were Orphans*', *Jouvert*, 7, 1 (2002, 26 July 2003), 7. <http://social.chass.ncsu.edu/jouvert/v7is1/ishigu.htm>.

9 Mike Petry, *Narratives of Memory and Identity: the Novels of Kazuo Ishiguro*, Aachen British and American Studies, 12 (Frankfurt: Peter Lang, 1999), p. 134; Barry Lewis, *Kazuo Ishiguro*, Contemporary World Writers Series (Manchester: Manchester University Press, 2000), p. 105; Shaffer, *Understanding*, p. 99.

10 See Shaffer, *Understanding*, p. 91; Finney, 'Figuring the Real', p. 4.

11 Lewis, *Kazuo Ishiguro*, p. 36; Shaffer, *Understanding*, p. 21.

12 Cf. Petry, *Narratives of Memory and Identity*, p. 14, n27.

13 Allan Vorda, 'Stuck on the Margins: an Interview with Kazuo Ishiguro', *Face to Face: Interviews with Contemporary Novelists*, ed. Allan Vorda (Houston: Rice University Press, 1993), pp. 3–35, 16.

14 See Vorda, 'Stuck on the Margins', p. 16.

15 See Wachtel, *More Writers* pp. 25–6; Vorda, 'Stuck on the Margins', pp. 14–15.

16 John Martin McLeod, 'Rewriting History: Postmodern and Postcolonial Negotiations in the Fiction of J. G. Farrell, Timothy Mo, Kazuo Ishiguro, and Salman Rushdie', PhD thesis, University of Leeds, 1995, p. 124; Petry, *Narratives of Memory and Identity*, p. 10.

17 Jean-François Lyotard, *The Postmodern Condition: a Report on Knowledge*, trans. Geoff Bennington and Brian Massumi (Minneapolis: University of Minnesota Press, 1984), p. xxiv.

18 See McLeod, 'Rewriting History', p. 125.

19 Brian W. Shaffer, 'An Interview with Kazuo Ishiguro', *Contemporary Literature*, 42, 1 (2001), 1–14, 4.

20 Brian McHale, *Postmodernist Fiction* (London: Routledge, 1987), p. 10.

21 John Carey, 'Few Novels Extend the Possibilities of Fiction. This One Does', Review of *When We Were Orphans*, *Sunday Times* [London], 2 April 2000, 45.

22 Alden Mudge, 'Ishiguro takes a Literary Approach to the Detective Novel', *Book Page* (September 2000, 10 July 2003). <http://www.bookpage.com/0009bp/kazuo_ishiguro.html>.

23 See Finney, 'Figuring the Real', p. 6.

24 Kazuo Ishiguro, *When We Were Orphans* (2000; rpt. London: Faber, 2001), p. 159.

25 Maya Jaggi, 'In Search of Lost Crimes', Review of *When We Were Orphans*, *The Guardian* (1 April 2000, 7 August 2003), 3. <http://books.guardian.co.uk/bookerprize2000/story/0,377734.00>.

26 See Wong, 'Like Idealism is to the Intellect', p. 319.

27 See Shaffer, 'Interview', p. 9; Wong, 'Like Idealism is to the Intellect', pp. 319–20.

28 See Jessica Chapel, 'A Fugitive Past', *The Atlantic Online* (5 October 2000, 10 July 2003). <http://www.theatlantic.com/unbound/interviews/ba2000-10-05.htm>; Finney, p. 15.

29 See Shaffer, 'Interview', pp. 4–5; Mudge, 'Ishiguro takes a Literary Approach', p. 2.

30 See Shaffer, 'Interview', p. 5.

31 See Jaggi, 'Search', p. 3.

32 Maya Jaggi, 'Kazuo Ishiguro Talks to Maya Jaggi', *Wasafiri*, 22 (1995), 20–4, 22.

33 See Finney, 'Figuring the Real', pp. 8, 12–13.

34 Benjamin Anastas, 'Keeping it Real'. Review of *When We Were Orphans*, *The Village Voice*, 4–10 (October 2000, 10 July 2003), 2. <http://www.villagevoice.com/issues/0040/anastas.php>; Finney, 'Figuring the Real', p. 11.

35 See Shaffer, 'Interview' pp. 5–6; Wong, 'Like Idealism is to the Intellect', p. 321.

36 Fredric Jameson, *The Political Unconscious: Narrative as a Socially Symbolic Act* (Ithaca: Cornell University Press, 1981), p. 102.

2

Ian McEwan: Contemporary Realism and the Novel of Ideas

Judith Seaboyer

My concern in this essay is to further an understanding of Ian McEwan's long fiction by positioning it within the genre of realist fiction in general and the novel of ideas in particular. Of course genres are always already contaminated: speculative and realist modes are conflated in McEwan's *The Child in Time* (1987) and an abstract concept of moral evil suffuses the otherwise realist *Black Dogs* (1992). While recognising this, I will define novelistic realism broadly in terms of a literary historical tradition that goes back to an eighteenth- and nineteenth-century focus on plot- and character-driven narratives, in which psychologically believable individuals function in familiar, everyday worlds rather than in fantastic or allegorical ones. Important generic precursors for McEwan, then, include not only central Modernist realists but, as Jack Slay has noted, the great reformist exponents of nineteenth-century sociopolitical realisms.[1] The novels considered here cross a zone of intellectual inquiry that extends over the last two decades of the twentieth century and into the twenty-first, and I am interested in the acuity with which McEwan observes, explores and analyses evolving contemporary subjects. In turn, those subjects serve as analogies for the public sphere as it is evolving in post-industrial British and European societies. This methodology, together with a finely-tuned ethical sense, and a sense of political urgency, recalls similarly analogical observation, exploration and analysis of subjects and society by Modernist reformists of the genre like Woolf, but also Victorian realists like George Eliot.

Novelistic realism is, as it has been since the time of the Victorian novel of ideas, as productively responsive to social, political and historical contexts as is the genre of the novel itself. It is, then, neither a conservative nor a safe choice of genre, since while realism has traditionally sought to provide an intelligible description of contingent reality, it has also, as George Levine has argued in *The Realistic Imagination*, served as a vehicle for radical investigations of the urgent dilemmas surrounding rapid change, including shifting identities. It observes but it also critiques. This means that McEwan – like Eliot – details both public and private spheres and outer and inner worlds but, and again the comparison with Eliot is apposite, he also scrutinises these spaces, seeking out unmapped parallels and tensions. It goes without saying that the 'ideas' McEwan addresses are different from those addressed in the nineteenth century. But because each period is remarkable for a vertiginous pace of social, economic, political and scientific change, it is often similarities that prove most striking. For example, three particular intertwined motifs and themes he works and reworks are familiar to readers of Victorian realism: the construction of gendered subjectivities; individual and communal ethics and moral responsibility; and the intersection of contemporary scientific knowledge with everyday life and thought. While these themes recur in McEwan's work, there is a marked shift in their deployment that dates from the publication of *The Comfort of Strangers* (1981), which I will argue is his first novel of ideas. In this darkly gothic text, he maintains the very particular psychological realism, expressed in intensely focused explorations of individuals and relationships within a claustrophobic private sphere, that made his early – and controversial – reputation.[2] But he also begins a transition towards a traditional realism in which the private sphere is not only mirrored in that of the public but is a way of addressing broader social and political issues.

The Comfort of Strangers is a sharply visualised realist observation of an uncannily ordinary middle-class, politically aware, thirty-something English couple on holiday in an unnamed labyrinthine city that is clearly Venice. Yet it is Venice as a textualised space, particularly as it is reworked by John Ruskin in *The Stones of Venice* (1851–53) and Thomas Mann in *Death in Venice* (1912). Both these conceptualise the city as a warning of the repercussions of moral decadence. *The Comfort of Strangers* traces Mary and Colin's unconsciously willed movement from sexual ennui to a renewed eroticism. Its foundation is the seemingly playful sadomasochistic fantasies they murmur to each other during lovemaking. But as they are inexorably drawn into a metaphorical labyrinth of 'ancient' gendered behaviours (p. 125) that has monstrosity and death at its heart, it becomes apparent that the fantasies are a screen for something else. At this level, the novel is of a piece with his earliest work, but the shift I have referred to, while 'tentative at this stage' (p. 125), is towards a parallel sociopolitical critique – in this case of the embedded patriarchal violence that McEwan saw as the invisible worm in the bud of a feminist drive towards sexual equality. It speculates that a perplex of cultural sadomasochism has been so entrenched historically and so successfully naturalised in the cultural unconscious that it subtly perverts 'normal' gender relations and consequently every aspect of culture. After Mary has been forced to witness Colin's ritual murder, she struggles to formulate a theory to explain sadomasochism as a counterindicated coevolutionary (biological and cultural) survival, but she loses the thread by which she might guide herself out of the labyrinth. McEwan's text itself is lost for answers, but in posing the question, it makes a 'tentative' move towards understanding. The ungraspable excess of Mary's trauma challenges the reader to bear witness not only to her witnessing but to her struggle through crisis towards recognition, since it is only once the deep historical structures that shape gender relations and render them dysfunctional are fully known that their power may be addressed. This element of McEwan's realism is both an ethical and an essentially dialogic move that, in the light of his later work, may be seen to reflect as much the influence of the biologist and neo-Darwinist Edward O. Wilson as that of Mikhail Bakhtin. McEwan has acknowledged his debt to Wilson, who argues that for the arts as for the sciences, 'asking the right question [may be] more important than producing the right answer', since the right question is an essential part of 'the process of locating new avenues of creative thought'.[3]

McEwan pursues similar avenues of investigation with increasing political force in the works that follow. *The Child in Time* (1987), like *Enduring Love* (1997), addresses the function of contemporary scientific thought in daily life. In each he enters into what Wilson terms the critical 'intellectual adventure' of achieving common ground through the consilience of the sciences and humanities (Wilson, pp. 6–7). *The Child in Time* is set in a slightly futuristic Thatcherite Britain; it may be defined as speculative fiction for this reason, but also because it plays with post-Newtonian ideas of SpaceTime, together with neo-Darwinian thought about the coevolution of biology and culture.[4] Through these means, McEwan contemplates psychoanalytic theories of psychic secrets and transgenerational haunting – a poetics of concealment as it has been theorised by psychoanalysts Abraham and Torok.[5] Intriguingly, he does this less to explore the shattering effects on the subject of the transmission across time and space of unspoken trauma than to explore and understand the transgenerational transmission of secrets that, while traumatic, have more to do with love and the moral responsibility I have linked to realism. At the same time, he interrogates the sociological power of the dead hand of nineteenth-century patriarchal child-rearing practices disingenuously marketed as Victorian family values but whose political purpose is to produce a nation of compliant docile bodies. Again, the experience of the private sphere is adumbrated in the public.

The event that drives the narrative is the unsolved and unbearably painful mystery of three-year-old Kate's abduction, and the resulting breakdown of her parents' relationship. The psychological realism is no less intense than that of *The Comfort of Strangers*, but as Stephen's and Julie's independent processes of mourning gradually succeed the death-like stasis of melancholia, McEwan takes a narrative stand against what he refers to in his novel *Atonement* as 'oblivion and despair'.[6] Love and optimism and new life are allowed to succeed. Causal realism, the way our understanding of reality shapes our sense experience of it, is as important to this narrative as psychological realism. In the course of his grieving, Stephen's perception of 'the changeless grid of time and space'[7] that 'monomaniacally forbids second chances' (p. 14) undergoes a shift. He is supported in his grief by a friend whose profession and passion is 'to reflect and teach' (p. 43) theoretical physics. Thelma extends Stephen's knowledge through 'tales of Schroedinger's cat, backward flowing time . . . and other quantum magic' (p. 43), enabling him to extend his 'peripheral vision'.[8] He begins to understand post-Newtonian SpaceTime in ways that help make sense of his lived reality. He undergoes hallucinatory experiences in which time is neither one-dimensional nor irreversible, and Thelma confirms that 'whatever time is, the commonsense everyday version of it as linear, regular, absolute . . . is either nonsense or a tiny fraction of the truth' (p. 117). The speculative element of the novel and its realism become difficult to separate: for all that we know relativity to be reality, we continue to perceive the world in Newtonian terms. *The Child in Time* is not science fiction; there is no question of the kind of 'second chance' that would see Stephen travelling through SpaceTime in order to alter the sequence of events that led to Kate's abduction. However, something very like time travel enables a second chance more familiar to novelistic realism. In one of his experiences of the bending of SpaceTime, Stephen undergoes a phylogenetic journey during which, conceived but as yet unborn, he observes his courting parents and, as he learns later, is observed simultaneously by his newly pregnant mother. The experience leads, eventually, to a redemptive understanding of a shared sociobiological history, and Stephen is able to occupy a SpaceTime that is haunted by his parents' love for each other and for him, his and Julie's love for each other, and the love they all have for the lost child. A more immediate effect is that as Stephen emerges from this hallucinatory experience, he risks his self-absorbed melancholia by making love to his estranged wife. He is aware that he and Julie are standing 'before the forking paths' (p. 63) where not only space but '[t]ime forks perpetually toward innumerable futures',[9] and 'that what was happening now, and what would happen as a consequence of now, was not separate from what he had experienced earlier that day' (p. 63). They are at one with each other and with 'biology, existence, matter' (p. 65) while they make love, but afterwards the vivid pain of Kate's loss causes them to retreat and by 'a perverse collusion in unhappiness, many months passed before they saw each other again' (p. 67). However, when they do meet, it is to experience reconciliation and the 'consequence' that is the birth of their second child. The baby is not a replacement but a repetition with a difference of the biological mystery of love and changeful continuity that signals a shift away from melancholia.

As I have noted, the role of science in society is a familiar theme in Victorian realism, although the kind of interdisciplinarity Wilson advocates and McEwan practises was, while challenging to the nineteenth-century world-view, more readily accepted. Not only were the sciences and what we have come to call the humanities less demarcated, but the revolution in perception that accompanied the development of evolutionary theory required a less specialised knowledge than does, say, quantum mechanics. Science was an object of public interest and concern, and what Freud recognised as the biological blow to 'the universal narcissism of men'[10] delivered by Darwinian theory was a topic of ardent debate in journals and newspapers. It was entered into by lay people as well as scientists and informed every aspect of society. In one of many literary examples, the social implications of evolutionary theory in general and Darwinian natural selection in particular become an essential part of the web that structures *Middlemarch* (1871–2).[11] Seeing McEwan's incorporation of contemporary scientific theory in the light of Eliot's consilient realism allows us to see *The Child in Time* as as closely allied to the literary history of realism as it is to that of speculative fiction.

Few readers of *The Innocent* (1989), McEwan's Cold War espionage thriller,[12] could forget the jarring juxtaposition of realism and surreal grotesque horror – and blackest comedy – that marks his English protagonist's 'innocent' complicity in the politics of private and public spheres. A struggle for power played out in the private sphere has uncanny resonances with the Great Game as it is being played out in occupied Berlin. In the name of democracy the Western Allies are teamed against the Soviets and the Cold War bugbear of communism, though the text foregrounds an even less innocent Anglo-American struggle for influence in Europe. Within the private sphere, the relentlessly realist peripeteia is a markedly unheroic fight between Leonard Marnham, the English protagonist, and Otto, a German ex-army sergeant. As the narrative develops it becomes clear that this fight, which ends in Otto's death and dismemberment, is a metaphor for the unheroic brutality exercised not only by the Third Reich but also by the Allies against civilian populations. And the bludgeoned and anatomised corpse of a corrupt, vicious and humiliated German veteran, divided between two suitcases for ease of disposal, is a telling figure for systematically carpet-bombed and defeated Berlin, parcelled out into Eastern and Western sectors.

The centre of consciousness is a twenty-five-year-old Post Office technician whisked from his parents' home in Tottenham to Berlin, where his electronics wizardry is to be put to use in the CIA–MI6 surveillance of Soviet communications. Leonard's first impressions of Germany in 1955 bring a visceral surge of patriotic pride that the narrative voice stresses it would have been 'impossible' to avoid. Within the prevailing discourses of power the nascent aggression of this shy, naïve man is not to be thought of as unusual. A product of the war and its propaganda, and ignorant of the suffering experienced by German non-combatants, he walks the pleasant reconstructed streets 'with a certain proprietorial swagger, as though his feet beat out the rhythms of a speech by Mr Churchill' (pp. 5–6). In this euphoric state he plunges into his first affair. For all that his love and respect for Maria are genuine, the aura of mastery that shapes his relation to the city is displaced onto her. A chain of linguistic associations ironically conflates the rhythms of Leonard's streetwalking and his lovemaking; in a trope as old as literature, city and woman are topographies to be mapped and subdued. In bed, Maria becomes 'German. Enemy. Mortal enemy. Defeated enemy' to Leonard's 'victorious and good and strong and free' (p. 93). He ingenuously imagines it is harmless to render her 'defeated' rather than 'liberated' (pp. 93–4), because it is only sexual play. He is oblivious to the disparity between their wartime experiences. He had been fourteen on VE Day and had followed the war from the safety of 'a Welsh village over which no enemy aircraft had ever flown' (p. 5), while Maria had been a young woman of twenty when the Russians liberated Berlin. By the time the lovers meet, she has survived sixteen years of war and occupation, the Blockade and the subsequent division of her city into two occupied zones, as well as a violent marriage, and divorce.

Leonard and Maria's psychosexual struggle leads to the scuffle that begins somewhere between bedroom farce and nightmare, and ends in Otto's gruesome murder. The horror lies less in the explicit description of the fight than in the efforts of the lovers to disguise their unintentional crime. First comes the precisely detailed dismemberment of Otto's body, and then Leonard's nightmare criss-crossing of the city, dragging the mutilated corpse in its two suitcases. Where he had swaggered, he now staggers under the concrete reality of his guilt, afraid of every passer-by. Forced to store the suitcases in his flat overnight, he falls into an exhausted sleep and in a 'waking dream' re-members the body-in-bits-and-pieces. But Leonard is no longer an innocent; unlike Shelley's Frankenstein, he knows even before he begins that all he can hope to produce is an embittered vengeful monster.

Sociologist Kai Erikson argues that 'trauma has . . . a social dimension' (p. 185): the shattering of communal bonds that is an effect of a blow inflicted on 'the basic tissues of social life' (p. 187) is no less far-reaching than that inflicted on the tissues of the individual body or psyche.[13] While trauma in the form of sexual violence, bloody murder, dismemberment and clandestine burial are the gothic-realist turning point for McEwan's narrative, it provides an elaborate extended metaphor for the kind of collective trauma Erikson outlines. In a *tour de force* illustrative of his consummate linguistic and narrative skill, McEwan goes some way towards addressing the questions surrounding patriarchal violence and its influence across private and public spheres that he raised in *The Comfort of Strangers*. A similar link may be made to his interrogation of the effects of a lack of imagination that finds its expression in an innocent patriotism that in its willed misreading of history is at best complicit in individual and national derelictions of moral and ethical responsibility.

Leonard flees Berlin in 1956, but a final coda redevelops the main composition. It is 1987. After thirty years' silence, recently widowed Maria has written to him from her home in Iowa, and the memories this triggers lead to his return to the scene of the crime. Once more, public and private spheres cunningly mirror each other, as rumours that the Berlin Wall is to be dismantled and the city reunified reveal the latent content of Leonard's long-ago overdetermined dream of the dangers of putting Otto together again. The buildings have been levelled, but the site of the surveillance operation remains a material repository of the past. Leonard lowers himself into the 'huge hole' that is all that remains, wondering what he expects to find: 'Evidence of his own existence?' (p. 261). On resurfacing, Maria's recollections and explanations that began this process fall into place. The experience realises Freud's archaeological analogy in which he likens his analysis of a hysteric to the excavation of 'a buried city' from which must be cleared 'pathogenic psychical material layer by layer' until 'a completely adequate set of determinants for the events concerned' is brought to light.[14] Older and wiser, Leonard plans his flight to Iowa, but the coda is ambiguous. Leonard has developed a heart condition and his struggle through the sticky heat recalls both his innocent youthful flânerie and the nightmare struggle to dispose of Otto's body. The novel ends with a wistful sense of belatedness that troubles individual and national dreams of reconciliation.

Black Dogs (1992)[15] circles around the two incommensurable questions which Geoffrey Galt Harpham notes 'dominate ethical inquiry' and are central, too, to the literary history of realism: 'How ought one live? and What ought I to do [in the situation I face at this moment]?'[16] Such shaping ideas may be traced through much of McEwan's *oeuvre*, but the intersection with *The Innocent* is particularly clear. Its realist focus is the repercussions of the Second World War (though there is a shift to the sociopathology of fascism) and in ethical terms it continues the problematisation of notions of innocence and complicity by means of a disquisition on the nature of evil. The dismantling of the Wall foreshadowed in *The Innocent* is witnessed two years later, in 1989, by *Black Dogs*' English narrator, Jeremy. The final section shifts back to Europe in 1946, with his recounting of the event that has haunted the narrative: his mother-in-law's transformative confrontation with the dogs. Further, *The Innocent*'s coda foregrounds a pressing moral urgency to remember; *Black Dogs*, as a fictional biography-turned-memoir-turned-'divagation' (p. 37), self-reflexively addresses contemporary anxieties surrounding the creation of coherent and stable personal and communal narratives from mis-remembered fragments of the past.[17] It is also about the ways in which the past infects the psychic and material present of individuals and of communities.

The generic contamination of this otherwise realist novel occurs, then, at the level of ideas. Moral evil, nebulous, resistant to interpretation, is symbolised by two enormous feral ex-Gestapo guard dogs abandoned in the countryside in the South of France in 1944 when the Germans were forced north to face the allied landings in Normandy. Two years later, half-starved and harbouring open sores, they stalk and attack a young Englishwoman as she walks alone on a deserted path in the Languedoc. For all their abject materiality, they embody and encode an uncanny menace that '[emanates] meaning' (p. 144) like an image from a medieval tableau. June expects to die, but through an unexpected and unrepresentable 'Presence' (p. 150) she conceptualises as God, she discovers the strength to drive the dogs off. They retreat, their mythic menace reduced to piteous yelping, but there is no suggestion that their defeat is other than temporary. Whether the repressed evil the weakened animals represent is a persistent trace that 'lives in us all' (p. 172) or whether its physical origins have their source in social inequities, the narrator, like June, concludes it 'will return to haunt us' (p. 174).

The contemporary dilemmas addressed in Jeremy's memoir of his mother-in-law include how we process and how we represent personal and public histories. But as the genre becomes unstable, as the focus digresses from the willed concretisation of 'the life' to the struggle to conceptualise the abstractions that have shaped that life, it becomes, too, Jeremy's means of confessing himself. He does so by means of an interrogation of the grand narratives of scepticism and faith as oppositional and equally unprovable absolutist belief systems, each of which functions as a means of sense-making, and as a law that provides an ethical foundation for a moral existence. The unconventional intellectual and philosophical positions of his parents-in-law seem rather simplistically conventionally gendered in that Bernard operates according to reason and June according to feeling; broadly, he is a historical-materialist, while she insists on the role of a spirituality that exists outside of material relations. In the context of McEwan's *oeuvre*, however, in which the feminine position is noticeably privileged, June's position might also be seen as contributing to a feminist redefinition of both the grand narrative of Christianity and male-dominated ethics. Jeremy outlines the couple's mutually exclusive positions and relates them to his own postmodern case: 'Rationalist and mystic, commissar and yogi, joiner and abstainer, scientist and intuitionist, Bernard and June are the extremities, the twin poles along whose slippery axis my own unbelief slithers and never comes to rest' (p. 19). When Jeremy is with Bernard, he feels June holds the key to what is 'missing from [Bernard's sceptical] account of the world' in which 'too much was closed off, too much denied.' When he's with June, he feels stifled by the 'unstated assumption . . . that faith is virtue, and, by extension, unbelief is unworthy or, at best, pitiable' (pp. 19–20). Yet he views his own atomised position as bereft: 'there was simply no good cause, no enduring principle, no fundamental idea with which I could identify, no transcendent entity whose existence I could truthfully, passionately or quietly assert' (p. 18). As he concludes his narrative, the ghostly presences of his parents-in-law put their closing arguments. June insists we each contain the potential for an evil practised in the private sphere that periodically erupts into nationalist hatred, and that until we address that, 'the sum of our misery will never diminish. . . . Without a revolution of the inner life, however slow, all our big designs are worthless' (172–3). Bernard retorts: 'Try having [an inner life] on an empty stomach. Or without clean water. . . . You see, the way things are going on this overcrowded little planet, we *do* need a set of ideas, and bloody good ones too!' (p. 173). By the end of his narrative, Jeremy not only remains unable to identify with either discourse, but has experienced at first hand the incommensurability of an overall system of ethics with the individual moral act. In the face of a specific instance of the unquestionable evil of child abuse, Jeremy challenges and pummels the abuser. As readers, we cheer, but immediately that personal moral choice is deconstructed. The binary opposition of good and evil collapses as Jeremy 'slithers' from the pole of avenging hero to that of murderous bully, and so is reminded 'that every (moral) choice in an ethical situation chooses against other alternatives' (Harpham, p. 398).

With *Atonement* (2001) the ethics of representation are even more strongly foregrounded than they are in, say, *Black Dogs*, or *Amsterdam* (1998).[18] As a thirteen-year-old, Briony Tallis insists, despite her own uncertainties, that she has witnessed the rape of her fifteen-year-old cousin by Robbie Turner. The Tallis family's cleaner's son, Robbie has grown up at once part of and not part of the household. Recognising his potential, Jack Tallis has paid for his education, and in 1935 he has just come down from Oxford with the best first in his year. He has plans for a degree in medicine, and he and Briony's older sister, Cecilia, are in the process of realising they are in love. Because of Briony's evidence, and because of her society's embedded class antagonism, Robbie and the life he has lived and the future he has been imagining into existence are 'vanished' as surely as if Briony had lobbed a literal rather than a metaphorical bomb (p. 202). Gaoled for three years, he is granted an early release to join the army as a private. In what seems the most likely of two versions of what follows, he dies during the retreat to Dunkirk, his and Cecilia's epistolary love affair becoming a figure for the endless deferral of desire. As the paratextual afterword reveals, Briony becomes a famous novelist, and *Atonement*, completed sixty-four years after her crime, is her last work. It is an effort to atone, to return to an originary state of at-one-ness with Robbie and Cecilia. She uses her authorial power to research and imagine into reality Robbie's life in prison and in France. Further, she writes her 'spontaneous, fortuitous sister and her medical prince' into literary immortality, using her Prospero-like power to 'conjure' comedy from tragedy. In the place of 'pitiless' 'bleakest realism,' (pp. 370–1) she inscribes comedy and consummation of bodily desire.

The afterword acts as a kind of exegesis of the text as writing, but from the first page, indeed from the epigraph, *Atonement*'s position in the literary history of realism is signalled by a vast chorus of canonical realist texts. It is not surprising, then, that the question of living an ethical life is central, but a number of allusions are even more to McEwan's point in that they are to novels about novel-writing and novel-reading. Richardson's *Clarissa* (1747–48), Austen's *Northanger Abbey* (1818) and Nabokov's *Lolita* (1955), for example, each underscores *Atonement*'s burning ethical questions: How (and what) ought one write? And how ought one read?

Atonement is performative in that while it is about the main character's desire to return to a state of 'at-one-ness', at the same time it *is* her act of atonement. However, the meaning of any performative utterance depends on its felicity, its appropriateness in context. The question becomes whether Briony's *Atonement* is simply an act of bad faith, or an act of love, or both, and whether the victims of her crime would have countenanced her efforts. From this perspective, Briony's use of an effaced third-person narration and free indirect discourse are problematised. Her desire to atone is complicated by her desire to arouse in us desire for her narrative. Part Two is exemplary of that seduction. Her moving identification with the mind of the man who was her victim is an atoning act of love and respect. But is it also a violation, a colonisation? If we as readers are seduced, if we are so immersed in the pleasure of the world Briony invents that, forgetting our literary training, we suspend disbelief and cheerfully disavow any distance between text and reality, do we risk becoming 'victims' of the text? Of course not; since Robbie, and indeed Briony, are fictions, there can be no violation – and yet. The process of being drawn into Briony's/McEwan's doubled narrative[19] is a little like the process of being seduced by the attractions of Milton's Satan, and thus, as Stanley Fish has argued, experiencing in small the seduction and fall of humanity. As we have seen, McEwan's realism holds up a nicely polished mirror to show us reality, but with *Atonement* he allows us to experience the ethics of writing and reading that reality.

FOR FURTHER READING

For a hard copy list of Ian McEwan's work up to 2001, see *Contemporary Novelists*, ed. David Madden et al., 7th edn (New York: St James Press, 2001). For a more up-to-date list on the internet, see the British Council website: <http://www.contemporarywriters.com/authors/>.

Levine, George, *The Realistic Imagination* (Chicago: University of Chicago Press, 1981).
McEwan, Ian, 'Interview with Jonathan Noakes', in Margaret Reynolds and Jonathan Noakes, *Ian McEwan: the Essential Guide* (London: Vintage, 2002).
Morrison, Jago, 'Unravelling Time in Ian McEwan's Fiction', in *Contemporary Fiction* (London: Routledge, 2003), pp. 67–79.
Slay, Jack, Jnr., *Ian McEwan* (New York: Twayne, 1996).
Wilson, Edward O., *Consilience: the Unity of Knowledge* (1998; rpt. London: Abacus, Little, Brown, 2001).

NOTES

1 Jack Slay, Jnr., *Ian McEwan* (New York: Twayne, 1996), p. 4. Modernism, a movement extending from late in the nineteenth century until some way

into the twentieth (how far into the twentieth is a matter of controversy), is characterised in part by formal innovation in literature and the other arts. For a good introduction to Modernism, see *Modernism: 1890–1930*, ed. Malcolm Bradbury and James McFarlane (1976; rpt. Harmondsworth: Penguin, 1991).

2 *The Comfort of Strangers* (1981; rpt. London: Picador, 1982). All quotations are from this edition; page numbers are given in the text. Two volumes of short stories (*First Love, Last Rites* [1975] and *In Between the Sheets* [1978]), and a first novel (*The Cement Garden* [1978]), preceded *The Comfort of Strangers*. Critically admired but widely condemned as obsessively perverse and violent, they gained McEwan the difficult-to-shake nickname 'Ian Macabre'.

3 See the Acknowledgements to *Enduring Love* (1997).

4 *The Child in Time* (1987; rpt. London: Vintage, 1992). All quotations are from the 1992 edition; page numbers are given in the text.

5 Nicolas Abraham and Maria Torok, *The Shell and the Kernel: Renewals of Psychoanalysis* (Chicago: University of Chicago Press, 1994). See especially sections IV and V.

6 *Atonement* (2001; rpt. London: Vintage, 2002). All quotations are from this edition; page numbers are given in the text.

7 Jonathan Boyarin, 'Space, Time, and the Politics of Memory', in *Remapping Memory: the Politics of TimeSpace* (Minneapolis and London: University of Minnesota Press, 1994), pp. 1–37, 6.

8 Ibid.

9 Jorge Luis Borges, 'The Garden of Forking Paths', in *Labyrinths: Selected Stories and Other Writings*, ed. Donald A. Yates and James E. Irby (New York: New Directions, 1964), pp. 19–29, 28.

10 Sigmund Freud, quoted in Gillian Beer, *Darwin's Plots: Evolutionary Narrative in Darwin, George Eliot and Nineteenth-Century Fiction*, 2nd edn (Cambridge: Cambridge University Press, 2000), p. 8.

11 See Beer, *Darwin's Plots*, Chapter 5.

12 *The Innocent* (1989; rpt. New York: Doubleday, 1990). All quotations are from this edition; page numbers are given in the text.

13 Kai Erikson, 'Notes on Trauma and Community', in *Trauma: Explorations in Memory*, ed. Cathy Caruth (Baltimore: Johns Hopkins University Press, 1995), pp. 183–99.

14 Sigmund Freud, 'Case 5', Josef Breuer and Sigmund Freud, *Studies on Hysteria. The Penguin Freud Library*, ed. and trans. James and Alix Strachey, vol. 3 (London: Penguin, 1974), pp. 206–7.

15 *Black Dogs* (1992; rpt. Toronto: Vintage, 1993). All quotations are from this edition; page numbers are given in the text.

16 Geoffrey Galt Harpham, 'Ethics', in *Critical Terms for Literary Study*, 2nd edn, ed. Frank Lentricchia and Thomas McLaughlin (Chicago: University of Chicago Press, 1995), pp. 387–405, 395.

17 See Jago Morrison, 'Unravelling Time in Ian McEwan's Fiction', in *Contemporary Fiction* (London: Routledge, 2003), pp. 75–9.

18 In five of McEwan's eight novels for adults, a central character is directly involved in writing or publishing. In *The Child in Time*, Stephen is a successful author of children's books; Jeremy is a publisher working on a memoir (*Black Dogs*); Jo is a science writer (*Enduring Love*); and Vernon Halliday is a newspaper man (*Amsterdam*).

19 McEwan has said of Briony that she is 'the most complete person I'd ever *conjured*' (Quoted in Noakes Interview, Reynolds and Noakes, *Ian McEwan*, p. 23; italics mine).

3

The Unnatural Scene: The Fiction of Irvine Welsh

Alan Riach

Behold, the heavens do ope,
The gods look down, and this unnatural scene
They laugh at.

Shakespeare, Coriolanus, V. iii

The opening paragraph of *Trainspotting* (1993) delivers unsuspecting readers to a domestic crisis of interpersonal, bodily, junk media-saturated, jargon-filled, freshly minted unnaturalness. Tension is high:

> The sweat wis lashing oafay Sick Boy; he wis trembling. Ah wis jist sitting thair, focusing oan the telly, tryin no tae notice the cunt. He wis bringing me doon. Ah tried tae keep ma attention oan the Jean-Claude Van Damme video.[1]

Who is being addressed here? What intimacies of care and sensitivity are being disclosed by this voice? How does the language convey the inured weariness of the character alongside his spontaneity and vitality? The atmosphere is febrile: physical debility, mental focus and the deliberate choice of cultural activity (watching an action movie on video), all suggest limitations of possibility yet every word speaks of energetic selection. Even the sweat seems energised. What sort of realism is this, if realism is the word?

The answer to the first question is plain enough: the reader. But the last question poses problems. Realism is normally associated with a depiction of reality, specific characters in social situations and relationships, presented as if through a transparent frame or focus. Developing through the nineteenth century alongside naturalism in theatre and figurative representation in painting, from Millet to Diego Rivera, realism in prose fiction held up for the reader's apprehension the secure contemplation of a reality fixed by a stable text. The great nineteenth-century classic realist novels – of which *Middlemarch* is a paradigmatic example – endorse this stability even as they describe or indicate change. The key characteristic of Modernism, a movement that lasted from the end of the nineteenth century until some time around the middle of the twentieth, was a disruption of this security through a disintegrated text where the reader's vantage point was no longer fixed but challenged, by the text itself.[2] The fiction of Irvine Welsh offsets the mimetic representation of reality by combining two apparently contradictory modes: an immediate vernacular voice, ostensibly an authentic representation of location-specific speech, and a narrative where unpalatable basic realities of economic and bodily imperatives are paramount.

To return, however, to the first question posed above, Welsh implicates the reader from the start. The reader's position is not one of mere contemplation but of linguistic, moral and social complicity. Therefore, while the subject of his writing – people in conditions of social squalor and economic poverty – connects Welsh to a long European tradition in the novel whose early epitome is Emile Zola, nevertheless Welsh's self-conscious linguistic technique derives from both Modernist experimentalism and the question of language in modern Scottish literature. The degree of self-awareness in Welsh's writing offsets any simple sense of linguistic verisimilitude in the novel's medium and drives itself further, into the entire Welsh phenomenon. We are not simply overhearing a character's voice or interior monologue. Rather, the voice assumes complicity in the reader. It is as if the character is both acting in a play and addressing the audience directly, at the same time. Vulnerability, fellow-feeling, selfishness, sympathy: all are evoked here and readers are responsive to a shared sense of culpable desire. The insinuating suggestiveness of that address runs right through all Irvine Welsh's fiction and inspires the popularity of his reception and readership. More than a decade after this debut, his hour at the Edinburgh International Book Festival in 2004 was sold out. In October that year, he was being referred to unironically in *The Herald* newspaper's Saturday magazine as 'the world's hippest author'.[3]

Welsh's language has its essential charm. In the paragraph quoted above, the elisions between writing and speech are evident: 'wis' is mimetic of pronunciation, as is 'Ah' for 'I', 'jist' for 'just' and 'tryin' drops the final 'g'. But 'lashing', 'trembling' and 'focusing' keep the standard spelling and 'thair' gives a visual reminder of the speaker's voice. It seems to offer no difference in sound from 'there' but say it out loud and it whines a little bit more, the tone implies self-righteousness, an appeal for sympathy, helpless sympathetic insight into Sick Boy's condition and a sense of responsibility. This language itself, and the narrator who uses it, are not without a sense of kinship and common humanity. The charm of this blend of fluency and quasi-eccentricity (it is both individuated and, as the book unfolds, the language of a community) is undeniable.

But the Scots language itself is a kind of rebarbative diction, full of ochs and achs, velar fricatives. To speak the tongue you have to use your tongue and throat and saliva – your body goes to work. It stands against the Latinate cerebral English of eighteenth-century gentility or the received pronunciation of the old BBC or the high nasal diction of condescending British politicians of whatever flag. Even without velar fricatives, the Scots tongue can sound harsh while yet capable of subtlety in nuance and tone. Alison

Kermack's poem 'Askinfurrit' is quick and clever, with fierce, combative intelligence: the poet is reading a newspaper article about 'whit iz / an whit izny / rape' when the doorbell rings:

> ah oapind thi doar
> an thi gy
> standin thare sayz
> yes?
>
> ah sayz
> wate a minnit
> yoo rang thi bell
>
> he sayz
> yoo oapind thi doar
> whidjy wont?[4]

The best poetry in Scots, say by William Dunbar, Robert Fergusson, Robert Burns or Hugh MacDiarmid, all moves with a quickness distinct from the magniloquent tradition of rhetorical English verse by, for example, Milton, Wordsworth, Derek Walcott or Ted Hughes. Speed is of its essence. A physical, bodily exhilaration is characteristic of Scots poetry. In Welsh's fiction, the narrative idiom embodies this quality of speed.

The question of language was at the heart of the debate about Scottish literature in the conflict joined between Hugh MacDiarmid and Edwin Muir in 1936, when, in his book *Scott and Scotland*, Muir famously evangelised the only future he saw for Scottish literature lying in the use of English, thus following the example of the great modern Irish writers Joyce and Yeats.[5] MacDiarmid's opposition to this was to emphasise the political validity of all forms of articulation in the arts – in any language, idiom, speech or form. Scots, Gaelic and English were all equally appropriate for artistic fashioning in literary work. His emphasis on the variety and validity of different voices has enhanced the authority with which post-Second World War Scottish writers – novelists and playwrights as much as poets – have been able not only to inhabit the characters and tonalities of their writing but also to foreground aggressively democratic idealism, from Welsh's Leith to Edwin Morgan's rhetorically self-conscious poem for the official opening of the reconvened Scottish parliament building, on 9 October 2004.

The notoriety achieved by the novels of James Kelman since winning the Booker Prize in 1994, for a sophisticated piece of literary fiction which uses the language that made Billy Connolly popular, has been followed by Irvine Welsh. This language is undeniably funny and wonderfully charged with angry energy. What is this charge? Where does this energy come from?

It is not from the subjects alone. Conditions of squalor, acts of indecency, morally repugnant behaviour, all these are described without the glamour of fantasy. If this implies a realist attention to social conditions, the literary artifice – typographical play – and experimental narration (for example, by the tapeworm, in *Filth*) counter the conscientious attention to social fact. Surreal realignments make the social point more forceful: international media stars speaking in broad Leith Scots voices ogle glossy magazines featuring stories about life in the housing schemes, speculate whether they might manage to holiday in Leith, in 'Where the Debris Meets the Sea', in *The Acid House* (1994). Story-telling through the principal character's dreams and nightmares, in *Marabou Stork Nightmares* (1995), departs from descriptions of the waking day. Nocturnal activities in unsteady light are normal practice in Welsh's fiction. None of these technical modes, narrative devices and contexts adheres to conventional canons of realism. Approaching Irvine Welsh's fiction with the idiom of its language and the slant of its address allows us to trace its trajectory in a vernacular tradition distinct from other aspects of the modern British novel and the realist tradition both in England and Scotland.

In *Trainspotting*, the main characters are a group of drug addicts whose disintegrating lives focus the narrative. The complexity of their interests and desires is depicted with brilliant economy, flair, humour and a serious acknowledgement of ethical questions. Spiritual cousins to *Pulp Fiction*, the notorious 1994 film written and directed by Quentin Tarantino, the characters of Irvine Welsh live in a world that is funny, violent, real, full of risk and hopeless precautions, generally disastrous but profoundly assertive, a truly gross barbaric yawp: a triumph of language. Though the American veneer of glamour is exposed more brutally as a flaky cosmetic sham, Welsh is not given to pessimism. In *Trainspotting*, a sub-chapter is entitled, 'Scotland Takes Drugs in Psychic Defence' – the stance is a familiar one: doomed but defiant.

Trainspotting was a wonderfully unpredicted debut. His second novel, *Marabou Stork Nightmares*, was beginning to look more insistently for ways to escalate the shock and scourge, and more or less succeeded, with child abuse, sodomy and rape, a brutalised and comatose narrator, upon whom a bitter moral revenge is enacted by one of his victims. Yet the targets of Welsh's satire, if apt, are easy: the hypocrisy of being straight, the sacred cow of piety, the falseness of the social order, the pretensions of stupidity. The sweeping judgement is that in the West, in the late twentieth century, drugs are humanity's context: drink, TV, film, work, careerism. Citation of James Bond and John Buchan's South African adventurer Richard Hannay, icons of reaction and conservatism, effects a reverse-colonisation of their significance. They are decadent heroes in an increasingly commercialised and heartless world, whose weave of distinctive national identity somehow effects a resistence to the Anglocentric hegemony and endorses the local affirmations Welsh's characters – even at their most wounded – vigorously enact.

At the heart of *Trainspotting* is the explanation of a defensive national strategy. Doomed and self-aware the main characters might be, but their insight and knowledge empower them to choose their own methods of self-destruction, rejecting the urge to accept the given: 'Choose mortgage payments; choose washing machines; choose cars . . . . Choose rotting away, pishing and shiteing yersel in a home, a total fuckin embarrassment tae the selfish, fucked-up brats ye've produced. Choose life' (p. 187). So far the sentiments might apply generally, but Welsh is explicit about not only the local but the national contexts: 'Some say that the Irish are the trash ay Europe. That's shite. It's the Scots. The Irish hud the bottle tae win their country back, or at least maist ay it' (p. 190). Intercutting the narrator's voice with that of his father and the voices from a television games show, Welsh dramatically highlights the contrasts between them: 'Scotland's goat eight per cent o the UK population but sixteen per cent o the UK HIV cases . . . *What's the scores, Miss Ford?* . . .' (p. 193).

Deplorable in some ways some may be, but all the characters in Welsh's *Trainspotting*, at some level, engage the reader's sympathy. The same cannot be said for Bruce Robertson, the central figure in *Filth* (1998), who is advertised on the back cover of the first edition as 'one of the most corrupt, misanthropic characters in contemporary fiction' – a careerist Edinburgh policeman whose worsening itchy skin disease around his chokingly malodorous genitalia speedily spreads in tandem with his vertiginous downward spiral of abuse of self and others. The hungry appetite for this abuse is almost all that keeps him going. Two tapeworms inhabiting his gut interrupt the text (literally) to disclose Bruce's childhood traumas and lament the mean and miserable state of his present existence. Yet again, the language is exuberant but the balance between sensationalism and the kind of compassion commanded in *Trainspotting* is tipped. The clever targeting of hypocrisy, as vicious careerism links with political correctness to outsmart Bruce's more straightforwardly vulgar violence does not exonerate *Filth* from exploiting its own lurid excesses. Behind it the spirit of Alex, Beethoven-loving thug in Anthony Burgess's novella *A Clockwork Orange* (1962) and Stanley Kubrick's film of the same name (1971), casts a cold eye.

In *Glue* (2001) and *Porno* (2002) Welsh returns to the arena of *Trainspotting* but has taken into account his own position, age and time over the decade since his debut. This creates a different sense of perspective, a heightened desperation in some of the characters, more careful tactics of evasion and self-preservation in others. *Glue* over-extends itself and the assertion of values of friendship and loyalty becomes sentimental and cloying, despite Welsh's efforts to offset it by varying the locations of the story and exploring the ironically self-serving aspects of the main characters' motivations. In the end, its build-up of emotional investment thins the characterisation and clogs the narrative verve. Tension wanes. The novel sags. However, the pace picks up in the self-consciously careful plotting of *Porno*, which reunites the characters from his first book, taking account of popular perception of them through the international success of the film version of the earlier book.

There is another problem though. The ambivalence of Welsh's exploitation of sensationalism is most evident in *Porno*. The depiction of women raises unanswered questions. Are we convinced that Welsh's writing is hard enough to depict the brutalisation of his characters without merely appealing to facile gratification? Is Welsh self-consciously progressive or does the extent of exploitation of sensationalism in *Porno* compromise its sense of indignation? The question admits no easy answer. (It is similarly vexed with reference to Alasdair Gray's novel *1982 Janine* (1984), where pornographic fantasy is also a major component, or to the depiction of the working-class world in William MacIlvanney's *Docherty* (1975), where reactionary family stereotypes are shown to endorse humanitarian values and a sexist society is presented as a location in which social ideals can nevertheless be fostered.) Authorial intentions are never enough to go on and in areas as socially volatile as those entered into in *Porno*, the co-ordinates are unreliable. Welsh is clearly enjoying his presentation of the making of pornographic films and the lurid pleasures of leering anticipation and fleshy engagement are described with at least as much involvement as irony. This is as true of his presentation of women as of men.

Women in Welsh's fiction are more strictly delimited by the directives of plot and their relationships with men than by their own character and motivation. The strongest of them – Dianne in *Trainspotting* and *Porno* for example – is attractive because of her cool self-determination, but the writing presents her (again, attractively, through juxtaposition of apparent vulnerability with evidence of self-assurance), predominantly from Renton's point of view. It is no great criticism of Welsh that his men are more convincing than his women but it suggests the limitations not only of the genres he is exploiting but of the ethos of social indignation he evokes. This is not feminist fiction. The priorities of his social vision marginalise the experiences of women. Mothers, girlfriends, lovers, victims, revengers, their roles are defined by the male protagonists. This is one of the worst aspects of *Marabou Stork Nightmares*, where the vengeance enacted by the raped woman upon the narrator seems entirely formulated in a moralistic scheme, not to emerge from her character but to be dictated entirely by the role Welsh requires her to play in the novel's trajectory.

This also is familiar enough in realist fiction, where social roles are often depicted according to masculinist priorities and strong women are shown pushing against such imperatives. Zola's *Nana* (1880), shockingly (if to our reading, discreetly), represents the life of a French prostitute, and the great women of nineteenth-century literature – Ibsen's Hedda Gabler in the naturalist play of that title (1890), Tolstoy's *Anna Karenina* (1873–7), Flaubert's *Madame Bovary* (1856–7), Kate Chopin's Edna Pontellier in *The Awakening* (1899), even Wagner's Brunnhilde and Sieglinde before her, in *The Ring* cycle of operas (1876) – all drive themselves against the priorities and orders of masculinist society and push the limits of social realist representation in work which, in its time, succeeded in discomforting – indeed, shocking – its readers.

We can trace another line of ancestry from Welsh back through punk rock. To paraphrase Steve Watts and Steve Xerri, punk rock was a release of dark energies, a feast of inversion in which all the positive, socially proper values of youth – freedom from cares, beauty, innocence, and so on – were transformed into parodic carelessness, incomprehensible canons of attractiveness, and a knowingness that transcended sexual precociousness and became a sort of gestural ennui: a scary carnival.[6]

This connects further back to Welsh's most distinguished predecessor in Scottish fiction, Alexander Trocchi, whose novels *Young Adam* (1954) and *Cain's Book* (1961) presented existentialist anti-heroes in a steadily glittering style, melding the outrageous shock of William Burroughs with the bitter clarity of Samuel Beckett. Unlike Burroughs, Beckett or indeed Welsh, Trocchi's fiction spurns humour. It is calculated and chill. Yet the kinship is clear and has been acknowledged by Welsh himself. It is underlined by the fact that the actor Ewan MacGregor played both Welsh's Renton, in the film of *Trainspotting*, and Trocchi's Joe, in the film of *Young Adam* (2003). Welsh notes, 'Trocchi was an empowering figure for those trying to escape the shackles of Scottishness. These tedious nationalistic issues that every Scottish writer is supposed to engage in are so limiting. . . . Trocchi was a much more appropriate role model because of his internationalist lifestyle and his attack upon Scottish parochialism.'[7]

Welsh is referring to the confrontation between Trocchi and Hugh MacDiarmid at the Edinburgh Festival of 1962, when Trocchi said, 'Of what is interesting in Scottish writing in the past 20 years or so, I myself have written it all.'[8] Increasingly, however, the opposition between Trocchi and MacDiarmid seems like a false paradigm of generational conflict. It was specifically in terms of *Scottish* writing that Trocchi set himself against MacDiarmid in the line just quoted. This asserted the validity of national identity and Trocchi's place within it. The internationalism Welsh identifies with Trocchi was as much MacDiarmid's prerogative, and their similarities are as significant as the contrasts between the historical eras in which they flourished. In their private correspondence, MacDiarmid's civility is matched by Trocchi's recognition of a revolutionary writer of an older generation.[9]

For the fiction of Irvine Welsh, realism has a specific meaning. We began by noting how the language of his narrative prose represented an insinuating engagement with readers' expectations. This is at a distinct remove from the mainstream tradition of English fiction and requires a contextualisation within Scottish traditions. In the mainstream tradition of the nineteenth-century Scottish novel, Sir Walter Scott set the pattern for narrative prose in English, reassuring readers with the legal authority of the language of dominant power, self-legitimising its own just perspective. Scots was confined to the speech of comic, wild or eccentric characters. Writing in Scots persisted, particularly in the north-east in the later nineteenth century, but it was not until the 1920s and 1930s that a different idiom was forged in terms of international literary art. MacDiarmid, in his experimentation with Scots as a medium for serious poetry as opposed to vernacular comedy, and Lewis Grassic Gibbon in the novel, opened the doors to a world in which the speech of people might be formed anew as literary artifice. Gibbon, in *Sunset Song* (1932), takes the Scots vocabulary and idiom of his native place as the narrative language. The intimacy of this language gives it authority, rather than the legalistic distance and judgmental height of utterance standard English would convey. And this is what Irvine Welsh inherits.

The argument is more familiar with contemporary referents, but it is worth noting the continuities from MacDiarmid and Gibbon to Kelman and Welsh. Perhaps Tom Leonard sums it up most effectively. What he has to say about language, class and the structures of power, hierarchies of authority and the actual, living voices of women and men, is essential. He tells us in one of the 'Unrelated Incidents' collected in *Intimate Voices: Selected Work 1965–1983*:

> fyi stull
> huvny
> thoata lang-
> wij izza
> sound-system,
> fyi huvny
> hudda thingk
> aboot the dif-
> frince tween
> sound
> n object n
> symbol,
> well,
> ma innocent
> wee
> friend – iz
> god said ti
> adam:
> a doant kerr
> fyi caw it
> an apple
> ur
> an aippl -
> jist leeit
> alane![10]

Realism, for Welsh, might be described as a responsibility to the characters he represents both in their social contexts and – crucially – in their language, combined with a responsibility to a readership which knows little of these things experientially. Most of Welsh's readers will not be of the company of the characters he describes. In this Welsh is clearly in a line of descent from Zola and other nineteenth-century writers whose novels, concerned as they are with the squalor of working-class life, might be criticised as subject-matter for the delectation of enlightened and better-off readers. Yet the infectious energy and speed of Welsh's language challenges this position of detachment whenever we read his work, and as Tom Leonard insists in the poem just quoted, the enactment of power in language is the most insidious form of exploitation and authoritative control. Welsh's fiction – whether he would acknowledge it or not – subscribes to MacDiarmid's judgement in his long poem *In Memoriam James Joyce* (1955), that 'All dreams of "imperialism" must be exorcised, / Including linguistic imperialism, which sums up all the rest'.[11]

The degree to which Welsh required to write himself into the modern *British* novel might be underscored by one final illustration. In *The Lay of the Last Minstrel* (1805), Walter Scott makes the ultimate patriotic identification of self and land which generations of nineteenth-century Scottish patriots believed might be contained by the Union: 'Breathes there the man with soul so dead, / Who never to himself hath said, / This is my own, my native land!'[12]

Robin Jenkins' novel, *The Changeling* (1958), presents in the boy Tom Curdie an immediate ancestor of Welsh's characters, and in the conversations between Charlie Forbes, Tom's teacher and the boy, there is a memorable clash of self-deluded idealism about the nature of Scotland's romantic past, the nation's landscape and natural beauties. Tom is a boy from the slums, to whom Scotland's natural beauty, extolled in Charlie's rhapsodies, is a misleading dream. This points forward inevitably to the scene in the film version of *Trainspotting* where the main characters arrive at a railway station and contemplate walking up a nearby hill. The view prompts Tommy to exclaim, 'Doesn't it make you proud to be Scottish?' The proposition is greeted with bitter invective by Renton:

> I hate being Scottish. We're the lowest of the fucking low, the scum of the earth, the most wretched, servile, miserable, pathetic trash that was ever shat into civilisation. Some people hate the English, but I don't. They're just wankers. We, on the other hand, are colonised by wankers. We can't even pick a decent culture to be colonised by. We are ruled by effete arseholes. It's a shite state of affairs and all the fresh air in the world will not make any fucking difference.[13]

Yet this is not a rejection of Scott's sense of identity but an attack on its affirmation, a corrective critique of the complacency or forced rhapsody associated with Scott's attitude which Charlie Forbes inherited and as such, it is perfectly aligned in a national tradition. Where Welsh differs from Scott, of course, and what Tom Curdie could never say, is in articulating Renton's rejection of the given and the assertion of the frustrated desire for something better. This comes through his sympathetic exploration of the repulsive unnaturalness of the inhabited world and prompted my Shakespearian epigraph. Laughter, the aesthetics of shock, the unnaturalness of language, behaviour and the entire social idiom are what Welsh heaves into service in a deeply traditional act of writing by which, to paraphrase John Berger, art teaches us to want better. All art helps us 'to refuse the inadequacy of the given. . . . Sometimes it mounts to a pitch of horror. Sometimes it gives permanent value and meaning to the ephemeral. Sometimes it describes the desired. . . . The only inspiration which exists is the intimation of our own potential.'[14]

The phenomenal popularity of the book was enhanced by the film (Danny Boyle, 1996), which used non-realist narrative techniques while simplifying the story and, as film does to some extent inevitably, glamourising it. The colour, speed, gamesomeness and effervescence demonstrated in the film-making and in the characters depicted brought it a long way from the paradigms of realism in fiction and film of a previous generation: *Saturday Night and Sunday Morning* (Allan Sillitoe's novel and the Karel Reisz film of 1960), *This Sporting Life* (similarly, both David Storey's novel and Lindsay Anderson's 1963 film), *Kes* (Barry Hines' book and Ken Loach's film of 1969), to name but three. Both in fiction and film, the gravity-bound self-apprehension of these earlier texts, their depiction of economic realities, constricting aspirations, stifling sexual energies, frustrating social hopes and delimiting imaginations, were replaced in *Trainspotting* by bright colours, mobile imaginative contortions, upward- and outward-swinging gestures enacting physical – and above all, verbal – attempts to escape the given, the imposed and the normative.

Trumping the conventional hokum of *Braveheart* (Mel Gibson, 1995) and *Rob Roy* (written by Alan Sharp, directed by Michael Caton-Jones, 1995) *Trainspotting* (film and book) could be seen as an aggressively oppositional antidote to the caricatures of Hollywood history. As it catapulted Welsh's fiction to the attention of an international cinema audience – an overlapping but different readership – it generated awareness of Scotland not as hills, heather, breathless chases, narrow escapes, martyrdom and aspiration towards ideals of freedom and self-determination, but of the nation's housing schemes, the unemployed and dispossessed (though martyrdom is also important in Welsh's story). A significant novelty was the fact that Welsh was writing not of Glasgow – where a distinct tradition of realist writing, often representing working-class experience, had been established through the fiction of Frederick Niven (1878–1944), Catherine Carswell (1879–1946), Dot Allen (1892–1964), George Blake (1893–1961), Edward Gaitens

(1897–1966), James Barke (1905–1958), George Friel (1910–1976), Robin Jenkins (b. 1912), Archie Hind (b. 1928) and, most notoriously, Alexander McArthur (1901–1947) and Kingsley Long's *No Mean City* (1935), which helped define the scenario of the Gorbals tenements, hard men, shrill women, razor gangs and violence – but of Edinburgh. While new departures in Glasgow writing flourished in the 1980s and 1990s in the fiction of Alasdair Gray, James Kelman and the poetry of Edwin Morgan and Liz Lochhead, post-industrial working-class Edinburgh seemed inarticulate, until Welsh.

Welsh's attacks on banal nationalism are activated by moral outrage and the kind of social indignation that comes from first-hand experience of degradation and indignity. His place in the tradition of Scottish fiction may seem exceptional due to his excessive employment of shock tactics but it is deeply implicated in distinctive national literary strategies for self-determination and social betterment. If 'realism' implies a literary vantage-point of height from which social conditions might be depicted for the benign, sympathetic but detached reader, Welsh's departure from this viewpoint takes him into the dynamics of ordure and engages an aesthetics of repulsion.

As a whole, Welsh's fiction has its *longueurs* (in *Glue*), self-indulgences (in *Ecstasy*, *Porno* and *Filth*), extremes of moral exclamation (in *Marabou Stork Nightmares*) and exploitation of sensationalism (everywhere). But these should be balanced against his sympathetic insight (the moment of recognition of Begbie's father in *Trainspotting* or the final moments of Bruce Robertson in *Filth*, when he wishes that his daughter might have had a different life), his gifts of storytelling and the pace of his narration (in *Trainspotting* and the stories of *The Acid House*, but also in *Porno*) and the insinuating complicity enacted by his language throughout his work. The securities and conventions of realism may seem to be endorsed by the verisimilitude enacted by this language but – artful or unconsciously extended – it is a different kind of fashioning, a gravitational belonging to a form of address which brings sympathetic engagement and moral judgement more closely together than the attempt at a kind of objectivity realised from the elevated place of judgement implied by the term 'realism'. The realism in his fiction is constructed by the language of his characters. At its best, this effects 'the intimation of our own potential'. It may seem constricting, trapping and locking us in, yet it may prove that even within ideologies that seem inescapable, there are strategies for liberation. That is why his people need all the words he can give them.

FOR FURTHER READING

For a hard copy list of Irvine Welsh's work up to 2001, see *Contemporary Novelists*, David Madden et al., ed. 7th edn (New York: St James Press, 2001). For a more up-to-date list on the internet, see the British Council website: <http://www.contemporarywriters.com/authors/>.

Craig, Cairns, *The Modern Scottish Novel* (Edinburgh: Edinburgh University Press, 1999).

Freeman, Alan, 'Ghosts in Sunny Leith: Irvine Welsh's *Trainspotting*', *Studies in Scottish Fiction: 1945 to the Present* (Frankfurt: Peter Lang, 1996).

Gifford, Douglas, et al., eds, *Scottish Literature in English and Scots* (Edinburgh: Edinburgh University Press, 2003).

Hodge, John, *Trainspotting & Shallow Grave* [screenplays] (London: Faber and Faber, 1996).

Jenkins, Robin, *The Changeling* (Edinburgh: Macdonald, 1958).

Oliver, Fiona, 'The Self-Debasement of Scotland's Postcolonial Bodies', *SPAN: Journal of the South Pacific Association for Commonwealth Literature and Language Studies*, 42/43 (April/October 1996), 114–21.

NOTES

1 Irvine Welsh, *Trainspotting* (London: Martin Secker and Warburg, 1993), p. 3. All quotations are from this edition; page numbers are given in the text.

2 Many books have been written on the Modernist movement. See, for example, *Modernism: 1890–1930*, ed. Malcolm Bradbury and James McFarlanes (1976; rpt. Harmondsworth; New York: Penguin, 1991). See also Jane Goldman's *Modernism, 1910–1945: Image to Apocalypse* (Houndmills, Basingstoke; New York: Palgrave Macmillan, 2004). As the titles of these books suggest, critics writing on the movement do not agree as to exactly when it began and ended

3 Though the journalist was reprimanding him for emotionalism at a concert in Dublin, the reprimand was made with reference to one of Welsh's fictional characters: 'Begbie would have nutted him for being such a wimp.' Lawrence Donegan, 'Exit', *The Herald Magazine*, 23 October 2004, 62.

4 Alison Kermack, 'Askinfurrit', in *Dream State: the New Scottish Poets*, ed. Daniel O'Rourke (Edinburgh: Polygon, 1994), p. 195.

5 Edwin Muir, *Scott and Scotland* (London: Routledge, 1936). Hugh MacDiarmid's response to Muir's assertion appeared in his introduction and editorial practice in *The Golden Treasury of Scottish Poetry* (London: Macmillan, 1940; rpt. Edinburgh: Canongate, 1993), which included poems in Scots and English and translated from Gaelic and Latin but carried nothing by Muir; and in the essay 'Scottish Arts and Letters: the Present Position and Post-War Prospects', from *The New Scotland: 17 Chapters on Scottish Reconstruction, Highland and Industrial* (Glasgow: The London Scots Self-Government Committee, Civic Press, 1942), rpt. in Hugh MacDiarmid, *Selected Prose*, ed. Alan Riach (Manchester: Carcanet, 1992), pp. 151–70.

6 Steve Watts and Steve Xerri, 'A Politics for Pop', *LTP: Journal of Literature Teaching Politics*, no. 3 (1984), 91–102.

7 Irvine Welsh, quoted by Allan Campbell, in 'Shooting Star', *Scotland on Sunday*, *Spectrum*, 28 January 1996, 1.

8 Alexander Trocchi, quoted by Allan Campbell, in 'Shooting Star', *Scotland on Sunday, Spectrum*, 28 January 1996, 1.
9 See Andrew Murray Scott, *Alexander Trocchi: the Making of the Monster* (Edinburgh: Polygon, 1991), pp. 122–3; and Hugh MacDiarmid, *New Selected Letters*, ed. Dorian Grieve, Owen Dudley Edwards and Alan Riach (Manchester: Carcanet Press, 2001), pp. 395, 398–9, 411.
10 Tom Leonard, 'Unrelated Incidents: 3', *Intimate Voices: Selected Work 1965–1983* (Newcastle: Galloping Dog, 1984), pp. 86–8.
11 Hugh MacDiarmid, *Selected Poems*, ed. Alan Riach and Michael Grieve (Harmondsworth: Penguin Twentieth-Century Classics, 1994), p. 276.
12 Sir Walter Scott, 'Scotland', from *The Lay of the Last Minstrel*, Canto VI, lines 10–36, in *Scotlands: Poets and the Nation*, ed. Douglas Gifford and Alan Riach (Manchester: Carcanet Press / Edinburgh: Scottish Poetry Library, 2004), pp. 100–1.
13 John Hodge, *Trainspotting & Shallow Grave* [screenplays] (London: Faber and Faber, 1996), p. 46.
14 John Berger, 'The Moment of Cubism', in *The White Bird: Writings*, ed. Lloyd Spencer (London: Chatto & Windus, 1985), pp. 159–88.

4

Angela Carter's Magic Realism

David Punter

In this chapter I would like to approach – or perhaps one should say 're-approach' – the set of questions surrounding the 'magic realism' of Angela Carter's texts. Perhaps it would be useful to begin with a standard definition, or one might better say description, of magic realism, to be found in Marion Wynne-Davies' *Bloomsbury Guide to English Literature*. It is:

> a term applied in literature primarily to Latin American novelists such as Jorge Luis Borges . . . Gabriel García Márquez . . . and Alejo Carpentier . . . whose work combines a realistic manner with strong elements of the bizarre, supernatural and fantastic. This technique has influenced novelists such as John Fowles, Angela Carter and Salman Rushdie.[1]

Perhaps, though, a more off-the-cuff description might be more illuminating, and here is one I heard at a recent conference: 'If a ghost sits down at your breakfast table and you are scared or terrified, *that* is horror or the "fantastic". If, however, you say, "Oh, here is a ghost, please pass the marmalade", *that* is magic realism.'

Some of these issues might be raised in the stories that make up Angela Carter's *The Bloody Chamber* (1979). For example, we could argue that one way in which the 'bizarre, supernatural and fantastic' invade the texts is that it appears to be as much the locations, the settings, that determine event and outcome as any of the desultory, often misunderstood actions undertaken by the characters themselves. The effect, as elsewhere in Carter, is for the characters often to seem as though they are characters from *somebody else's* story – not their own, nor even their apparent author's, but stories that come from a different, irreversible past, even if this past can be known only through a certain virtuality, a consciousness that has already in some sense been traumatised, and which is now moving in a dreamy afterlife in which the presence of a ghost at the breakfast table would be anything but surprising.

Thus, in Carter we keep coming across characters who find their chief purpose in being, in the end, involved in a *bricolage* of 'other', ghostly stories, of embedded tales according to which, apparently, we live and move and have our being. What story, we may ask, is Carter's heroine actually inhabiting – as one might, of course, inhabit a cell, or a Gothic castle, while knowing all the time, on some other scene, that one does not *live* there – as she approaches the location in the short story 'The Bloody Chamber' which we need to know – are allowed to know – only as 'his castle':

> And, ah! his castle. The faery solitude of the place; with its turrets of misty blue, its courtyard, its spiked gate, his castle that lay on the very bosom of the sea with seabirds mewing about its attics, the casements opening on to the green and purple, evanescent departures of the ocean, cut off by the tide from land for half a day . . . that castle, at home neither on the land nor on the water, a mysterious, amphibious place, contravening the materiality of both earth and the waves, with the melancholy of a mermaiden who perches on her rock and waits, endlessly, for a lover who had drowned far away, long ago. That lovely, sad, sea-siren of a place![2]

We might notice that 'his castle' becomes, in the course of a single paragraph (which is none the less divided at its midpoint, which encloses or is broken apart at a hiatus, an aporia or gap), 'that castle': an attempted deictic, we might say (meaning a denotation of time or place), which in its presumption of fixed 'location' in a world of virtual uncertainty seeks to draw the castle from the ambiguous realm in which it exists and to place it firmly *here* – or, indeed, 'there', or anywhere, but at any rate on dry land, while at the same time severing it from all that holds it as 'his' and casting it loose so that we might be able to see it as in some clearer relation to the protagonist.

But this would seem to be a doomed attempt. 'This' castle can no more have reality conferred on it by language than any other, but here, of course, there is a further, particular mystery; for the 'castle' is, it seems, momentarily 'at home' but, immediately, 'neither on the land nor on the water', undecidably hovering between a state of being at home *nowhere* or of being at home in some third realm, a realm which mediates between, slips and slides between, land and water, the dream-state, the moment under the moment (as Russell Hoban would put it); or the story under the story, the 'other' castle that always shadows any particular castle we see. This castle might be a place where – as according to the dim memories of a 'virtuality-slave' like Victor in Bret Easton Ellis' novel *Glamorama* – people remember us as *having been*; whether we remember having been there ourselves remains open to doubt, an unconfirmed rumour that we have, at some time in the past, played a role in somebody else's story. Such a rumour could, of course, menace the narcissism of the confirmed subject, the subject who inhabits the centre of his or her own story and according to whom all other 'actors' are mere 'bit-parts', in every sense of that term.

But one of the things *this* castle does do, at any rate, is to 'contravene' materiality; the mode of its existence – experienced or not, remembered or not, constructed or reconstructed – challenges the notion that any one 'moment' can be severed from its echoes, whether those be ruined echoes of the past or hallucinated echoes of the future. And that contravention of materiality is linked further with another mystery of the sign, in this case the melancholy of the mermaid, the melancholy of the being who would have life as it was and refuses to accept the weight of stories piled against her – who refuses to accept that the evidence presented to her, lies though it may all be, is the only evidence she is ever likely to see, and that the place in which she finds herself will continue to form her subjectivity no matter what alternative lies she would prefer to fashion for herself.

I am trying to point here to the way in which this castle, like other similar locations in the stories in *The Bloody Chamber*, figures as a ghostly, or phantomatic, 'character', albeit perhaps a non-organic one, in its own right; it cannot be fully 'inhabited', because it is a machine which is already playing and replaying its own stories. To be part of this castle we would have to 'fit in', which might not be so very different from the adoption of a persona involved in playing computer games. In terms of 'magic realism', we might say that it is more 'real' than the mere accidents, in terms of human relationships, that might happen to or within it. It 'outlives' – it outlives the specificities of our lives, it outlives the 'game' and will always be available as the site for another game which might at first glance appear quite different but which will reveal itself as a version of the same game, played according to the same claustrophobic rules; and it would be in this sense – no doubt among others – that Carter's magic realism could be seen to prefigure whatever it is that we now call 'virtual reality', with its panoply of 'locations' that remain the same no matter how many times one inserts 'character', no matter how many times one 'plays the game'.

To support this idea (as well as, inevitably, re-call attention to the Gothic roots of these 'locations'), we could momentarily consider another castle. This one is the setting for Iain Banks' *A Song of Stone* (1997):

> The castle has a full reserve of memories, their living-on a special sort of death. . . . I saw so many dances here. . . . The great hall resounded like a skull, abuzz with wheeling thoughts, dissimilar and same. The patterns of their music took hold of them, held them, there in its gloved hand, at once fused and confused, and scattered them about the brighter hallways, their laughter like the music for a dream. The halls and rooms are empty now; the balconies and battlements hang dim, like handholds in the voided dark. In the darkness, in the face of memory, the castle seems now inhuman. Blocked windows mock with the view they no longer afford; here there is a stair's stone spiral disappearing into a blank ceiling where an old tower was levelled, long ago, and here cramped rooms open randomly off one another, implying a passageway, centuries abandoned and reshaped, an appendix within the castle's bowels.[3]

The inhabitants of this castle, it needs to be immediately said, are far from heroic; indeed, they are variously unpleasant, and it is possible that the continuous warfare which reduces them to refugees on their own lands provides a better way of living – at least for some – than the feudal stultification they mourn or the restricted codes of elegance to which they claim once to have had access.

But no matter; they are not important. What is important is the castle, and they, like their enemies, are mere functions of it. Here again is a castle that 'contravenes', and what it contravenes here are the notions of what it might be like to be 'full' or 'empty', notions perhaps of the full or empty sign, the 'full reserve of memories' vis-à-vis the empty halls and rooms. The castle's past and present slide together, although here it seems that they do not fit with exactitude; all that can be provided is a series of 'handholds', perches (like rocks on which mermaids may sit) in the enveloping darkness; to seek security here – of memory, of physical existence, of the generations – is to risk being 'thrown off' by the castle, being forcibly ejected, or abjected, as unworthy of the stories it wishes to weave around you.

And this may also be relevant to what happens in another story in Carter's *The Bloody Chamber*, 'Wolf-Alice', where again it is unclear where the memories lie, or who is acting out what more antique script:

> In the lapse of time, the trance of being of that exiled place, this girl grew amongst things she could neither name nor perceive. How did she think, how did she feel, this perennial stranger with her furred thoughts and her primal sentience that existed in a flux of shifting impressions; there are no words to describe the way she negotiated the abyss between her dreams, those wakings strange as her sleepings. The wolves had tended her because they knew she was an imperfect wolf; we secluded her in animal privacy out of fear of her imperfection because it showed us what we might have been, and so time passed, although she scarcely knew it. (p. 122)

One of the questions one would address to a passage like this would again be about memory and reconstruction. It would not here be a case of trying to recount a synthesised 'whole'; such an attempt would do violence to the hesitancies, the delicacies, the terrible anxieties of the text. It would rather be a matter of trying to respond to a sense of the 'abyss between her dreams', and it is here, I suggest, that Carter's fictions provide an extraordinary link between the multiple forgettings of folk-tale and the equally remarkable forgettings which are characteristic of a culture based on virtual reality, immediate information access and the corresponding 'inattention' which comes to replace human memory at every point.

Where would any secure ground of 'knowledge' be in this scenario? Despite the assertions made in 'Wolf-Alice', there could be no verifiable evidence of why wolves might behave as they do; nor is the notion of 'animal privacy' in any way transparent – indeed, the story seems to show that the very idea of privacy is peculiarly human, that it plays no part in what might be termed 'animal transactions'. What is exposed, then, in Carter is a possible limit of what has been termed by Nicholas Royle among others the necessity of textual telepathy; in the cases of 'characters' who are living out

– or living in – the contexts of myth and legend, then, to attempt to insert
the readerly self is simultaneously to challenge the assumptions by which we
claim to recognise the 'self-in-the-text'.

The wolf, of course, behaves like a wolf; the human behaves like a human.
Wolf-Alice behaves, and can only behave, like Wolf-Alice; no further reduction is possible. And so at the end of the story – 'her' story, or the story about
her, or (without wishing to be too complicated) the story about the story
about her (of which she, of course, not being human, can have no readerly
knowledge) – she can only behave in a way that fails to yield (to) interpretable meaning, even while the phantomatic tracery of the writing inevitably
embroils her in the work of interpretation, as subject, as object and as part
of a story woven around the incomprehensible being of the wolf and the even
more incomprehensible being of the 'wolf/human limen'.

Wolf-Alice polishes a mirror:

> As she continued her ministrations, this glass, with infinite slowness, yielded
> to the reflexive strength of its own material construction. Little by little, there
> appeared within it, like the image on photographic paper that emerges, first,
> a formless web of tracery, the prey caught in its own fishing net, then in firmer
> yet still shadowed outline until at last as vivid as real life itself, as if brought
> into being by her soft, moist, gentle tongue, finally, the face of the Duke. (p.
> 126)

Only an animal tongue, we might say, has the patience, the organic 'consistency', to achieve this kind of picture; only an animal perception can remain
(so we suppose, from within our limited human vocabulary) entirely
unknowing of what it is doing while it is doing it. And only an animal
tongue, Carter here appears to be saying, can produce an image which is not
'constructed' but simply brings into manifest being what is already latently
'there'. We might again be reminded of abysses and dreams, of the nature of
the dreamwork: what is it that washes over the latent content of the dream
to supply it with a manifest outline? What, to put it into a different rhetoric, would it be that would imbue virtual reality with some element less
virtual, and how threatening would that 'magic' be?

One answer may be supplied, or at least hinted at, in Carter's 'The Lady
of the House of Love', in *The Bloody Chamber,* at a moment when sensuous reality seems altogether too vivid, too strong in its life, to satisfy, and
where instead it appears to be merely a function of an inevitable ruin:

> A great, intoxicated surge of the heavy scent of red roses blew into his face as
> soon as they left the village, inducing a sensuous vertigo; a blast of rich, faintly
> corrupt sweetness strong enough, almost, to fell him. Too many roses. Too
> many roses bloomed on enormous thickets that lined the path, thickets bris-
> tling with thorns, and the flowers themselves were almost too luxuriant, their
> huge congregations of plush petals somehow obscene in their excess, their

whorled, tightly budded cores outrageous in their implications. The mansion emerged grudgingly out of this jungle. (p. 98)

This mansion is, one might say, one of many mansions; to take only one example, it is (or inhabits a land very near to) the Caribbean mansion of Jean Rhys' *Wide Sargasso Sea*, the location within which the 'hero' becomes aware that his previous perceptions have all fatally flinched before the luxuriant, that his desires are revealed as pallid, bloodless in the very moment of their potential fulfilment. It is the mansion, the 'location', in the context of which it becomes necessary to reach for a different, dismissive vocabulary of the 'corrupt'; for how else can the thin line of reason remain intact, how else will it not quail and fall before a version of 'fullness' which challenges the very notion of representation?

If we were to try to be clearer, we would need to ask about the implications of these 'implications' which the text mentions. One of these implications, again bearing in mind the more obvious implications of Rhys' story (which tend towards showing precisely how a 'character' can find himself displaced in the midst of what may, apparently, but on another scene, be his 'own' story) may be that representation itself is in a continuous, but usually repressed, sense of being outraged at being potentially submerged, humiliated, at the hands of its 'real' adversary. For a story-teller, for a hearer or reader, there are always 'too many roses'; but more to the point, there are also 'too many roses' for those who are actually required to 'inhabit', to live inside those stories.

'Sensuous vertigo', then; we might relate this to a passage in Carter's *The Magic Toyshop* (1967), where Finn is (perhaps) seeking to 'amuse' Melanie. 'There is too much', she says several times in the environment of his magic theatre: 'She was in the night again, and the doll was herself. Her mouth quivered'.

> Finn saw her distress and his own loose mouth turned down in sympathy, like the moon on its back. To her intense dismay and astonishment, he suddenly hurled down the room in a series of cartwheels; he made a whizzing plaything of his devilish masked self, a fizzing Catherine wheel, flashing arms and legs, landing on his hands before her, his upside-down false face obscured by hair both false and real, tumbling over his *papier-mâché* cheeks.
>
> 'Laugh at me', he said. 'I'm trying to amuse you'.
>
> He kicked his filthy heels in the air.
>
> 'I want to go home', she said hopelessly, bleak as November. She buried her face in her hands.[4]

Finn is, of course, here disguised; indeed, so thoroughly disguised that the very question of where is up and where is down is multiply obscured. His very body has 'gone uncanny'; it no longer makes sense as a steady, *lisible* (readerly) text, it makes you want to go home. His behaviour, his travesty of the body, his carnivalesque sacrifice of his own physical integrity, these are all 'too much' for Melanie – just as in Carter's *Nights at the Circus*, Fevvers' physical being is 'all too much' for anybody, too much by virtue of its crossing of biological boundaries, but too much also by virtue of sheer size – grandeur or grossness, depending on the readerly perspective. In the face of the huge flying woman, as in the face of Finn (or, in this case, of what may or may not be the face of Finn), a certain vertigo is induced, it becomes impossible to establish coordinates, or to remember to what part of whose story you might belong.

In the case of *Nights at the Circus* (1984), one might want to recall that it ends in a moment when all is enveloped in laughter:

> The spiralling tornado of Fevvers' laughter began to twist and shudder across the entire globe, as if a spontaneous response to the giant comedy that endlessly unfolded beneath it, until everything that lived and breathed, everywhere, was laughing. Or so it seemed to the deceived husband, who found himself laughing too, even if he was not quite sure whether or not he might be the butt of the joke.[5]

Here, in the first sentence, we might feel ourselves in the presence of a profoundly 'comic' ending, in the sense of one that is redeemed by the power of laughter. But the second sentence undermines and destabilises this apparent act of reconciliation; no jokes exist without the possibility that one might be the 'butt' – and indeed, in the very final sentence of the book – ' "To think I really fooled you!" she marvelled. "It just goes to show there's nothing like confidence" ' – the entire question around which the book appears to be built – whether or not Fevvers 'really' has wings – is reopened as a matter of conjecture and rebeginning rather than subjected to determinate closure.

And this, perhaps, can lead us into further consideration of the situation in 'The Lady of the House of Love':

> Wearing an antique bridal gown, the beautiful queen of the vampires sits all alone in her dark, high house under the eyes of the portraits of her demented and atrocious ancestors, each one of whom, through her, projects a baleful posthumous existence; she counts out the Tarot cards, ceaselessly construing a constellation of possibilities as if the random fall of the cards on the red plush tablecloth before her could precipitate her from her chill, shuttered room into a country of perpetual summer and obliterate the perennial sadness of a girl who is both death and the maiden. (p. 93)

To be both death and the maiden, to gather into (or perhaps 'unto', in a phrasing which the scenario, the 'location' of the story, invites) oneself – or to have thus gathered – the multiple signifiers of corruption and purity, of terror and promise, of what may come after the end and what may be there before the beginning, all this is certainly sufficient to induce a certain vertigo, which here we would probably need to construe not in the crude version of a 'fear of heights', but rather as the more challenging, and revealing, anxiety about losing one's own sense of the perpendicular and the stable, finding oneself weightless and shorn of gravity, at the mercy of a world whose own 'small mercies' have been abruptly withdrawn.

Whose story is the story of this 'queen of the vampires'? The story of Miss Havisham, traumatised and condemned to live in the 'other' world of repetition, the world where no action propels forward, where one is always already back at the beginning, even while the beginning flakes away all around you? Or the story of the queen's own ancestors, 'demented and atrocious' – but these are themselves, of course, mere stories, the portraits can provide no verifiable evidence, except in so far as they are themselves representations of the life of the castle, the mansion itself, signs, projections, emanations of a longer, broader story within which their own lack of freedom is now again 're-represented' in the fixity of their delimitation within the picture frame.

The main character in the 'Little Red Riding Hood' folk-tales is similarly the wood, as Carter tells us in the splendid second-person narration of the opening of 'The Erl-King', in *The Bloody Chamber*:

> The woods enclose. You step between the first trees and then you are no longer in the open air; the wood swallows you up. There is no way through the wood any more, this wood has reverted to its original privacy. Once you are inside it, you must stay there until it lets you out again for there is no clue to guide you through in perfect safety; grass grew over the track years ago and now the rabbits and the foxes make their own runs in the subtle labyrinth and nobody comes. (p. 84)

Swallowing and gulping, striving for air in the face of panic – vertigo is certainly here; but here it is the wood which swallows, which envelops you in its own stories, or potential stories, stories written on the trees. In a very different context, Derek Walcott also writes of ways in which the wood, the forest, is continually telling stories which we cannot properly hear or interpret, for we have lost our way – as the result of the previous imprinting of different stories, to be sure, in this case the 'different stories' of colonisation, but the uninterpretable 'difference' of the stories that trees might tell remains across a wide swathe of different contexts (and the phrase 'wide swathe' has its own colonial resonances):

> For no one had yet written of this landscape
> that it was possible, though there were sounds
> given to its varieties of wood;
>
> the *bois-canot* responded to its echo,
> when the axe spoke, weeds ran up to the knee
> like bastard children, hiding in their names,

whole generations died, unchristened,
growths hidden in green darkness, forests
of history thickening with amnesia . . .[6]

I would want to link the phrase 'thickening with amnesia' back to the question of what might come to replace the atrophying concept of memory, and to see the erosion of memory, folk-tale, legend under the pressure of colonial change as a violent inversion of the softer and perhaps less resonant collapse of memory under the impact of the technology of virtuality. Within this complex constellation (within which, again, it is evidently useful for the corporate controllers of the world's stage to encourage amnesia, indeed to sell the various drugs, of various kinds, which will promote it and thus destroy the memory of what it might mean, in any context, to be 'native'). Carter's reworking of folk-tales might appear not so much feminist, or even ecological (although those are certainly horizonal interpretative strategies), but performative of the possibility of a strange recuperation; but a recuperation which may only work if it induces us to recognise that we too – as readers and as human actors – are only bit-part players on a wider – bizarre, supernatural, fantastic – scene. There are issues arising from this to do with narcissism, not only as a psychological condition but also as a socio-political goal; but they would be too complex to pursue here.

Like Easton Ellis, however, and like Walcott, I suggest that Carter's texts have a major concern with amnesia, with what might get forgotten – but also, of course, and absolutely paradoxically, with what might already have been forgotten, with what might now only continue to exist in a 'virtual' half-life, or afterlife. A certain type of privacy, and the associated reworking of the ancient figure of the labyrinth, would be relevant to this, but there would be two larger paradoxes to consider.

One would have to do with the phrase in the 'Erl-King' passage above, 'and nobody comes'. The paradox here, obviously, is transparent: if nobody comes, then nobody tells the tale; nevertheless, the tale gets told, somehow. It tells itself or the trees tell it. It would, perhaps, be convenient to imagine that all trace of these old tales could be wiped (out), that when the screen is blank nothing is happening, or that erasure from the 'system' (technological, organic, political) can be permanent. But if there is one point at which the technology of virtuality converges with Freudian thinking, it is, to the distress of many a politician and other 'public figure' (whatever that opposite to 'privacy' may mean), that nothing ever disappears. E-mails re-emerge from the mechanical unconscious, trees continue to bear messages, and even to disseminate them, they reassert their continuity with paper even in an economy which claims to be approaching the realm of the paper-free. It is not possible to wipe away all the traces, or the tracery, or to be sure that nobody will ever come.

The second, and my final point, emerges from a paragraph from 'The Erl-

King' shortly after the one quoted above: 'A young girl would go into the wood as trustingly as Red Riding Hood to her granny's house but this light admits of no ambiguities and, here, she will be trapped in her own illusion because everything in the wood is exactly as it seems' (p. 85). No trickery of the light, no magic in the realism, no succumbing to the hallucinatory power of tumbling clowns or deranged vampires; everything 'is exactly as it seems'. To go back to Ellis' *Glamorama*, and to its peculiar protagonist Victor, one last time: he is the apotheosis of depthlessness. To use the cant phrase, 'What you see is what you get'; Victor is in permanent, culturally sanctioned denial of his own past, even of the continuity of his own life. In a sense we might say that his 'perpendicularity', his lack of complex dimensions, is precisely what demands a matching vertigo in the reader.

What Carter is saying here is, perhaps, of a piece with this fear of cultural reductivism, yet it is also subtly different. To be exactly what it seems, the world would have to stand between such reduction and the manic roaring in the ears of vertigo, of being exposed to 'too many roses'; a balance would have to be struck on this difficult, geometry-defying terrain. But if everything is 'exactly as it seems', why would this simultaneously imply that we are trapped in illusions? Because, to use the most obvious key from Carter's own work, we have to run the tricky course between admitting to the unyieldingness of the woods, the immoveable fixity of the castle on the one hand, and on the other the ceaseless restlessness of desire; which may be an illusion but nevertheless makes the world go round – not in the sense of vertigo but in the sense of a necessary, life-giving mercy, although the two senses are, of course, irretrievably interlocked. If, in this sense, it stopped, then we would all fall down, the woods would grow around us, and nobody, indeed, would ever come.

FOR FURTHER READING

For a complete list of Angela Carter's fiction, see:
<http://www.isfdb.org/cgi-bin/ea.cgi?Angela_Carter>.

Ellis, Bret Easton, *Glamorama* (New York: Alfred Knopf, 1998).
Hoban, Russell, *The Moment under the Moment* (London: Cape, 1992).
Rhys, Jean, *Wide Sargasso Sea* (London: André Deutsch, 1966).
Royle, Nicholas, *Telepathy and Literature: Essays on the Reading Mind* (Oxford: Blackwell, 1991).

NOTES

1 Marion Wynne-Davies, ed., *Bloomsbury Guide to English Literature* (London: Bloomsbury, 1989), p. 693.
2 Angela Carter, *The Bloody Chamber* (London: Gollancz, 1979), p. 13. All quotations are from this edition; page numbers are given in the text.

3 Iain Banks, *A Song of Stone* (London: Abacus, 1997), pp. 35–6.
4 Angela Carter, *The Magic Toyshop* (London: Heinemann, 1967), p. 68. All quotations are from this edition; page numbers are given in the text.
5 Angela Carter, *Nights at the Circus* (London: Chatto and Windus, 1984), p. 295. All quotations are from this edition; page numbers are given in the text.
6 Derek Walcott, 'Homage to Gregorias', in *Collected Poems 1948–1984* (London: Faber and Faber, 1992), p. 195.

5

Facticity, or Something Like That: The Novels of James Kelman

Laurence Nicoll

> The world is not what I think, but what I live through.
> Maurice Merleau-Ponty, *The Phenomenology of Perception*[1]

Although recent critical appraisal of James Kelman's fictions has expanded, moving beyond the view that Kelman's work is informed by problematic notions of 'Scottishness', there is still too little attention paid to the relationship between Kelman and existentialism. Kelman frequently describes himself as operating from within an existentialist tradition, yet this declamation is rarely, if ever, taken seriously. This is perhaps unsurprising, given that existentialism is something we associate with the 1940s and 1950s. None the less, here I want to trust the teller; here I want to indicate some of the ways in which Kelman's texts, principally his novels, can be read as contributing to and drawing from the existentialist tradition.

Existentialism is a notoriously elusive term, employed, often loosely, to demarcate a divergent range of literary and philosophical discourses. The use of the term is further complicated given its rejection by some of those – Heidegger, Camus – to whom the term is usually ascribed. Amongst philosophies, existentialism is also unusual in that its popularity owed, and owes, as much to fictional and theatrical exposition as it does to more formally philosophical writings. My use of the term here then is, of necessity, a crude conflation, intended to capture both the literary and philosophical senses of the word. Broadly, though, we can state that existentialism concerns itself with a number of problems, a number of issues – both ontological and epistemological – but central to these, particularly visible in the thought and fiction of Sartre, is a radical notion of freedom. It is, I want to argue, precisely this radical conception of freedom that underwrites and sustains Kelman's work. This commitment to an existentially inspired freedom distances Kelman too from the realistic/naturalistic modes of, say, Balzac and Zola. For Zola, realism amounts to the insistence that identity, character, is *necessarily determined* by society and historical circumstance. Kelman cannot be deemed a realist in this respect, for this would mean abandoning the central existentialist notion of a freely chosen and freely choosing self.

Kelman's question is not, then, how are we shaped by society, but rather, given this or that society, what freedom, what possibilities, does an individual have?

Freedom, though, is not solely a thematic concern, not simply a matter of content, for it is present too at the level of form. An existentialist philosophy, when distilled and translated into an aesthetic practice, necessitates the adoption of and, crucially, the *rejection* of, a number of literary practices and techniques. Accordingly, this chapter is divided into two sections. The first presents an examination of these practices and techniques, whilst the second looks at existentialist themes through a more detailed analysis of Kelman's 1989 novel, *A Disaffection*. I focus upon this novel, because here, it seems to me, Kelman's existentialism is both clearly operative and clearly visible, and yet scarcely considered in much of the critical commentary devoted to the work.

The first notably existentialist component of Kelman's fictional technique is his attitude to plot. All of Kelman's fictions feature minimal or considerably reduced plotting. Robert Hines, the eponymous main character of *The Busconductor Hines* (1984), seeks to give up his employment and, perhaps, emigrate to Australia. The novel, however, ends as it begins with Hines aboard his bus, still tracing and retracing the same routes. In *A Chancer* (1985), Tammas does little other than gamble in a variety of settings. Patrick Doyle, Kelman's disaffected secondary school teacher, ponders a number of philosophical questions, contemplates suicide and resigning his position, but never translates these contemplations into action. Plot seems to increase in *How Late it Was, How Late* (1994). Sammy Samuels wakes up hungover, is arrested and either goes blind or feigns blindness (it is noticeable that within the novel this is never conclusively resolved). The remainder of the novel is occupied with Samuels' attempt to get home and his dealings with local government departments. The novel suggests a kind of micro-Odyssey: as Samuels journeys his way around Glasgow, he too searches for an absent Helen who seems to be, have been, either his wife or his girlfriend. Homer's grand epic narrative, a plot peopled by gods and heroes, is thus percolated into an unemployed man's attempt to negotiate a single city.

Translated Accounts (2001) decreases even these bare outlines of plot, for there is no conventional sense of story here at all. Instead, we are simply presented with a deeply ambiguous set of documents or reports, written and translated by anonymous figures, ostensibly concerned with a not altogether clear collection of events that have taken place in an equally anonymous country (or countries). In an interview with Kirsty McNeill, Kelman explains the principles behind his Spartan plots:

> I think the most ordinary person's life is fairly dramatic; all you've got to do
> is follow some people around and look at their existence for 24 hours, and it
> will be horror. It will just be horror. You don't need any beginning, middle

and end at all. All you have to do is show this one day in maybe this person's life and it'll be horror . . . . There's no need to be saying or thinking "When's the murder or bank robbery going to happen?" No such abnormal event will occur – the kind of event that seems to motivate almost all mainstream fiction whether in book or screen form. In reality these events are abnormal. The whole idea of the big dramatic event, of what constitutes 'plot', only assumes that economic security exists. The way that literature generally works in our society you never have to worry about these very routine horrors, the things that make up everyday reality for such an enormous proportion of the population. In the Anglo American literary tradition there's almost no concrete reality, no economic detail. All kinds of abnormal events and dramatic plots are required, there's got to be folk appearing out of closets, long lost sisters and brothers, a father who's a murderer, all that sort of junk.[2]

This quotation contains a number of points that warrant elaboration. Firstly, and crucially, Kelman locates drama within the everyday. Ordinary life on an ordinary day supplies sufficient material for literary (re)presentation. The use of 'everyday' suggests further a correlation between Kelman's literary principles and the philosophical principles that underpin existentialism. For both Heidegger and Sartre, philosophy begins, and ought to begin, with an analysis of, to use Heidegger's locution, 'average everydayness'.[3] In *Being and Nothingness*, Sartre's complex arguments are often exemplified by the seemingly trivial – the actions, events and objects encountered in a café. So, whilst philosophical existentialism involves a reconfiguring of the concerns and procedures of philosophy, moving away from systematic abstraction towards an exploration of the diurnal, so too Kelman's fictional existentialism expunges the extraordinary to maintain itself amidst the ordinary, the Gogolian *poshlost*.[4]

If the rejection of extravagant or convoluted plots is a preliminary step toward an everyday existential realism and a movement towards an examination of everyday being, then Kelman's insistence upon 'concrete reality' leads us to a further related point. In existentialist thought, all being is necessarily situated, necessarily concrete, has a *here*, has a *this*: hence the locution 'being-in-the-world'. But, and this is a point that nationalist interpretations of Kelman's work often bypass, whilst all being must necessarily take place somewhere, the where itself is utterly, supremely contingent. Thus, although Kelman's first four novels utilise Glasgow as a setting, this is not to suggest that there is some set of essential Glaswegian, far less Scottish, experiences that Kelman is trying to depict and dissect. Glasgow is sufficient, rather than necessary: Kelman reminds us that when reading his work it 'should be kept in mind that Glasgow can be any other town or city in Great Britain, including London, Edinburgh, Cardiff, Cambridge, Newcastle or Ramsgate'.[5] This quotation suggests that what is sought is a specific account of a general urban experience, the capturing of the existential relationship between an individual and his or her contingent setting. *Translated Accounts* (2001) more forcefully demonstrates this last point, for within the novel all temporal and geographical markers are absent. The novel is literally set *some*where and this shearing of locational specificity helps effectively foreground what is existentially important: being-in-situation.

This and other factors within Kelman's literary strategies bear comparison with the positions that Sartre develops throughout his critical essays and in his 1948 text, *What Is Literature?* Sartre is constantly and consistently suspicious of the metaphysical implications of certain aspects of narrative construction. He identifies these with his 'bourgeois' elders: 'The novels of our elders related the event as having taken place in the past. Chronological order permitted the reader to see the logical and universal relationship, the eternal verities. . . . A past was delivered to us which had already been thought through'.[6] Sartre does not simply negate the work of his antecedents and offer nothing in compensation. His suggestion is that fiction ought to 'restore to the event its brutal freshness, its ambiguity, its unforseeability', ought to retain the 'strangeness and opacity of the world' (*WIL*167, 87). Sartre's desire for 'unforseeability' and 'ambiguity' becomes possible only through a narrative with a non-teleological plot. A novel that works its way through to a consistent ending, where events are neatly rounded off, becomes, for both Sartre and Kelman, deeply unrealistic, anti-existential. Life, while it is being lived, is simply not like that, for life contains unexplained events, chance happenings, unknown and unforeseen repercussions.

The use of a linked and progressive plot then suggests precisely what Sartre rejects: an unambiguous life, a past already thought through. Furthermore, a novel built around such a plot conveys a foreordained or immutable quality and thereby inhibits and disables the freedom that an existentialist work seeks to exhibit and sustain. In place of progressive, plot-driven narratives Kelman substitutes a series of contiguous episodes and events. *A Chancer* (1985) in particular is composed of a number of vignettes placed side by side, the only unifying factor being the presence of Tammas (and this episodic quality is aided by sections of the novel having been published earlier as short stories). These events and situations do not unfold, though, in the sense of becoming clearer, but rather simply accrete and accrue. Like Kafka, Kelman seems content to let a basic existential situation expand and deepen. Unforseeability is not, however, solely a matter of adopting more realistic plotting, for it also implies a number of narrative proscriptions. Noticeably, Kelman employs neither prolepsis, narrative foreshadowing, nor flashback. The first technique implies that the future is already known, already decided and settled, while the latter imputes a causal link between past and the present. Both techniques suggest determination. For similar reasons, narrative tense becomes equally important. So, although Kelman usually favours a past tense, he never opts for the remote past, thereby ensuring a certain immediacy, the sense of an unfolding present and an undecided future. Ultimately, the refusal to accept and utilise a coherent and systematic means of narration is analogous to the existential refusal to accept those ideological or philosophical systems that attempt to totalise and comprehend individual human existence.

Perhaps, though, the most readily recognisable Kelman signature is his blending and compression of narrative. Given existentialism's focus upon individual consciousness, one would expect a solely first-person mode of narration. Kelman, though, deploys what is usually termed a third-person singular voice.

> Aye. And Sammy was on the pavement and he didnay stop till he made it to the tenement wall; it was a shop window, his hand on the glass; he was breathing fast; fuckt, drained, knackt, totally, felt like he had run a marathon. Fucking tension, tension. When ye done something. Every fucking time. Strain into the muscles; everything, every time; just so fucking tense, every part of yer fucking body. And he needed across the new street, he knew where he was, he thought he did, and there was another street now round the corner round this corner, where he was standing jesus christ alfuckingmighty. The traffic was roaring. Oh my my my my, fuck sake, my fucking.[7]

The 'Aye' with which the passage begins is either a voiced affirmation, or an internal thought. There is, then, a seeming transition: the use of 'he' in the second sentence marks a movement from the first person to the third person, but this too is ambiguous, for it is possible that this is either Sammy Samuels commenting upon himself, or the voice of a narrator. The introduction of 'didnay' introduces an additional complication, for, as with the ensuing 'fuckt' and 'knackt', the printed word indicates and mimics the manner of pronunciation: the written and the verbal interpenetrate. Further, if this is the voice of a narrator, then the narrator shares the accent of the character. These ambiguities are activated and made possible because Kelman refuses to demarcate clearly the shift between registers. This is achieved partly through the omission of quotation marks and authorial indicators such as 'he said', but also because the narrative voice is pressed down into, wrapped around and interfused with the character voice. This intermingling has both Joycean and Chekhovian precedents, but it confirms and conforms to a given of atheistic existentialism, for it is at the same time a refusal of omniscience. Kelman cannot opt for a conventional third-person narrative, with an author/narrator who views his characters from above, for this would convert the author into a divine orderer, a 'God'.

Rejecting this position entails too the rejection of an interpolating narrator, that is, a narrator who intercedes, contextualises and explains. For an existentialist, the world is not something that is to be, or can be, known; rather it is something encountered, something one lives through. A narrator who hovers over his characters, inserting himself into the text to modify, correct and substantiate, implies also a certain value system, a certain sense of hierarchy. By obliterating this distinction, Kelman decisively distances himself from, among others, William McIlvanney. The latter, although also notably influenced by European existentialism, employs exactly the narrative technique that Kelman criticises. *Docherty*, for example, contains an omniscient third-party voice rendered in standard English, but character voices are given in the demotic. This suggests either a certain verbal and intellectual deficiency, characters are unable to speak and intellectualise events for themselves, or, a denial of freedom: characters are simply *not* permitted to speak and intellectualise events for themselves.

Narrative, then, needs to be carefully monitored, carefully voiced and phrased, lest it becomes complicit in delivering an anti-existential text. Kelman describes his adoption and rejection of various narrative positions as an attempt to construct a value-free text, a 'clean' narrative:

> . . . that's what I was trying to do in *A Chancer* – to get something that was 'Let me state a fact here'. So nobody can say that's your opinion because you're working class or middle class. It had to be something that is so cold, so straight black and white that no-one can deny it as a *fact*. So in a sense, getting rid of the narrative voice is trying to get down to that level of pure objectivity. This is *the* reality here, within this culture. Facticity, or something like that. (*IKM*4–5)

This desire for a 'cold', almost disinfected prose has a number of literary precedents. There are notable similarities with the French 'new novelists' of the 1950s, in particular Alain Robbe-Grillet, for whom prose ought to achieve the neutral, objective quality of a scientific report, but also with Albert Camus' *The Outsider*, which demonstrates a similar disdain for unnecessary or distorting literary colour. Notice, though, that for Kelman, such techniques are deployed to establish a particularly existential quality: facticity.

Facticity, a term used by Kierkegaard, Heidegger and Sartre, denotes the finite and concrete aspects of human being. Facticity refers to the givens of human reality: the fact that I was born in a certain year, to particular parents, in a particular place and so forth, but also in a particular time, in a particular social milieu. Facticity encapsulates the concrete thisness, the particular world, into which being is thrown. The maintaining of a factical sense explains why Kelman dispenses with both metaphor and simile. These literary techniques are rejected for they seek to present the world as something other than it is. To state that something is 'like a', is to move away from what it *is*. Yet what it is, is exactly what is at issue. The existentialist idea of being as a 'thrown facticity', indicates that being is both contingent, but also unavoidably placed, situated, within a concrete and specific set of circumstances. Thus Kelman's narratives invariably begin in the midst of things. Consider the opening of *The Busconductor Hines*:

Hines jumped up from the armchair, she was about to lift the huge
soup-pot of boiling water. She nodded when he said, I'll get it.
. . . What a weight, he said.
   I put in too much . . . She had returned to the oven for a smaller pot
of water which was also boiling . . .She murmured, almost inaudibly.
   What?
   She glanced at him.
   Sorry; I thought you were eh . . . He prised the lid off his tobacco
tin and began rolling a cigarette. Before putting the empty pots back
into their place in the kitchen-cabinet she wiped them dry with the
dishtowel. Then she undressed. She stopped, and walked to draw the
venetian blind at the window above the sink. Hines smiled. Passing
helicopters eh!![8]

Facticity and concretion are established immediately the novel opens. The
passage begins with the subject followed by an active verb, subject and verb
suggesting the existential couplet of being and doing. A number of sentences
– 'I put . . . She glanced . . . He prised . . . She stopped' – convey processes,
the cumulative effect of which is to suggest and reinforce the notion of activity disclosed by the opening clause. The frequent use of the definite article
provokes the situational specificity which one would expect from an existentialist text, and, as with all of Kelman's novels, the opening is immediately
determinative, the passage lacks any aetiological moments; there is no antecedent causal state. We do not know why Hines has jumped until we move
further into the narrative. Similarly, Hines' wife is initially indicated by the
pronoun 'she' and only as the tale progresses do we learn her name.
Noticeable, too, is an abandonment of character description: we are given
no details of physical appearance.
   Dostoevsky's Underground Man, Rilke's Laurid Brigge, Camus'
Meursault, Sartre's Roquentin, Kafka's K: none of these characters is physically described. Kelman too eschews the detailing of physical attributes, for
a focus upon properties is implicitly a focus upon essence. If, however, as
existentialism has it, existence precedes essence[9] then the ascription of character predicates – fat, thin, tall, handsome – is equivalent to the ascription
of essential qualities. An existential narrative needs to show, reveal character as dynamic and fluid – something chosen, constructed through action,
rather than something given and eternally fixed. This movement away from
external description is supplemented and complemented by a rejection of
psychology. More specifically, a rejection of psychology as explanation. For
an existentialist, psychology is neither a repository nor a cause of character
– hence Sartre's opposition to Freud. Character must be shown to be
mutable, open and able to change through its own volition, not the product
of antecedent drives and complexes. *A Chancer* is perhaps the clearest
example of this, for although we accompany Tammas, we are never given

direct access to his inner life. Neither his hopes nor his desires are made present, and whatever the content of his occluded consciousness, he achieves a presence and is revealed to the reader only through his actions.

If a commitment to an existentialist aesthetic engenders a number of related narrative positions, it also suggests a number of themes. Again, operative here are the notions of freedom and contingency. *A Chancer* relies upon cards and gambling as a metonymic reproduction of a life of contingency, and both *The Busconductor Hines* and *How Late it Was, How Late*, feature protagonists whom we might describe as struggling freedoms. All of Kelman's texts deal at some level with the fundamentally insecure and tenuous aspects of human reality, but it is perhaps with *A Disaffection* that Kelman most fully and forcefully engages with existential themes. The calmly declarative opening – 'Patrick Doyle was a teacher. Gradually he had become sickened by it' – compresses plot into two compact sentences, which in turn propel the narrative forward. If Doyle was a teacher, what is he now? How, why, has he become sickened? These questions remain unanswered, for in suitably existentialist fashion, Kelman is less interested in causes and more interested in consequences. Patrick's sickness, rather like that of Dostoevsky's Underground Man, has distinctly metaphysical symptoms. Curiously, given that the novel contains several explicit and implicit references to Kierkegaard, critical attention has often sought to connect Patrick Doyle with George Friel's *Mr Alfred MA*. But the inclusion of Kierkegaard ought instead to direct us to *Either/Or*, the first part of which, Part A, is written by a secondary school teacher who has resigned. Kierkegaard's text dramatises and presents two possible modes of being – the aesthetic and the ethical – which in turn roughly correspond to the Romantic and the existential. *A Disaffection* takes up these opposing life-modes, but instead of allocating each to a separate character, deposits them within one: Patrick Doyle. What Kierkergaard's *Either/Or* presents as a choice, as competing alternatives, *A Disaffection* presents as an *agon*, a contest. This contest revolves around the central symbol of the novel: the electricians' pipes that Doyle finds at the outset of the narrative. For Doyle, these pipes come to represent 'some kind of escape',[10] and thus become symbols of what the German Romantics described as *Sehnsucht,* the longing for a lost sense of wholeness. This sense of loss is perpetuated through Doyle's repeated references to nostalgia. With its Greek roots – *nostos*, 'return', *algos*, 'pain' – the noun encapsulates Doyle's troubled quest for some sense of reconnection, some recoverable sense of rootedness. This is in turn translated into a desire for a form of Romantic transcendence, a desire for reintegration and the achievement of the kind of harmony that Doyle associates with the Pythagoreans: 'One grabs a pair of pipes from the rear of an arts centre and proceeds to blow sounds, and these sounds seem so perfectly stated that the pipes themselves are henceforth transformed, they are become transcendental objects, instruments of music! instruments of something greater than anything previously experienced, anything acted upon with you' (*D*67).

The quest for transcendence is seen here, but Doyle's desire to lift himself out of his factical and earthbound existence is flawed and failing. It proves unsustainable, simply momentary: 'He is going to take this pair of electrician's pipes and create harmony – no he isni' (*D*115). Doyle's other source of longing, both Romantic and romantic, is his married colleague, Alison Houston. Within the novel, Alison functions in a way analogous to Tadzeu in *Death in Venice*, in that she serves as a screen upon which Doyle's imagination projects. *A Disaffection* reconveys a central tenet of Mann's text in that it depicts the consequences of an excessive Romantic imagination. Hence, too, Doyle's identification with Goethe's Werther and his mention of Suzette Gontard – the latter the wife of a Frankfurt banker with whom the poet Hölderlin had an affair. Doyle equivocates between viewing Alison as a person – 'Fuck sake she is just [a] woman and that's that. No paragon there' (*D*89) – and as an object, a form, a solution.

> She was beautiful . . . he had never for one real and genuine minute imagined she could ever arrive here in this place, his house . . . quietly studying the book in hand, taking the weight of her body onto her left foot, the right leg bent at the knee. It was one of these poses, good kind of poses, classic; he could imagine being a sculptor and motioning her to the side a little, and back a little and so on, capturing the shadows of the folds in her coat, these long spiral shapes – curved cuboidals. (*D*138)

Sculpted by Doyle's Romanticised imagination, Alison is transformed into a Platonic form. Again, however, Doyle's imagination is defeated. When in Miller's Bar Patrick touches Alison's hand, she becomes physical – Doyle realises that 'she was human after all' (*D*228) – and she tells Doyle that it is not possible for them to have a relationship. Alison's rejection of Patrick is then a rejection of the possibility of either physical or metaphysical communion or redemption. As Richard Kearney points out, 'while [existentialism] inherits the romantic cult of subjectivity, it exposes the existential limits of man's creative powers. As such, existentialism tempers the initial optimism of romantic idealism. It clips the wings of the transcendental imagination and lays bare the everyday obstacles which obstruct its flights and fiats. [Existentialism] brings imagination back to earth'.[11] With a thump. What Doyle seeks to evade, then, is the reality of his condition. Doyle's Romantic longing becomes an instance of Sartrean bad faith, for Doyle seeks to evade what he is: free. For Heidegger, it is part of our ontological make-up that we are essentially 'unhomely' – that is, we are unrooted, without essence. Doyle only grasps the negative aspect of this; he fails to see that if we are not fixed and final, if we are not an already decided and determined pattern of behaviour, then that enables us to fashion ourselves. In this context, an early conversation in the staffroom over whether one should drink and drive, assumes a greater significance than its ostensible subject matter would suggest:

> It was a case of either/or, the drink or the car.
> Patrick gaped at him. Is that the truth?
> Yeh.
> For fuck sake.
> It would be impossible for him! said Alison. (D40–1)

As it proves to be. Kierkegaard's either/or is not simply an invitation to choose between two options; rather it is an invitation to accept and choose the very possibility of choice, and, therefore, accept the responsibility of self-determination. Doyle never quite manages this. Or, perhaps he does, for in typical fashion, Kelman does not close the narrative, which simply ends with Doyle running away from some unidentified policemen.

What I have tried to show here is that existentialism, far from being a peripheral and ancillary concern, constitutes and contributes much to Kelman's fictions. The identification and investigation of problematic freedom is not, then, simply an instance of Scottish postcolonialism setting itself against its English colonial master. Kelman's existentialism is instead a return to the problematic self locked within its problematic everyday, a return to those issues of individual freedom with which philosophical existentialism began. The subject which Foucault thought washed away on some nameless beach in the 1960s, still persists within the practices and themes of modern fiction.

FOR FURTHER READING

For a hard copy list of James Kelman's work up to 2001, see *Contemporary Novelists*, ed. David Madden et al., 7th edn (New York: St James Press, 2001). For a more up-to-date list on the internet, see the British Council website: <http://www.contemporarywriters.com/authors/>.

Craig, Cairns, 'Resisting Arrest: James Kelman', in *The Scottish Novel Since the Seventies: New Visions, Old Dreams*, ed. Gavin Wallace and Randall Stevenson (Edinburgh: Edinburgh University Press, 1993), pp. 99–114.
Macquarrie, John, *Existentialism* (Harmondsworth: Penguin, 1972).
Milne, Drew, 'James Kelman: Dialectics of Urbanity', *Writing Region and Nation: Proceedings of the Fourth International Conference on the Literature of Region and Nation*, ed. James A. Davies et al. (Swansea: University of Wales, 1994), pp. 393–407.
Nicoll, Laurence, '"This is not a nationalist position": James Kelman's Existential Voice', *Edinburgh Review*, 103 (2000), 79–84.
Various, *Kelman and Commitment*, *Edinburgh Review*, 108 (2001).

NOTES

1 Maurice Merleau-Ponty, *The Phenomenology of Perception*, trans. Colin Smith (1945; London: Routledge, 1962), pp. xvi–xvii.

2 Kirsty McNeill, 'Interview with James Kelman', *Chapman*, No. 57 (Summer 1989), 1–9, 9. Hereafter cited as 'IKM'; page numbers are given in the text.

3 Martin Heidegger, *Being and Time*, trans. John Macquarrie and Edward Robinson (1927; Oxford: Blackwell, 1962), p. 94.

4 The term translates as 'banality', 'tawdriness', 'paltriness'. For Kelman's use of Russian fictional models, see my 'Gogol's Overcoat: Kelman *Resartus*', *Edinburgh Review*, 108 (2001), 116–22.

5 James Kelman, 'The Importance of Glasgow in My Work', *Some Recent Attacks: Essays Cultural and Political* (Stirling: AK Press, 1992), pp. 78–84, p. 80.

6 Jean-Paul Sartre, *What is Literature?* trans. Bernard Frechtman (1948; London: Methuen, 1967), p. 167. Hereafter cited as *WIL*; page numbers are given in the text.

7 James Kelman, *How late it was, how late* (London: Secker & Warburg, 1994), p. 54. All quotations are from this edition; page numbers are given in the text.

8 James Kelman, *The Busconductor Hines* (Edinburgh: Polygon, 1984), p. 9. All quotations are from this edition; page numbers are given in the text.

9 This locution is, strictly speaking, only applicable to Sartre. The formulation registers Sartre's hostility to traditional conceptions of human being, in which every person has a given nature, or set of qualities – an essence – that determines what they are, what they value and what they will be. Sartre reverses this: our values, our choices and desires are generated by ourselves; first we exist, and *then we choose* what we wish to be.

10 James Kelman, *A Disaffection* (London: Secker & Warburg, 1989), p. 136. Hereafter cited as *D*; page numbers are given in the text.

11 Richard Kearney, *The Wake of Imagination: Toward a Postmodern Culture* (London: Routledge, 1994), p. 196.

6

One Nation, Oneself: Politics, Place and Identity in Martin Amis' Fiction

Daniel Lea

Money: a Suicide Note (1984) and *London Fields* (1989) are Amis' most political novels, vituperative castigations of the materialistic attitudes promoted by Thatcherite capitalism. Unlike the formalistic experimentalism of some of his later work (notably *Time's Arrow* [1991]) and the characteristic emotional detachment that appears elsewhere in his fiction, these are committed and angry novels. Amis derides the conspicuousness of the Thatcherite yuppie generation, the consumerism that shamelessly affirms its self-perpetuation whilst disavowing any broader social responsibility. A devotee of free market economics, *Money*'s John Self lives out a fantasy of capitalist exorbitance protected from the reflections of conscience by the seductive reassurance of money.[1] He can know himself only through his possessions, his material and psychic parameters irreducibly entwined, their substance determined only by his affluence in comparison with others. Self is a grotesque parody of superfluous consumption, shorn of morality and self-restraint. But Amis' political engagement, his insistence on the interdependencies and responsibilities that permeate even this attenuated cultural framework, point towards a broader remit of social satire. Despite their metafictional flourishes these novels belong to the tradition of the 'condition-of-England' novel, the tradition beginning with such novels as Benjamin Disraeli's *Sybil* (1845) and Elizabeth Gaskell's *North and South* (1855).[2] Amis' novels lie firmly within the conventions of nineteenth-century realism: they present a mimetic rendition of the objective realm for the purposes of social commentary. Employing a nineteenth-century realist form deliberately problematises that realism however, as, for Amis, the concept of a singular nation and a singular reality is no longer tenable in the era of late capitalism. Both novels postulate the explosion of nationhood and selfhood into an amorphous abstraction that allows the interpenetration of self, other and, most spectacularly, cultural product. Wresting selfhood from the influence of a homogenising capitalism becomes an impossibility given such hybridisation, yet one context for Amis' criticism is the emergence of the right-wing insistence that free-market expansionism is not incompatible with definitions of unique local and national identity. Such an insistence is explicit in the One Nation rhetoric of Margaret Thatcher's early Conservative administrations.

Upon election in 1979 the Thatcher administration put in train a series of economic policies which broke fundamentally with the broadly Keynesian model of previous governments and advocated a free market economy with limited state intervention. Over-reliance on the welfare system was discouraged in this model in favour of self-help, self-reliance and financial self-empowerment.[3] The imperative for economic control by the state was largely relinquished to the trends of a market that embraced the dynamism of capitalist exchange. Existing social divides were addressed by the impact of 'trickle-down' economics which presupposed that greater national affluence would inevitably be dispersed throughout the entire economy, with disadvantaged areas benefiting from the buoyancy of the metropolitan business world. In this way Thatcher broke from the Conservative tradition of the 'One Nation' ideal, replacing it with a political relativism that openly acknowledged divisions in the economic fabric of the nation.[4] At the same moment that the fissures in social provision were disclosed the rhetoric of unity was employed to cohere fragmented constituencies within an overtly nostalgic nationalism, tying individuals and communities to a form of Britishness that by the 1980s was increasingly anachronistic. As Ulf Hedetoft and Hanne Niss have pointed out, the discourse of Britishness as stable and identifiable became vitally important to the Thatcher administration around the time of the Falklands War in 1982 but was rendered most hyperbolically and fervently in the defence of economic policies which appear to be at variance with its assumptions.[5]

For Amis the hypocrisy of the Thatcherite dichotomy lies in the *faux-naif* assumption that an absolute, culturally cohesive national identity can co-exist with the sprawling, indiscriminating momentum of capitalism. One central premise of both *Money* and *London Fields* is that traditional conceptions of place-identity, particularly where they are tied to ideas of nationhood, are meaningless, given the increasingly pervasive influence of globalised media and business concerns. The expansion of multinational corporations and the subsequent spread of a competitive free market arguably destabilise conventions of cultural difference. With the products of pan-continental companies consumed in world-wide markets, and aggressively publicised through the ubiquity of media networks, the individuality of those national markets is seen by Amis to be jeopardised. Mass retailing depends upon the standardisation not only of product but of desire, and advertising relies upon cross-cultural semiotics for maximum effect. The resulting democratisation of cultural interpretation ultimately impacts upon the distinctive qualities of the individual consumer nations. Capitalism, Amis contends, necessitates the homogenisation of the territories into which it expands, extirpating cultural difference and bringing codes of self, community and national formation within the logic of its symbolic order. *Money* explores the collision of capitalism's impulse to dissolution with its main character's residual need to define himself in relation to concrete modes and spaces of belonging.

John Self represents a form of cultural amalgam, positioned between his nation of birth (England) and his primary nation of business (the United States). The novel alternates between London and New York and Self is at home in both and neither. Much of the novel is devoted to his spiritual home-lessness and his frustrated desire to find a space of belonging which endows him with a stable past and historical origin. In New York he creates a surro-gate 'home' in his hotel room and establishes an eccentric, familial, bond with the bell-hop, Felix, based upon outrageously inflated tips. In London, his search for a private space is undermined by the influence of his quondam partner, Selina Street, whose pleas to be allowed to live in his flat challenge his sense of inviolable space and rootedness. Even his genuine familial rela-tionships offer little in the way of stability or history. The man he has always assumed to be his father is revealed to be an impostor, who not only pro-vides Self with a carefully itemised bill for his upbringing, but also arranges a contract beating to be enacted on his 'son'. Self is incapable of defining himself in the terms of any stable origins, yet at the same time, he is willingly alienated from means of self-definition through his devotion to a money-greed which paralyses his ability to judge value in terms other than the finan-cial.

From the biological dictates of his decaying body, through his onanistic attraction to pornography, to the alienated and staccato nature of his rela-tionships with others, his existence is suffused with the influence of material greed. At its most basic level the corruption of capitalism is seen in the parlous condition of Self's body, a site of degeneration as a result of his life-style, but also reflects a deeper psycho-social malaise. An ongoing dialogue with his unresponsive body revolves around a litany of physical defects including a rotten tooth, hair loss and an excess of body fat. The deteriora-tion of his body is explicitly related to external influences that challenge the integrity of his physical boundaries. At one point he complains:

> My clothes are made of monosodium glutamate and hexachlorophene. My food is made of polyester, rayon and lurex. My rug lotions contain vitamins. Do my vitamins feature cleaning agents? I hope so. My brain is gimmicked by a microprocessor the size of a quark, and costing ten pee and running the whole deal. I am made of – junk, I'm just junk. (p. 265)

Self is a man-made man and his body is the product of artificial elements which introduce the corruption of capitalist exchange into his somatic centre. The boundaries of his self are seen as permeable, his body is an exten-sion of the world in which it exists; not only does he indulge in a culture of junk, but that junk penetrates and contaminates his bodily space rendering him internally, as well externally corrupted.

Self's corporeal degradation is paralleled by the wrangling of his fragmented subjectivity that expresses itself through multivocality. He isolates
four distinct voices, all of which are limited and conflictual. Dominating
these vocal registers are the persistent 'jabber of money' and the voice of pornography (p. 108). His third voice is a vaguer gesture towards a melancholia at the passing of time; it is the 'voice of ageing and weather . . . the
ever-weakening voice of stung shame, sad boredom and futile protest' (p.
108). His final voice prompts him to abandon work and embrace a life of
self-confession. This final voice he finds most threatening, for it intimates a
suppressed need for something beyond the protective cordon of money. All
of these voices, however, 'come from somewhere else' and are experienced
as fundamentally alien and involuntary (p. 108). Yet Self has no alternative
means of vocalising his alienation or lack of self-control. The voices which
come from elsewhere are those of an imperialistic capitalism that has infil-
trated his private culture and replaced any 'authentic' voice with a ventrilo-
quial script. His narrative is the product of these voices, and does not present
us with an objective view of the world at large – the view put forward in a
nineteenth-century novel of social realism, a condition-of-England novel.
Instead, it is the highly subjective account of a character whose inner voices
speak of a distinctly idiosyncratic contemporary world.

As with the insistent calls of money and pornography, the third and fourth
voices reveal themselves to Self not as intimations of his humanity, but as
mere psychological traps laid for him by capitalism to guard against any dis-
sension from the ideology of self-reliance. The process of ageing represents
his failure effectively to 'buy time', and he is possessed by dread at the prospect of his impotence in a world of conspicuous power. The voice which
encourages him to absent himself from the world of money is similarly dismissed as an unwilled impulse for self-reflection, which he believes to be tan-
tamount to moral weakness. Self is incapable of disentangling the genuine
desire to escape money from the emotions he believes to have been engineered by money itself to retain him as its slave.

Self is a consumer *par excellence* who has fully assimilated the grammar
of supply and demand into his *Weltanschauung*, meaning that his judgements
can only ever be filtered through the focus of economic compulsion. He sees
with the eyes of capitalism and interprets with its logic. His intellectual independence, which supposedly pre-exists his commercial adventurism, actually
becomes the servant of that system; his independent self is usurped and evis-
cerated by the imperialistic dictates of profit. Given this colonisation it is
redundant to conceptualise a separate identity, whether individual or
national, outside money, for such an identity is fatally compromised. He is
thus a perfect example of why Thatcherism's ideal of discrete national and
economic subjectivities is flawed. Indoctrinated by the ideological imperative
for self-reliance and competitive survival, Self is incapable of envisaging
himself as an indissoluble part of a national or collective identity which is

distinct from the influence of capitalism. Self espouses no national identity and depends upon frequent trans-Atlantic relocation to avoid further complications in his notion of home. He belongs in no traditional sense and stands alienated from any defining culture. Yet Amis suggests that Self represents the condition of the contemporary self – detached, homeless, fluid.

Culture as commodity represents the ultimate phase of money corruption for Amis, as it displays an insidious interpolation of money into national self-image and individual identity. Cultural and social dictates reiterate a predominantly economic *status quo* within an increasingly uniform global market-place. Discrete national and individual identity cannot co-exist with the demands of free unlimited markets precisely because the existence of those markets depends upon the voluntary submission of governments to unified economic practices. To contend that capitalism is an economic system of the state becomes self-defeating, for rather, the state exists as a means for capitalism to thrive, a body upon which it parasitically feeds. Given a relationship where politics is motivated and perpetuated by economics, the idea of an essential identity which defines Britain as distinct from the rest of the world is futile.

The limitations of Thatcherism's conflation of nation and international politics are seen most clearly in the framework of references to the wedding of Prince Charles and Lady Diana Spencer in 1981. This event becomes a symbolic reference point for the narrative and increasingly so for Self, whose initial indifference gives way to a compelled curiosity. The wedding displays the British as a separate people with a long monarchical history, and as an attenuated part of a global community where ownership of a national heritage is seriously compromised by international media coverage. On a microcosmic level the wedding functions as a focus of national togetherness, concretising the political discourse of Britishness. Macrocosmically the wedding reveals how monarchy and heritage have become commodified and sold to a global market as a living performance of history. Self views the ceremony as a moment of hopeful self-assertion by the British, representing a subcutaneous collective identity which reacts triumphantly against a pressure for uniformity: 'London feels like Blackpool or Bognor or Benidorm in bad weather. This is history: the subjects of England converge on the capital, to honour the nuptials of the heir to the throne. This is history, and they want a piece of it. . . . They are loud and happy. Their time has come . . .' (p. 240). Masked by the stentorian tone of his narration is Self's own romantic idealisation of the marriage. His treatment of Lady Diana lacks his customary cynicism, and it is implied that the wedding constitutes a new beginning for both couple and country. This is reiterated as he watches the television broadcast of the event with Martin Amis:

> Lady Diana cruised slowly up the aisle, her tottering dad at her side and the
> pocket bridesmaids smirking in her wake . . . She is nineteen years old, just

starting out. There she goes now, gathering herself into the carriage while the horses stamp. All England dances. I looked at Martin again and . . . I saw a grey tear glint in those heavy eyes. (pp. 262–3)

In this acknowledgement of the potentiality of youth there exists a hope for escape from the greed which appears ubiquitous and all-consuming. The hyperbolic 'all England dances' attests to the communal impact of a national event which appears to define the British within a paradigm of an independent nation-state. However, the ownership of that event by a geographically, historically, culturally and ideologically defined people is illusory. The event is relayed worldwide by media networks and British 'ownership' is at best tangential, because it becomes a global rather than a parochially national experience. The royal wedding becomes a media spectacular in which the paraphernalia and pomp of monarchical tradition are an added attraction to the pantomime of history. The anachronistic retrospection of this presentation emphasises further the degree to which the power of the individual nation-state has become atomised and irrelevant. Influence no longer resides with monarchical structures but exists outside and across national boundaries in the collisions between capitalism and the expanding market. It is ultimately this marriage that has the greater consequences.

London Fields (1989) reveals its political antipathies ironically through the adoption of a detached indifference to the workings of administrative machinery, focusing instead upon the accreted consequences of political and public mistakes. The novel is more formally subversive than *Money*, revealing Amis' growing interest in the limits of representation and the flexible metafictional interface between author, text and reader. Though postmodern in so far as it draws attention to its own constructedness as a literary text, deliberately placing the creative acts of reading and writing at the heart of the narrative, *London Fields* gestures towards the realist tradition in its employment of an, albeit severely compromised, omniscient narrator. Unlike *Money* it revels in its indeterminacy, teasing the reader with the epistemological inverse of a detective fiction and continually shifting characters between contexts, locations and subject positions. Yet for all its formalistic flair *London Fields* retains a strong political sensibility. The novel clearly reflects contemporary concerns about global warming and the nuclear stand-off between the United States and the Soviet Union. Yet there is an overriding interest in the deeper causal roots of these catastrophes, which seem to Amis to be planted in a similar money-greed and selfishness to that which characterised John Self's world. *London Fields* portrays the consequences of a culture of capitalist greed where future security has been ransomed in favour of the 'panting present' (*Money*, p. 207). Where Self is the egotistical monster created from a forceful ideological imperative of self-promotion, identity in *London Fields* is problematised by schizophrenic crises of definition which in turn reflect back upon the condition of political abstention. *London Fields* presents the impossibility of forming a stable individual or national identity in the context of global destabilisation, where the individual is simultaneously aware of her/his position within an immediate environment and as part of a global community responsible for its own destruction. Inevitably the result of this dichotomy is a fragmented subjectivity which is manifested in a desperate search for control of individual actions and the proximate environment.

The ability of individuals to control their actions is a recurring trope. Indeed, a lack of control is seen as fundamental to the ailing condition of the planet, for on both individual and collective levels human existence is characterised by despair and impotence. All areas of the text are dominated by a brooding inevitability (the destruction of the planet; the murder of Nicola Six; the death of the narrator Samson Young) and yet there is simultaneously a competing anarchical instinct which undermines the stability of progression towards the *dénouements*. The unpredictable, protean nature of Young's double narrative perfectly evinces this chaotic seam within a broader framework of inexorability; Nicola is destined to die, but the murderer's identity is not fixed. This authoritarian/carnivalesque dichotomy is typical of the narrative structure of *London Fields* which opposes moments of control with an impotence in the face of events. From the obsessive control which Young demands over the events of the narrative, through Nicola's coercive direction of the actions of Keith and Guy, to the discipline that Keith exerts over his darts practice, each character seeks control of the world around them. Yet these isolated performances of power are all jeopardised by the awareness of the futility of these actions. Throughout the novel Amis presents worlds which are falling apart and which require meticulous ordering to provide a degree of meaning and purpose. The permanence of that order is revealed as illusory, however, for the conditions of apocalypse are irreversible, and temporary control is achievable only on the understanding of that transience. Nicola is able to manipulate Keith and Guy through sexual temptation only because her death is predetermined and her actions appear to bear no direct consequences. At several points near the end of the novel, the possibility of her escaping death and altering the novel's conclusion is raised, but this eventuality is dismissed as impossible. Control is achieved solely through the inevitability of her death, and escape is a chimera.

In the same way that *Money* represents the collision between notions of belonging, so *London Fields* presents a similar schizophrenic contest between form and formlessness and between place-belonging and placelessness. The ambivalence which underscores subjectivity in *Money* is replicated in the later novel through the co-existence of a self bounded by a locality in space and time, and a self that belongs to a global community, guilty of the destruction of that very community. Issues of identity in *London Fields* revolve around conflicts between place and role and suggest that identity can only ever represent itself through instability. This is manifested most clearly in the novel in the area of role-playing which, although ostensibly voluntary, is in fact a compulsive response to the search for cohesive selfhood. All four of the principal characters are chameleonic and are forced to adopt performative roles. The most overt of these is clearly Nicola, who variously plays an erotically teasing vamp, a child-like *ingénue*, an artistic muse and a compliant murder victim. Equally, however, Keith has several personae: darts-disciple; helpful handyman; thief, and most strikingly, the debonair parvenu created for a television documentary. Guy, the most stable and idealistic character, nevertheless falls into the roles of faithful and unfaithful husband. Samson Young plays the narrator whose alternative life is a character in his own drama. The novel consists of the continual oscillation of these characters between their dramatic parts and registers the jolting interchanges as identities become melded before separating. In such a self-consciously metafictional novel the interplay of character roles is partly a knowing acknowledgement of the narrativity of a notional reality, but it also has important connotations for the novel's representation of control and chaos.

Playing roles becomes a necessary means of controlling or wishfully creating an environment within which these characters can belong. The assumption of personae is not a gratuitous act of ludic invention deriving from the firm knowledge of a stable central identity, but exactly the opposite – an unavoidable fluctuation between possible identities as a result of a central vacuum. The players of *London Fields* do not have static selves from which they temporarily deviate, but consist of a fragmented collection of partial selves which alternate freely. The barriers between performed roles are no longer solid therefore, but allow an endless interpenetration. By performing within a particular role the character can attain a form of control, both of their self and their environment, but that dominance is enacted within a wider context of flux and chaos.

The pattern of conflicting identities is further destabilised by representations of place and particularly the role of place in concretely defining the self. Characters are carefully placed within specific contexts – Young in Asprey's flat; Nicola in her chic apartment; Keith in his tower block and Guy in his mansion – and yet their characters are equally defined by their transgressive excursions into other contexts and they assume different roles as they transfer. In his own house Guy is a wealthy, influential bureaucrat; in Young's flat he is the aspirant, yet timid, writer; in Nicola's apartment he is the romantic idealist. Nicola becomes a social worker in Keith's flat and a nanny in Guy's house. Keith shifts between being a willing sex slave at Nicola's, an unreliable child-minder at Guy's, and a thief/entrepreneur at Young's. This fluidity across the boundaries of role and place further jeopardises the possibility of achieving a fixed and unchanging subject position.

Given this continual fluctuation of place and role, the rigid immutability of Young's idealisation of London Fields is significant. Young identifies himself with a utopian image of a romantic, pastoral landscape, a place to which he increasingly desires to go:

> I must go to London Fields, before it's too late.
>
> If I shut my eyes or even if I keep them open I can see the parkland and the sloped bank of the railway line. The foliage is tropical and innocuous, the sky is crystalline and innocuous. In fact the entire vista has a kiddie-book feel. There in his van putts Postman Pat: Postman Pat and his black-and-white cat. It is all outside history. Vicars, spinsters, parkies, gardeners, widows so old, so long-widowed, that they have reverted to a state of virginity. The only hard evidence of sex is the children – and, in the distance (and not so hard), soft hills in the shape of breasts.[6]

This arcadian vision of stability and order contrasts sharply with the shifting incoherence of the London in which Young lives. Significantly, it is described as existing 'outside history' and is thus invulnerable to the degeneration of the novel's ontological reality.[7] As such it is an imaginative response to a situation which is beyond the control or influence of the impotent individual. Young withdraws into a world of childish fantasy where knowledge of sex is displaced into the environment, and where an idyllic freedom of play is beneficently indulged by an established hierarchy. Invoking the presence of vicars, park-wardens and the implicitly worldly-wise widows functions as a wistful sign of regret at the absence of authority-figures, prepared to take responsibility for the ongoing crisis. Yet this pastoral is not simply conjured up to express a desire to escape to the perceived security of an ideal, holistic past; it also articulates a need to establish roots of belonging in a specific place. Away from the flux and chaos of his lived reality, Young imagines his ownership of a private place within which the vagaries of self-definition are replaced by calm knowledge of a pre-existing role.

Given the representation of individual identity as a conflict between multivocal selves as a result of world-historical changes, it inevitably follows that the means for portraying those events are necessarily problematised by that same multivocality. The narrator's efforts to provide a structured, chronologically logical narrative of Nicola's murder are hampered by the inability of conventional narrative form to represent the unrepresentable. At one point Young complains: 'Perhaps because of their addiction to form, writers always lag behind the contemporary formlessness. They write about an old reality, in a language that's even older' (p. 238).

The formlessness of experience necessitates the application of a logical and formal process in art, but what characterises Young's narration are its immediacy, mutability and alleged responsiveness to external events. Through Young's double narrative Amis presents a struggle between narratorial control and narrative chaos. Young's desperation to produce a final work of lasting and ineffable quality leads him not only to found the novel in an immediately proximate reality, but also to connive with his characters to manipulate the contingent nature of that reality. The consequent destabilisation of the barriers between fiction and reality reveals the crisis status of the novel, which, in Amis' view, has historically depended upon a stable conception of a 'real' world. With that stability increasingly equivocal, the fundamental *raison d'être* of the novel is foregrounded, as are the elusive notions of literary value and truth. The questionable relevance of literary form to an experiential formlessness is discernible in the nascent rivalry between Young and his one-time sponsor Mark Asprey, which revolves around the relationship between truth and art and its relevance to an audience which has obstinately ignored the truth of their own planetary self-destruction.

Again Amis returns to the entropic consequences of human negligence and irresponsibility. Truth has no relevance because it has been so monumentally degraded by the instincts of greed and by the demand for instant self-gratification regardless of the consequences. In such a scenario the writer or artist is faced either with producing populist ephemera, or with obsolescence. Asprey's detached approach to his texts is seen as one way of circumventing that obsolescence; the writer distances her/himself from the 'real' world and constructs purely imaginative fantasy. Young is unable to distance himself sufficiently from the 'reality' of his world and is consequently embroiled in a continuum where narrative, narration, fiction and reality are inseparable. Attempting to produce something of enduring value, Young has closely based his novel on a world around him, believing that a form of truth is contained in that reality. Effectively he has ceded his imaginative power to the tangibility of a subjective reality, and in doing so he has compromised his own ability to control and influence events. The distance between author/narrator and between plot/characters is collapsed, rendering him unable to extricate himself both from responsibility for the pattern of events and emotional involvement in those events. The author/narrator becomes incapable of controlling his text if he intends that text to be in any way tangentially connected to a reality. Therefore on a structural level *London Fields* articulates the same dialogue between control and chaos that characterises the narrative response to global deterioration. In a condition of individual impotence in the face of global chaos, narrative inevitably tends towards the formless in sympathy with contemporary incoherence.

The implications of a political reading of this fluctuation between control and chaos are clear. The absence of a controlling political force which provides guidance and authority is crucial to this novel, for it is interpretable as a renunciation of responsibility for events set in train by now absent governments. Whilst less overtly critical of the brutality and rapacity of capitalist free-market politics than *Money*, *London Fields* continues obliquely to attack the principles of money-greed which radically bisects the nation into a 'slum-and-plutocrat' duality (p. 137). Yet the localised eruptions of individualised greed of *Money* are superseded by the global impact of an acculturated greed in *London Fields*. The wholesale indifference necessary for the unalleviated process of political and environmental degradation is seen to derive from increasingly atomised and solipsistic ideologies which naturalise self-interested actions as favourable over collectivity. Given the ubiquity and homogenising impact of capitalism on individual state economies, Amis does not lay blame directly with Thatcher for the ideological imperative of self-gratification. The macro-political context in which Amis sets his novels belies the credibility of economic independence being the preserve of the nation state. Capitalist imperialism renders all politics globalised, reducing the influence of temporary governmental administrations to the negligible. Amis' specific rejection of Thatcherism derives from its refusal to acknowledge the secession of a collective national identity to the individualistic dictates of capitalism. Discourses of Britishness become rhetorical performances of an anachronistic idealism which fails to accommodate the altered conditions of contemporary world politics. As *Money* and *London Fields* illustrate, national identity can no longer be defined by rigid geographical or historical boundaries but exists in a complex continuum of fluid interchange and negotiation. Subjectivity mirrors this pattern of fragmentation, inevitably resulting in crisis and schizophrenia. Thatcherite conceptions of cohesive and discrete selves are, for Amis, exercises only in self-serving political expediency.

FOR FURTHER READING

For a hard copy list of Martin Amis' work up to 2001, see *Contemporary Novelists*, ed. David Madden et al., 7th edn (New York: St James Press, 2001). For a more up-to-date list on the internet, see the British Council website: <http://www.contemporarywriters.com/authors/>.

Diedrick, James, *Understanding Martin Amis* (Columbia: University of South Carolina Press, 1995).
Kavanagh, Dennis, *Thatcherism and British Politics: the End of Consensus?* (Oxford: Oxford University Press, 1987).
Lane, Richard J., Rod Mengham and Philip Tew, eds, *Contemporary British Fiction* (Cambridge: Polity, 2003).
Taylor, D. J., *A Vain Conceit: British Fiction in the 1980s* (London: Bloomsbury, 1989).
Tredell, Nicolas, *The Fiction of Martin Amis* (Cambridge: Icon Books, 2000).

NOTES

1 Martin Amis, *Money: a Suicide Note* (London: Penguin, 1985), p. 91. All quotations are from this edition; page numbers are given in the text.

2 The phrase, 'the condition-of-England question', was coined by Thomas Carlyle in *Past and Present* (1843).

3 For a detailed analysis of Thatcherite economic intervention, see Martin Holmes, *Thatcherism: Scopes and Limits, 1983–1987* (Basingstoke: Macmillan, 1989). See also Stephen Edgell and Vic Duke, *A Measure of Thatcherism: a Sociology of Britain* (London: HarperCollins Academic, 1991).

4 For fuller discussions of the impact of Thatcherite economic policies on national integrity, see Bob Jessop, Kevin Bonnett, Simon Bromley and Tom Ling, *Thatcherism: a Tale of Two Nations* (Cambridge: Polity, 1988); and Peter Riddell, *The Thatcher Era and its Legacy* (Oxford: Blackwell, 1991).

5 Ulf Hedetoft and Hanne Niss, *Taking Stock of Thatcherism* (Aalborg: Publications of the Department of Languages and Intercultural Studies, Aalborg University, 1991), pp. 67–9.

6 Martin Amis, *London Fields* (London: Penguin, 1989), p. 323. All quotations are from this edition; page numbers are given in the text.

7 London Fields has a geographical reality as an area of parkland in Hackney in north-east London, yet Young's romantic construction of a rural past is at best a fantastical recreation of that physical reality. The idealised amalgam of London Fields reflects both Young's desperate desire for stability in a decentred world, and the ambivalent multiplicity of Amis' empirical London, existing between past and present, fiction and reality, ideal and degraded actuality.

PART II

Postcolonialism and other -isms

7

Abdulrazak Gurnah and Hanif Kureishi: Failed Revolutions

Bruce King

As the term 'postcolonialism' changed from its original meaning, from an historical period (used to avoid the misleading 'colonial', 'indepen-dence', 'post-independence' chronology) it took on various cultural and political significances, most of which are concerned with the continuing effects of Western imperialism on Others, and with cultural resistance to those who hold power in the West. As the term has become fashionable it has been applied to all 'minority' struggles against a dominant order, and even to all post-invasion periods of history. It is not uncommon to hear of classical or medieval postcolonial studies. Like most once cutting edge ideas that have been around too long, 'postcolonialism' has become a cliché, a 'received idea' enshrined in the cultural vocabulary. It is unlikely that any student of literature can avoid some version of 'post-colonialism' or 'postcolonial resistance theory'.

I want to look at two writers to show how misleading it can be to apply such generalising terms as Third World, Black, postcolonial or Muslim, to most authors and to the complexities of art. Indeed, literature often seems to be written against such simple-think. The two writers I have in mind are Abdulrazak Gurnah (b. 1948) and Hanif Kureishi (b. 1954), and my title comes from two rather different revolutions that have been part of their background and shape their subject matter and themes. One revolution might be thought 'postcolonial', but the actuality is different from what is usually claimed for such political changes. The other is the counter-culture of the 1960s and 1970s. My reason for including the two writers in the same essay is that they both have been slotted into such categories as 'Muslim', 'Black British', 'immigrant' or 'postcolonial', whereas their novels show the particularities of history and how individual lives differ.

For centuries Zanzibar was controlled by descendants of the Sultan of Omar who interbred with local Africans. Gurnah, originally from Zanzibar, is from part of the Arabised elite that dominated Zanzibar for centuries until independence and a revolution brought Black Africans to power. Zanzibar subsequently became part of Tanzania. Critical studies of Commonwealth, Postcolonial and New English Literatures are generally concerned with

European imperialism and its aftermath, whereas most of the world has a history involving many people and cultures. *Paradise* (1994) portrays the complexities of East African societies on the eve of the First World War. There are Arab traders backed by Indian financiers who dominate the region and deal in cloth, hides, manufactured goods and slaves. The latter are Swahili-speaking Africans, themselves divided into many tribes. The Germans claim the area but they are seldom present, nor are their enemy, the British. The story is seen through the eyes of Yufu who at the age of twelve becomes a slave of a trader after his merchant father cannot pay off his debts.

Besides its portrait of an area of Africa dominated by Arab expansionism which was being challenged by European imperialism, and the portrayal of continuing Arab involvement long after slave trading was banned elsewhere, the novel is also about alienation and freedom. Yufu and others are uprooted as slaves and must learn to adjust to another society. The paradise of the title refers to the trader's garden which Yufu enjoys but which turns into a personal hell as he attracts the attention of the trader's first wife and he falls in love with the trader's second wife; with his loss of innocence, his life as a slave becomes dangerous and he flees the garden. Home, however, depends on memories; Yufu can no longer remember the past. His parents dead, he joins the soldiers the Germans recruit to fight the British. Life is a journey; there is no paradise to which we can return, only dangers, trades, changes in status.

Rather than creating polarities between native and alien culture, Gurnah claims that African writers naturalise international influences.[1] His novels show that Africans have always been part of the larger, changing world. *Paradise* is related to Conrad's *Heart of Darkness* in the Arab trader's journey to the interior of Africa, and to Achebe's *Things Fall Apart* in offering a view of the last moments of a part of Africa before it underwent European colonisation. Like Achebe's novel it offers an alternative history of Africa to that of Western imperialists. It is, however, not a pre-colonial paradise. In explaining the origins of the town where he lives the trader claims:

> 'You'll be thinking: how did so many of these Arabs come to be here in such a short time? When they started to come here, buying slaves from these parts was like picking fruit off a tree. They didn't even have to capture their victims themselves, although some of them did so for the pleasure of it. There were enough people eager to sell their cousins and neighbours for trinkets.'[2]

Gurnah's fiction is rich in ironies, parallels, historical detail and allusions to other works of literature. The writing has a powerful intensity and complex vision. The style is in places imitative of Arabic and Swahili, although not to the degree of Achebe's Iboised English in *Things Fall Apart*.

One of Gurnah's themes is the need to have ambitions to define oneself. Ambition caused people to explore their world, journey outwards and may end in a failure, but those who lack ambition become victims of family, friends, those in power and their own depression. He writes about individuals who are uprooted, alienated, unwanted and therefore are, or feel, resentful victims, yet their condition offers possibilities unlike those who do not attempt to change their lives. Although the effectiveness of the novels is that their focus is on outsiders, and that the narration remains within or near their consciousness, the stories are set within a history of empires and racial discriminations, including modern Zanzibar in which feudal elites after national independence were replaced by revolutionary thugs. Postcolonial liberation may be the replacement of one unjust local order by another.

Memory of Departure (1987) tells of a young man, Hassam Omar, of a part-Arab African family which is headed by a brutal, often drunken father, who beat his eldest son to death, and who earlier in life sold young men to Arabs for sexual purposes. There is now a revolutionary Black Socialist dictatorship in Zanzibar and anyone with Arab blood is treated as a public enemy. Hassam passes his examinations but cannot afford to go to university, which could be his way out of the slums in which his family now lives. At the conclusion Hassam is a sailor on a ship transporting poor migrants between countries as he tries to find a means to reach a part of the world where he might make something of himself. *Memory of Departure* examines the problem of being 'unhoused'; houses owned by others are unsafe from their whims and desires. Ambitions to improve one's life are frustrated by lack of means and opportunities. Gurnah shows a world in which various individuals and groups are in competition and in which achievements easily crumble without support.

Besides treating of migration and journeys, Gurnah's novels examine the relationship of memory to identity; his stories are of exiles and immigrants caught between memories of the past and their present life. *Memory of Departure* was the first of several novels which seem based on autobiography. Gurnah came to England in 1968 and worked as a hospital orderly in Canterbury from 1970 to 1973, then qualified for a Certificate of Education (1975) and a BEd (1976) from the University of London, before teaching at a secondary school in Dover, Kent, 1976–78. He later earned a doctorate and taught at universities. *Pilgrim's Way* (1988) tells of a Black former student who works as a hospital orderly in what appears to be Canterbury, faces various indignities and recalls his past. He was part of the local elite in Zanzibar and fled after the Black revolution against the Arabs. He came to England with his father's savings, which were not enough, and he failed his examinations. He is stranded in England, encounters racial prejudice and is several times threatened by hoodlums. He is bitter, isolates himself from others and feels humiliated by his work, while being unwilling to admit to those at home what his life has become. This is Gurnah's version of Dostoevsky's *Notes from Underground* with a bitter, resentful character at a low point in his life. The thwarting of the African's ambitions makes him resentful of others and turns him towards living alone in a rotting, filthy house.

Admiring Silence (1996) could be *Pilgrim's Way* two decades later. It consists of the dispiriting memories of a forty-two-year-old unnamed African of part-Arab descent. Since he moved to England in the late 1960s he has taken up with and is losing interest in an English woman who is the mother of his teenage daughter. Feeling discontented, alienated, surrounded by racial prejudice, he invents his past, the past of his family and that of Zanzibar. Trying to keep his worlds apart he never tells his family about Emma, his English woman. After twenty years of being away he returns on a visit to Zanzibar; it is a disillusioning society symbolised by overflowing, broken, stinking, filthy toilets. His supposed memories were lies meant to comfort him in exile. Zanzibar is an impoverished place of inter-racial quarrels ruled by those who seek revenge on the formerly ruling Arabs. The narrator returns to England, but Emma has found someone else and he is at home in neither place.

The title of *By the Sea* (2001) refers to the coast of Tanzania and to the British seaside town where one of the two narrators of the novel now lives as a political refugee. As the novel opens he is being interrogated at Immigration and pretends not to speak English. The organisation and sentences of the opening paragraph do not read like normal English prose and often in the following pages the narrator will make minor mistakes in usage and think in Swahili or Arabic. By the end of the novel the narrator has met, learned that he is distantly related to and formed a friendship with another exile who regarded him as an enemy. We learn the complicated family histories of both men, the pettiness, treacheries and hatreds of the formerly dominant part-Arab community, and how the subsequent Black power revolution in Zanzibar punished those with Arab blood while destroying the economy and imposing a tyrannical, corrupt, single-party state. Being part of a diaspora recounting its past allows the men to understand what made them.

Dottie (1990) shows the dangers of obsession with past hurts. Dottie's mother, a Black prostitute, died when the girl was in her teens. After her mother's death Dottie, with a crazed dedication, tries to keep her younger brother and younger sister away from what she feels is a white world intent on humiliating them. Often what she does is wrong and self-defeating. While the story of Dottie might be seen as a criticism of Black British separatism, it portrays a side of Black England that has mostly been ignored The novel shows that British 'Blacks' have complex family histories that need to be traced and told. Dottie's grandfather was a Pathan who ran away from his tyrannical brother and in helping the British during their empire building ended up in Cardiff where he married a Somali woman. This is part of England's history, which includes Africans, West Indians and other people of colour who in various ways came to England and formed part of an unnoticed, unrepresented underclass.

In contrast to Gurnah's concern with Zanzibar, exile, memories and racial resentments, Kureishi's plays and screen plays of the 1980s were part of an angry response by writers to Thatcher's government and its dismantling of the Welfare State. They were also among the first works to look at how British life was changing with the presence of large numbers of Asian immigrants, the class distinctions among the immigrants, and how the children of immigrants were becoming part of English society. Of mixed race, with a Pakistani father and a white British mother, and raised in Bromley, Kent, Kureishi was not concerned with matters of decolonisation, migration, exile and cultural conflict. His subject matter was life in England, including how to leave the dreary suburbs for London, where he hoped still to find the lingering joys of the 1960s counter-culture. Although his early plays were intended as criticisms of Thatcher's effect on society, Kureishi felt the excesses of the Left and the Welfare State were partly responsible for England's problems. Like such theorists as Paul Gilroy, he saw that, by contrast, popular music represented the liberating energies of a cultural revolution, a form of protest that gave the working class a chance to become rich and famous, helped integrate racial and sexual minorities, and changed notions of Englishness.[3] The counter-culture of the 1960s is the ideal of many of Kureishi's characters.

His semi-autobiographical novel, *The Buddha of Suburbia* (1990) opens with a clarion call to a new era. It is one of those grand beginnings (with echoes of Melville's Ishmael, Bellow's Auggie March, even Mark Twain's Huck Finn), filled with energy and introducing a major author and a new voice embodying the personal with generational and national themes:

> 'My name is Karim Amir, and I am an Englishman born and bred, almost. I am often considered to be a funny kind of Englishman, a new breed as it were, having emerged from two old histories. But I don't care – Englishman I am (though not proud of it), from the South London suburbs and going somewhere. Perhaps it is the odd mixture of continents and blood, or here and there, of belonging and not, that makes me restless and easily bored. Or perhaps it was being brought up in the suburbs that did it. Anyway, why search the inner room when it's enough to say that I was looking for trouble, any kind of movement, action and sexual interest I could find, because things were so gloomy, so slow and heavy, in our family, I don't know why. Quite frankly, it was all getting me down and I was ready for anything'.[4]

Karim is not a product of cultural conflict like his father, who came to England from India in 1950, twenty years previously. Karim, at seventeen, is a product of the cultural revolution of the 1960s of pop music, instant fame, sexual freedom, drugs, multiracialism, multiculturalism. *The Buddha of Suburbia* is not primarily about identity, but about desire and liberation and their costs, especially the wounding effect of change on family and those with whom one has emotional ties.

Buddha offers several contrasting portraits of desire and liberation and their effects. There is Karim's father, Haroon, who like Kureishi's own father, is from a well-off Bombay Muslim family, came to England as a student, married a white working-class woman, and settled into a dull, secure job at a time when most of the family moved from India to Pakistan. Now a father of two grown children, Haroon is bored, disappointed and turns to Oriental philosophy with its message of conquering cravings by wishing nothing, especially not divorce: 'In the suburbs people rarely dreamed of striking out for happiness. It was all familiarity and endurance: security and safety were the reward of dullness' (p. 8). In one of the many whimsical ironies that make the novel amusing, Haroon's platitudinising appeals to the ageing hippiedom of the suburbs where, under the guidance of a tempting, ambitious Eva, he becomes famous as a guru whose vaporising people pay to hear. Soon the father is intertwined with Eva, divorces his wife, who collapses but eventually remarries, while bisexual Karim finds mutual satisfaction with Charlie, Eva's son. Charlie in his clothes, hair style, speech and music keeps up with the changing fashion from David Bowie-glitter to Johnny Rotten-punk, and becomes famous.

Karim follows Eva and Haroon to their new flat in West Kensington where Eva and Karim begin their advancement through the opportunities London offers. Eva contacts a former lover, a theatre director, invites the famous, and soon has a career as an interior decorator, while Karim, now the focus of the novel, becomes a brown sex object in the theatre director's awful play, from which he moves on to a major role in a play by a famous avant-garde, theatre director (for whom he is also a brown sex object, as he is for the director's wife). This takes him to New York where Charlie has become a jaded rock star of world-wide tours; eventually Karim achieves his own national fame as an actor in (anti-climax) a soap opera.

The Buddha of Suburbia is a version of the Balzacian novel about the provincial who comes to the metropolis and the ways and costs of making it. Rather than an orphan without a past, Karim is the new breed produced by divorces and a multiracial England. The novel renews modern literature's celebration of the rebellion of desire against its socially and morally imposed limits – as represented by youth versus age, the bohemian against the bourgeoisie, the gay and bisexual rather than the heterosexual, the orgy in contrast to marriage. It treats such themes as part of the aftermath of the great counterculture revolution that began in the 1960s with it sexual and narcotic revolutions, the breakdown of the nuclear family and the racial reshaping of cities.

While the novel's amusing ironies are indebted to British social comedy, they show how people change. It is absurd to expect consistency of behaviour. Anwar, Haroon's best friend who followed him to London, becomes a hen-pecked grocer, goes on a Hindu hunger strike to assert his authority as a Muslim patriarch, and forces Jamila, his feminist Marxist daughter, into an arranged marriage. She is sent from Bombay a deformed, useless, ambitionless husband who regards the marriage as a way to support his reading of middle-brow fiction – Changez demands the complete works of Conan Doyle as part of his dowry. Jamila refuses to have sex with Changez, who makes use of a Japanese prostitute instead. Jamila has sex with Karim, then becomes a lesbian, joins a commune where she has a child who is parented by her doting, continually cuckolded husband. So the love-less arranged marriage does result in affection and an heir, although in untra-ditional ways. The situation, even the tenderness, is amusingly absurd, as there is a tension in Kureishi's work between the enterprising individual's desires and the comforts and security of family and the communal.

Although Karim is not a product of cultural conflict, he is a product of the British class system. The famous rock musicians he admires have emerged from working-class or middle-class suburban families like his own. Karim has also been affected by racism in British schools: 'I was sick too of being affectionately called Shitface and Curryface' (p. 63). He regards his father's belief in the superiority of England and its way as a colonial mental-ity. Racism, however, is seen by Kureishi as white working-class resentment at immigrant competition and achievement, while professional class liberals are often patronising.

The Black Album (1995), Kureishi's portrait of post-swinging London, is set in 1989, the year of the publication of Rushdie's *Satanic Verses*. The lib-erations of the 1960s, the ideologies of the 1970s, massive immigration and Thatcherite economics have resulted in acid raves, slavish followers of any-thing anti-Western, universities in which no one reads, sex without love, dis-appointed feminists, increasing unemployment, angry minorities, angry white men and the collapse of liberal culture. Things have fallen apart, the best lack conviction, there is social, emotional and intellectual anarchy, while fanatics demanding unthinking obedience gain followers among the angry and disillusioned.

Shahid's father rejected Asia and Islam, but a boom-bust-everyone-for-himself economy, working-class resentment, postcolonial theorists and the expedient muticulturalism of some Labour Party politicians have destroyed the national consensus. Shahid is thought Pakistani by skinheads and Muslims. Shahid attends a college staffed by poorly qualified teachers, most disillusioned 1960s radicals, for whom their brighter students write about the cultural significance of Prince recordings while the others take drugs or burn books. Shahid is caught between the fading but well-practised attrac-tions of Deedee Osgood – a college lecturer who teaches him many new pleasures, ranging from designer drugs to masturbation and voyeurism while cross dressing – and Riaz, leader of a group of Islamic fundamentalist toughs who claim that any free thought or individuality leads to Western decadence, inaction, lack of respect for and betrayal of the Third World, especially Islam. Deedee is an example of why the Muslim students turn towards fun-damentalism from liberalism.

In an analogy to *Satanic Verses*, Shahid rewrites some of Riaz's poems and is forced to flee for his life with Deedee who, having tried to discuss Rushdie's book in her class, is hiding from Riaz's gang. But Kureishi is too much a fan of popular culture, and knows contemporary British taste too well, to have an unhappy ending. A now televised Riaz moves from book-burning and violence towards mainstream ethnic politics, while Deedee and Shahid are invited to a private party after a Prince concert. As in much recent British fiction the period is filled in by alluding to its fashions – Fred Perry and Paul Smith shirts, Chrissie Hynde singing 'Stop Your Sobbing'. If the tone and structure of the novel feel mishandled and unfixed that results from the rapidly shifting Ecstasy-influenced high speed hallucinatory style which the novel imitates. *The Black Album* is a plea for real literature, scepticism, and, yes, even England, in contrast to those who regard them with scorn as the products of elitism, liberal decadence, and racist imperialism.

After 1995 Kureishi's fiction turned away from large portraits of the nation and ethnic themes. His later books are about self-doubt, the onset of middle age, and the breakdown of long-term relations and moral rule. Such fiction concerns the loss of youthful excitement, dreams and love as one ages, becomes experienced, and finds the once open world closing. Instead of the liberated, hedonistic, subversive 1960s, and the opportunities it offered, his characters grow older and are faced with the responsibilities and boredom of settled lives. As desires for change and renewal are expressed through sexual relationships and where one lives, such topics as race, social justice and personal advancement are replaced by stories of couples uncoupling, moving, and the costs.

Kureishi had become someone asking where have the youth excitements of the 1960s and 1970s gone? His lament for the passing of unrestricted pleasure was mixed with asking how people lived together, how it was possible to restrict desire, how love could last without betraying the soul of a now ageing rebel. If the desire for fame, variety and renewal are causes of change, the main stimulus is sexual excitement. *Intimacy* (1998) is a complaint at being locked into a loveless, sexless, unaffectionate relationship. It is about the desire for reawakened excitement and the pains of breaking up. The reader's empathy with the male narrator, however, is undermined by the novel's many ironies. The left woman, although sharp-tongued, is not what the narrator claims; he turns down her offers of sex, affection, concern. He has been consistently unfaithful, keeps her awake by scratching his bottom in bed throughout the night, and he likes comfort and order but refuses to help around the house. Another irony is the lack of attractiveness beyond youth and sexual excitement of the object of desire. An uneducated suburban runaway with no mind or interests beyond playing in a rock band, she sleeps around, drifts through life, moving from place to place.

The prose of *Intimacy* approaches the aphoristic and epigrammatical, with short lyrical outbursts, while following the shifts in mood and focus of the narrator's mind. The registers and tones vary from the intellectual and moralistic to the erotic and obscene, but there is always control, precision, economy and rhythm as the novel records the nuances, politics and ethics of personal crisis. Larger emotions sit alongside such realities as cleaning the children's bottoms when they dirty themselves. This is a story about growing up and the conflict between desire and responsibility. The narrator's drug-taking and wish to return to the purple haze of the early 1970s seem pathetic. He has never married the mother of his children, feels no responsibility towards her, and appears to lose little beyond a place to hang his fashion-able clothes. This is not a novel about conflicts of ethnic identity; when the parents of the narrator enter the picture it is as the voice of a rejected world of responsibility. Except for their names we would not even think of them as part of a different cultural past.

Gabriel's Gift (2001) treats a similar situation from a child's perspective and is one of the few places in Kureishi's fiction which concludes with rec-onciliation rather than everyone going in their own direction. An ageing rock musician, Rex, wastes his time at the pub with other has-beens until his woman, Christine, kicks him out. She becomes a waitress to support herself while he lives in a seedy bedsitter. Gabriel is hurt by the situation, cannot understand why his parents cannot get along, and eventually brings them together in marriage. The father learns that the excitements of youth cannot be regained, and that loneliness is worse than being bored by a partner. This is also a book about art. Gabriel has learned about art from his father, has visions and becomes a painter. There is a possible allegory in the names of the characters and in Gabriel's function as an artist (his nickname is Angel) who imitates reality and, through various ironies, it is his art which brings his parents together. Romance is counterpointed by such ironies as Christine thinking Rex is searching for something on the floor when he kneels to propose to her.

In his early works Kureishi encapsulated much of what people felt and did in the 1970s and 1980s. In the later works he became a voice of a genera-tion as it moved into middle age. His writing changed from political and cul-tural themes to the personal, especially the isolated life of an artist. He became concerned with how people live together. If pop culture provided a model for limitless rebellion, Gabriel's art of drawing brings about the need to accept life and aging – not exactly 'post-colonial resistance'. Indeed, it is difficult to understand why postcolonialism should be applied to both the novels of someone writing about self-exile from Zanzibar and the novels of a British writer of part Pakistani (actually Indian) descent who writes about life in England and the difficulties of accepting life's limitations.

FOR FURTHER READING

For a hard copy list of the works of Abdulrazak Gurnah and Hanif Kureishi up to 2001, see *Contemporary Novelists*, ed. David Madden et al., 7th edn (New York: St James Press, 2001). For a more up-to-date list on the internet, see the British Council website:
<http://www.contemporarywriters.com/authors/>.

Griffiths, Gareth, *African Literature: East and West* (London: Longman, 2000).
Lee, A. Robert, 'Long Day's Journey: the Novels of Abdulrazak Gurnah', in *Other Britain, Other British: Contemporary Multicultural Fiction*, ed. Robert A. Lee (London: Pluto, 1995).
Moore-Gilbert, Bart, *Hanif Kureishi* (Manchester: Manchester University Press, 2001).

NOTES

1 *Essays on African Writing Volume 1: a Re-evaluation*, ed. Abdulrazak Gurnah (Oxford: Heinemann, 1993), p. ix.
2 *Paradise* (London: Hamish Hamilton, 1994), p. 131. All quotations are from this edition; page numbers are given in the text.
3 *Dreaming and Scheming: Reflections on Writing and Politics* (London: Faber and Faber, 2002); see, in particular, 'Eight Arms to Hold You', pp. 105–20. Paul Gilroy has argued that 'popular culture has formed spaces in which the politics of "race" could be lived out and transcended in the name of youth' (*There Ain't No Black in the Union Jack* [London: Hutchinson, 1987], p. 167).
4 *The Buddha of Suburbia* (London: Faber, 1990), p. 3. All quotations are from this edition; page numbers are given in the text.

8

Salman Rushdie's Fathers

Hermione Lee

I

> Children make fictions of their fathers, re-inventing them according to their childish needs. The reality of a father is a weight few sons can bear.[1]

So speaks the narrator of *The Moor's Last Sigh* (1995) in the process of discovering that the businessman father Abraham Zogoiby, whom he has sidelined during his childhood under the dominance of a powerful mother, is the embodiment of evil and of corrupt power. Many of Rushdie's characters discover who their real fathers are in the course of their fictional lives, or come to terms with 'the reality of a father'. That is often what makes the 'weight' of their stories, in both personal and political terms. If you were to argue (as the novelist Elizabeth Bowen does)[2] that there is something childish in all writers, especially in a writer as fascinated by childhood as Rushdie, in love with stories and folktales and movies for children, then you could say that the adult Rushdie continues to 'make fictions' of his father. Fathers in Rushdie are unreliable, demanding and frequently metaphorical. They threaten or fail their sons; they battle with the rival power of the mothers; they need to be loved, but may not be loveable.

Fatherhood in Rushdie may itself be a kind of fiction. In *Fury* (2001), the enraged dollmaker Malik Solanka, son of an absentee father and a stepfather who abused him, dressed him as a girl, and gave him dolls to play with, watches the film *Solaris* in horror: 'He'd known a man like this, he thought, a man who lived inside a delusion of fatherhood, trapped in a cruel mistake about the nature of fatherly love. He knew a child like this one, too, he thought, running towards the man who stood in the role of father, but that role was a lie, a lie'.[3] Solanka is the latest in Rushdie's procession of sons who don't know their own fathers – or fathers who don't know their own sons. His novels are full of composite ancestries, illegitimacies, mongrels, orphans and all kinds of dubious parentage – not to mention dubious parenting. This is especially true in the two novels which form a kind of pair, *Midnight's Children* (1981) and *The Moor's Last Sigh* (1995). Rushdie is a plotter of Dickensian elaboration, and (as often in Dickens) his plots hinge on family complexities: inheritances, rivalries, feuds, ancestral quarrels. The emphasis on dynasties is not just personal; it has everything to do with postcoloniality and the politics of the countries he is writing about. But it also feeds into a fictional preoccupation with the slipperiness of parentage and with the desirability of illegitimacy. Better to be a changeling, or a baby switched at birth, or an orphan, or a bastard, than to be imprisoned inside the immutable destiny and inherited weight of family life.

In *Midnight's Children*, Saleem Sinai famously turns out not to be the child of the wealthy middle-class Muslim family, the Sinais, with German and Kashmiri origins, whose history we so painstakingly trace in the first part of the novel, but the swapped, illegitimate baby of a Hindu street singer's wife Vanita, who dies in childbirth, and the Anglo-Indian landlord, the outgoing vestige of colonialism, William Methwold, in whose property the Sinais are tenant-squatter-inheritors. Saleem's double, mixed parentage, and his birth at the stroke of Independence, make him not the child of his father and mother but a child 'fathered . . . by history',[4] and that is the point of the novel. He inherits all the fictions of parentage and – like the newly independent India – is allowed the freedom of 'inventing new parents for myself whenever necessary' (p. 108). And he is part of a world in which everyone invents and reinvents their parentage. His father, Ahmed Sinai, in order to impress the landlord, invents a romantic Muslim ancestry for himself ('Mughal blood, as a matter of fact'), complete with ancestral curse (p. 110). The fictional family curse becomes as much a reality as anything else in this fiction of self-inventions. Methwold, the real father, leaves his own 'curse' on the fictional father Ahmed. After his departure, Ahmed, living on in his property, begins to fade and grow pale and turn into an Englishman, along with many other post-Colonial Indian businessmen, who, in taking over from the British, 'were becoming very, very pale indeed!' (p. 178). So, Ahmed Sinai, Muslim Indian businessman, inherits the pigmentation and attitudes and behaviour patterns of the outgoing British colonialists; and Saleem Sinai, child of independence, inherits everything that pours into Indian history in the ticktock down to 1947: Kashmiri, Hindu, Muslim, British, high and low, fantasy and reality, myth and history. The family in *The Moor's Last Sigh* will be pieced together out of similar kinds of historical mishmashes: Chinese and Portuguese, Jewish and Arab and Spanish strains are mixed into the Zogoiby dynasty, with explosive results.

The father in *The Moor's Last Sigh* is 'the most evil man that ever lived' (p. 417), a monster of corruption and power, a Mafia-style figure in control of the most dangerous, illicit trade in drugs and armaments in India, who is secretly making a nuclear bomb. The father in *Midnight's Children*, by contrast, is a helpless and hopeless figure. That is the more usual status of fathers in Rushdie. They are unmanned by their creator, and turned into figures in retreat; they are often innocent and credulous. Ahmed Sinai sinks into drink and ineffectuality, is temporarily rescued by love, and then has a disabling stroke. When he and his family are ruthlessly exterminated by the narrator (well before the end of the novel), his elegy is to a comically ineffectual character: 'Ahmed who always lost his way and had a lower lip which stuck out and a squashy belly and went white in a freeze and succumbed to abstraction and . . . fell in love too late and died because of his vulnerability to what-falls-out-of-the-sky' (p. 343). In *The Ground Beneath her Feet* (1999) there are two inadequate fathers, the grand Parsi Sir Darius Xerxes Cama, father of Ormus the singer, who withdraws from fatherhood into cricket, studies of mythology, drink, silence and reclusiveness, and the local historian and builder Vivver Merchant, father of Rai, the narrator, who means well as a father but is too trusting and unworldly to succeed. He can always be sold a cheap watch 'and think it an Omega', and his son can always beat him at cards.[5]

Between them these two inadequate fathers undermine the Indian legends of divine paternity: 'As we grow, we lose our belief in our progenitors' super-human nature. They shrivel into more or less unimpressive men and women' (p. 58). Rai's disillusionment has tenderness in it too, and Rushdie's fallible fathers invoke some pity, and love. The children's story *Haroun and the Sea of Stories* (1990), written for Zafar, Rushdie's son by his first marriage, in the first year of the fatwa, is about a father who needs help. Haroun, the son of the story-teller whose gift for story-telling has failed him, rescues his father and returns his gift to him. The son acts out of guilt, because the father's gift fails when the son criticises him for the unimportance of just 'making things up'. 'Storytelling is the only work I know', the father pleads 'piteously' to the son; the son shouts back: 'What's the point of it? *What's the use of stories that aren't even true?*'[6] It is an outburst he will regret.

Life-giving complicity between father and son is here bound up with the imaginative freedom of story-telling: father and son must give each other permission to find some usefulness in fiction. The rescue of the father by the son involves their sharing fictional adventures which bring them together 'like two children': that is, father–son relationships can only work where there is a casting-off of authority and a mutual playfulness. But this is only possible in the light, fairy-tale, happy-ending world which Rushdie deliber-ately constructs in *Haroun* as an antidote to his own imprisonment and as a consolation for his young son. The emotional interdependency between father and son is much darker in the adult novels.

Fatherly love (as much from fathers to daughters as to sons) can be the kind of curse which Ahmed Sinai rashly boasted about. One of the inspira-tions for *Shame* (1983), a novel concerned with the politics of family dynas-ties in Pakistan, was the story of a father's love for a daughter which was also a curse. The narrator tells us the terrible story, set 'not so long ago, in the East End of London', of a Pakistani father's murder of his beloved only child, a daughter, because of her love affair with a white boy and the dishon-our she has brought on the family – so that 'only her blood could wash away the stain'. The narrator (who has recently become a father himself) is appalled to realise that he found himself 'understanding the killer' because he too has 'grown up on a diet of honour and shame'.[7]

Rushdie, who intervenes frequently in *Shame* as himself, invokes his own fatherhood as a means of understanding the cultural politics of family life, which he finds appalling, archaic and understandable. Family feeling, in this bold critique of a particular religious ideology, is shown to be capable of leading to injury, warfare and destruction. One of the most vivid parts of *Shame* is the relationship between the playboy leader, the Prime Minister Iskander Harrapa (who is overthrown by his rival and relation by marriage, Raza Hyder) and his daughter Arjumand Harappa, known, because of her ferocious inviolability, her determination to live life like a man, and her undeviating devotion to her rascally father, as the 'Virgin Ironpants'. During her father's less-than-spotless life she treats him with 'a reverence bordering on idolatry'; after his death she builds around him an 'Alexandrine god-myth' (p. 126). Resemblances between this father-and-daughter couple and Prime Minister Bhutto and his daughter Benazir were evident (the country in *Shame* 'both is and is not Pakistan'). Bhutto was deposed and executed by General Zia in 1979; his daughter followed in his footsteps in governing Pakistan until she too was thrown out. Arjumand's inability to think any ill of her father, frequently criticised by her mother, Harappa's wife and widow, is one of the many strands of dangerous family self-deceptions that fill this novel, and clearly embodies what Rushdie thought of Benazir, whom he mocked in a review in 1988 as still being 'Zulfikar Ali Bhutto's little girl, still unwilling to admit that the martyred parent even committed the tiniest of sins'.[8] The parallel between Arjumand's invidious idolising of her father – so dangerous to their nation – and the London Pakistani father's despotic, destructive idolising of his daughter, is shockingly emphatic.

'A father is both a warning and a lure' (p. 133), says the narrator of *Shame,* speaking in his characteristic tone of unmediated autobiographical reflection. Certainly Rushdie's own relationship with his father edges into a great deal of his fiction (as do his feelings for his own sons, for instance in the sentimental treatment of the three-year-old Asmaan in *Fury*). What Rushdie tells interviewers about his father is that he was a lawyer who moved from Delhi to Bombay, had a son and three daughters, sent his son to school in Rugby and then to Cambridge, moved his family to Karachi in the early 1960s, did not initially approve of his son's ambition to be a writer, and died in the 1980s during the writing of *The Satanic Verses*. Rushdie's fictions provide a composite picture of a recognisable father. Alcoholic fathers who make their family's life hell recur in more than one novel. Ahmed Sinai, in *Midnight's Children*, enters, every evening at six, 'the world of the djinns' (an intentionally painful pun), and his behaviour at the breakfast table is increasingly affected by 'the irritable exhaustion of his war with the bottled spirits' (p. 132). Ormus' father, Sir Darius, in *The Ground Beneath her Feet*, is also a drinker, and takes out his own disappointments in life on his children: 'He was a father who loved his sons and came to be hated by all of them because of the harangue that never ended, the critique that reached no final summation but surged on through the days of their youth' (pp. 52–3). One of the two, bifurcated main characters of *The Satanic Verses* (1988), Salahuddin Chamchawala (who changes his name to Saladin Chamcha when he goes to England) quarrels with his father, the tricky, possessive, domineering Changez Chamchawala, over everything: nationality, religion, his father's second marriage, his father's control of him and their conflicting desires. Their life-long quarrel is told as fairy-tale, but this is the dark opposite of the benign fairy-story world of father and son in *Haroun*. In a parody of the catechism ('Ithaca') section of Joyce's *Ulysses* (a gesture towards the father–son substitution that takes place at this point in *Ulysses* between Bloom and Stephen, towards Stephen as Ireland's prodigal son, and towards Joyce as one of Rushdie's literary fathers), the narrator interrogates the son's resistance to his father:

> Of what did the son accuse the father? Of everything: espionage on child-self, rainbow-pot-stealing, exile. Of turning him into what he might not have become . . . . Of succumbing to Allah-worship. . . . Above all, of magic-lampism, of being an open-sesamist. Everything had come easily to him, charm, women, wealth, power, position. Rub, poof, genie, wish, at once master, hey presto. He was a father who had promised, and then withheld, a magic lamp.[9]

These composite loving, critical, boozing, disappointed, domineering fathers seem closely linked to Rushdie's own life, especially in the short story 'The Courter', in the volume *East, West* (1994), and in the death of the father in *The Satanic Verses*. 'The Courter' (the title refers to the family ayah's mispronunciation of the English word 'porter') seems to be, unusually, unmediated autobiography. The main story is the relationship between the ayah and the porter (both 'enforced exiles', one from India, one from Eastern Europe). But the background is a phase of Rushdie's own life. The story describes how his family lived for a time in the early 1960s in a block of flats in Bayswater, his father having decided to bring the family over from Bombay at the start of Rushdie's time at boarding-school at Rugby. 'Like all his decisions', says the unappeased narrator, 'it was neither explained to nor discussed with anyone, not even my mother'.[10] This father, too, is described as a compulsive and bad-tempered drinker. There are terrible quarrels between the boldest of Salman's sisters and the father. Like Saladin in *The Satanic Verses*, the son feels himself 'coming unstuck from the idea of family itself. . . . I looked at my choleric, face-pulling father and thought about British citizenship. . . . I might soon have a British passport and then, by hook or by crook, I would get away from him. I would not have this face-pulling in my life' (p. 202). In his imagination, he strikes the father dead. At school, on the occasion of Kennedy's assassination, encountering an American boy who tells him that the nation has been orphaned, he sympathises: 'I know how you feel. . . . My father just died, too' (p. 208). But the narrator's sixteen-year-old desire to leave his home and kill his father is mediated by a wry, wise, older narrator, who now recognises that the father cannot be so easily escaped from: 'At sixteen, you still think you can escape from your father. You aren't listening to his voice speaking through your mouth, you don't see how your gestures already mirror his; you don't see him in the way you hold your body, in the way you sign your name. You don't hear his whisper in your blood' (p. 202).

The narrator gets his British passport and is set free to 'make choices that were not the ones my father would have wished'. But his later self comments: 'I . . . have ropes around my neck, I have them to this day, pulling me this way and that, East and West, the nooses tightening, commanding, *choose, choose*. . . . I refuse to choose' (p. 211). These ropes tug underneath all of Rushdie's writing, most violently in the best scene in *The Satanic Verses* (obliterated, for a long time, by the novel's incarceration under the fatwa). One of the key plots – indeed the heart – of *The Satanic Verses* is the alienation between father and son which provokes Saladin Chamcha's name-change and exile from home, and his eventual return to his father's deathbed. Before the fatwa, when it was still possible for him to discuss the formal and psychological workings of the novel, Rushdie described Saladin's return to India, after his attempt to assimilate to British culture, as a vital moment of 'redemption', of facing up at his father's deathbed 'to the big things about life', like 'love and death'.[11] He has acknowledged that the writing of this scene was closely interwoven with his own life: 'In the first draft the father still dies, but the son gets there too late. The central relationship is deliberately left unresolved and unresolvable. The big difference between the first and final ending is that my own father died'. He then moved the scene towards resolution. 'It was a big risk for me'.[12]

As in other, more nakedly autobiographical accounts of the deaths of fathers, like Philip Roth's *Patrimony* (1991) or Blake Morrison's *And When Did You Last See Your Father?* (1993), Saladin's witnessing of his father's death from cancer is unsparingly physical. The son, for the first and last time, is in charge of the father's body, and witnesses all the torments and humiliations of his dying. He shaves him, gives him his medicines, takes him to the lavatory, supports him while he tries to eat, sees the diarrhoea beginning, holds a cup to his mouth as he vomits, carries him to the car for the hospital, watches while the doctors pound his chest, watches his corpse being washed, watches him being lowered into the grave: '*The weight of my father's head, lying in my hand. I laid it down; to rest*' (p. 529). The powerful scene returns us to that first quotation from *The Moor's Last Sigh*: 'The reality of the father is a weight few sons can bear'. And this account of the death of the father ends with 'reality': 'The world, somebody wrote, is the place we prove real by dying in it' (p. 533). The son comes to terms with the physical reality of death; he gets his last lesson from his father, a lesson in courage, and he grasps his fundamental link with his father, one of the few places in Rushdie's work where fairy-tale, myth, misapprehension and self-deception, do not cloud and confuse this relationship.

II

In those two autobiographical treatments of the father, issues of nationality and identity are part of the tension in the relationship. Saladin Chamcha has changed his name and his place of habitation because he wants to be as unlike his father as possible. He is burning with an 'implacable rage' which 'boil[s] away his childhood father-worship' and which makes him determined 'to become the thing his father was-not-could-never-be, that is, a goo-dandproper Englishman' (p. 43). Although I have so far been deliberately dwelling on the emotional, familial even autobiographical side of Rushdie's struggle with fathers, so as to emphasise the powerfully realist, character-driven aspects of his fiction (which often get obliterated by a critical emphasis on magic realism, or postcoloniality, or hybridity), it's clear that this is also a metaphorical and political conflict. The struggle with the literal, personal father invokes the conflict with origins that forms the story of any migrant or émigré. It may stand in, especially in *Midnight's Children*, for the struggle of an independent nation to emerge out of a patriarchal colonial history, or for the loss of the vision of the 'founding fathers'.[13]

A political reading of fatherhood as a metaphor for nationhood has especial force in *Shame*, which directs some savage ridicule at dynastic rule, and in *The Moor's Last Sigh*. Here, the narrator, trying to give a sense of his father's 'demon king' qualities, has a long meditation on the image of a 'National Father' in India. There is no popular tradition of 'Father India', he notes. ('Mother India' is a rival, and vital, subject in Rushdie's fiction.[14]) Popular movies in India are an unerring touchstone for national myths, and 'nobody ever made a movie called *Father India*'. But he once saw a 'trashy extravaganza', a Bollywood imitation of James Bond called 'Mr India', which had an arch-villain called 'Mogambo', who may have 'provide[d] us with an image of the National Father after all', a 'thousand-fingered puppet-master' sitting like a dragon in his cave. (The image points ahead to the berserk dollmaker in *Fury*, who takes some of his characteristics from the foul-mouthed puppet-master in Philip Roth's *Sabbath's Theatre*.) The narrator of *The Moor's Last Sigh* recognises, in the conflict between Mr India and Mogambo, 'the life-and-death oppositions of many movie fathers and sons. Here is *Blade Runner*'s tragic replicant crushing his creator's skull in a lethal filial embrace; and *Star Wars*' Luke Skywalker in his ultimate duel with Darth Vader' (pp. 168–9).

Rushdie's own anxieties about the father–son relationship may have made him especially alert to the Indian cultural preference for myths of 'Mother India' over 'Father India'. But the father-son psychodramas which so often play out in his fiction are almost always staged, also, as political allegories.

He has written with loathing about the family dynasties which have had such power in the political history of India and Pakistan. *Midnight's Children* and *Shame* expend great energy on the grotesque family struggles for power in those histories. And in his non-fictional political comments, Rushdie, like other left-wing critics of politics in India and Pakistan, has firmly maintained that dynastic rule is bad for democracy. Writing on the Nehrus and the Gandhis in 1985, Rushdie said: 'the facts indicate that Family rule has not left Indian democracy in particularly good shape.'[15] Fatherhood is frequently used as a metaphor for political despotism, most sinisterly (and most dangerously to the author) in the caricature of the Ayatollah Khomeini as the Imam in *The Satanic Verses*, a grotesque fundamentalist tyrant, who is also a ferocious and despotic father: 'His son . . . bows before his father like a pilgrim at a shrine. . . . The Imam is a massive stillness, an immobility. He is living stone. . . . He is pure force, an elemental being; he moves without motion, acts without doing, speaks without uttering a sound. He is the conjurer and history is his trick' (p. 210). Like the ruler of the sad city of Khattam-Sud in *Haroun*, he is the dark tyrant whose power can bring into being the 'Untime of the Imam' – otherwise known as a fundamentalist theocracy.

Fathers act as loud political metaphors in Rushdie's work. But they also provide a way of thinking about writing. Theories and studies of postcolonial writing frequently use the concept of patriarchy or patriarchal rule to make clear what is being written against, or resisted, or subverted, in postcolonial literature. The project in postcolonial writing (and literary studies) of 'reconstructing the canon' has been described as a reaction against 'the privileging hierarchy of a "patriarchal" or "metropolitan" concept of literature'. The postcolonial enterprise has been called 'the subversion of patriarchal literary forms', and when postcolonial literature is seen as a form of 'counter-discourse', or 'writing back' (a phrase itself borrowed from Rushdie), it is often said to be reacting against paternalistic ideas. In postcolonial studies, Rushdie is cited as an example of a 'migrant' writer who displays a rich, polyphonic, hybrid array of literary borrowings, adaptations, mutations, appropriations and disruptions: all techniques 'for dismantling authority'.[16]

Rushdie is a novelist who 'writes back' to a large number of literary fathers. Reviewers, reaching for their inevitable comparisons, bring out whole hosts of (male) literary progenitors: Gunther Grass, Laurence Sterne, Franz Kafka, N. V. Gogol, Miguel de Cervantes, Herman Melville, François Rabelais, Gabriel García Márquez, James Joyce, Samuel Beckett, Flann O'Brien. The list of what Rushdie has called his chosen family extends from Latin American magical realism, European satire, modernism and surrealism, to Indian myth, children's stories, and Western and Asian movies. This hotchpotch of paternal influences makes its presence strongly felt in his narratives, and he has been at pains to acknowledge some of his literary fathers, as in his much-quoted tribute to Gunther Grass and the 'midget drummer' of *The Tin Drum*, who taught him (as he says in *Imaginary Homelands*) to 'argue with the world' and never to forget that 'writing is as close as we get to keeping a hold on the thousand and one things – childhood, certainties, cities, doubts, dreams, instants, phrases, parents, loves – that go on slipping, like sand, through our fingers' (p. 277).

Tributes to literary fathers are always ambivalent – as Freud, or Harold Bloom, will tell us. Rushdie's list of filial debts to Grass includes 'childhood' and 'parents' as things we should try to keep hold of, but which also keep slipping away. He also learns resistance and bloody-mindedness from him. So he learns from his literary father to throw off all fathers. All Rushdie's novels express a preference for being what Rai in *The Ground Beneath Her Feet* calls 'semi-detached' (p. 72). All involve a desire – as much 'migrant writing' does – for an anti-authoritarian weightlessness and rootlessness, for the shedding of all fathers (which may also co-exist with a desire to go home again).[17] 'In every generation', says Rai, 'there are a few souls, call them lucky or cursed, who are simply *born not belonging,* who come into the world semi-detached . . . without strong affiliation to family or location or nation or race'. The world, he argues, erects a system of taboos and prohibitions against rootlessness, but in our dreams we 'soar, we fly, we flee'. 'In our myths, our arts, our songs, we celebrate the non-belongers, the different ones, the outlaws, the freaks' (pp. 72–3).

Rushdie is committed to representing the histories of nations, places and families, but, at the same time, he is dedicated to a fictional ideal of outlawry and non-belonging. One of his literary fathers is Rudyard Kipling, whom he has written about with an interesting mixture of suspicion, resentment and admiration. Kipling – as others, including Edward Said, have noted – is a difficult patriarchal figure for postcolonial writers.[18] Rushdie often mentions Mowgli (especially in *The Moor's Last Sigh* and *The Ground Beneath Her Feet*). The wolf-child, estranged from his family and brought up by animals in the jungle, alienated from the human race and yet belonging to it, is the invention of the Anglo-Indian writer whom Rushdie rightly diagnoses as 'a personality in conflict with itself, part bazaar-boy, part sahib' (*IH*74). The narrator of *The Moor's Last Sigh*, in a passage about his father, calls himself a perpetual outsider, a Mowgli (*MLS*241). The narrator of *The Ground Beneath her Feet*, saying goodbye to his country ('India. . . . my fable, my mother, my father and my first great truth'), steals a phrase from Mowgli to define his self-exile: 'I go – I hunt – alone' (*GBF*248–9). It is entirely characteristic that Rushdie should express his rejection of fathers, his determination to be an outcast, through a literary quotation which suggests that he carries the weight of his fathers always with him.

FOR FURTHER READING

For a hard copy list of Salman Rushdie's work up to 2001, see *Contemporary Novelists*, ed. David Madden et al., 7th edn (New York: St James Press, 2001). For a more up-to-date list on the internet, see the British Council website: <http://www.contemporarywriters.com/authors/>.

Ashcroft, Bill, Gareth Griffiths and Helen Tiffin, eds, *The Empire Writes Back: Theory and Practice in Post-Colonial Literatures* (London: Routledge, 1989).

Boehmer, Elleke, *Colonial & Postcolonial Literature* (Oxford: Oxford University Press, 1995).

Hodge, Bob and Vijay Mishra, 'What is Post(-)colonialism?', in *Colonial Discourse and Post-Colonial Theory: a Reader*, ed. Patrick Williams and Laura Chrisman (Brighton: Harvester Wheatsheaf, 1993), pp. 276–90.

Nasta, Susheila, 'Introduction', *Reading the 'New' Literatures in a Postcolonial Era* (London: The English Association, 2000), pp. 1–16.

Rutherford, Anna, *From Commonwealth to Post-Colonial* (Coventry: Dangaroo Press, 1992).

Said, Edward, *Culture and Imperialism* (New York: Vintage, 1993).

Slemon, Stephen and Helen Tiffin, eds, *After Europe: Critical Theory and Post-Colonial Writing* (Coventry: Dangaroo Press, 1989).

NOTES

1 Salman Rushdie, *The Moor's Last Sigh* (London: Jonathan Cape, 1995), p. 331. All quotations are from this edition; page numbers are given in the text.

2 Elizabeth Bowen, 'The Roving Eye', *Afterthought: Pieces About Writing* (London: Longman, Green, 1962), p. 194.

3 Salman Rushdie, *Fury* (London: Jonathan Cape, 2001), p. 220. All quotations are from this edition; page numbers are given in the text.

4 Salman Rushdie, *Midnight's Children* (London: Jonathan Cape, 1981), p. 178. All quotations are from this edition; page numbers are given in the text.

5 Salman Rushdie, *The Ground Beneath Her Feet* (London: Jonathan Cape, 1999), p. 77. All quotations are from this edition; page numbers are given in the text.

6 Salman Rushdie, *Haroun and The Sea of Stories* (Cambridge: Granta Books, 1990), pp. 22, 27; italics original. All quotations are from this edition; page numbers are given in the text.

7 Salman Rushdie, *Shame* (London: Jonathan Cape, 1983), p. 115. All quotations are from this edition; page numbers are given in the text.

8 Salman Rushdie, *Imaginary Homelands* (Cambridge: Granta Books, 1991), p. 57. All quotations are from this edition; page numbers are given in the text.

9 Salman Rushdie, *The Satanic Verses* (London: Jonathan Cape, 1988), p. 69. All quotations are from this edition; page numbers are given in the text.

10 Salman Rushdie, *East, West* (London: Jonathan Cape, 1994), p. 181. All quotations are from this edition; page numbers are given in the text.

11 'Salman Rushdie: an Interview by Catherine Bush', *Conjunctions: 14* (New York: Collier Books), 20 October 1988, 7–20, 17.

12 Interview with Sara Rance, *The Observer*, 3 May 1992, 54.

13 'The project of India, what the founding fathers of the country – Nehru and Gandhi – had brought into being was a country which was internationalist . . . socialistic . . . secularist . . . That's the India that I was born into and that's the idea I try to write about . . . And what's happened is . . . that idea really hasn't survived' ('Underground but Unbowed', interview with Sarah Crichton, *Newsweek*, 5 February 1995, p. 53). For fathers and 'pluralism' in *The Satanic Verses*, see Ishrat Linblad, 'Salman Rushdie's *The Satanic Verses: Monoism contra Pluralism*', in *From Commonwealth to Post-Colonial*, ed. Anna Rutherford (Coventry: Dangaroo Press, 1992), pp. 83–90.

14 For an analysis of the film 'Mother India', see Vijay Mishra, 'The Text of "Mother India"', in *After Europe: Critical Theory and Post-Colonial Writing*, ed. Stephen Slemon and Helen Tiffin (Coventry: Dangaroo Press, 1989), pp. 138–42.

15 Salman Rushdie, *Imaginary Homelands* (Cambridge: Granta Books, 1991), p. 52. All quotations are from this edition.

16 The phrase 'subversion of patriarchal literary forms', appears in *The Empire Writes Back: Theory and Practice in Post-Colonial Literatures*, ed. Bill Ashcroft, Gareth Griffiths and Helen Tiffin (London: Routledge, 1989), p. 176; 'counter-discourse' appears in Susheila Nasta's introduction to *Reading the 'New' Literatures in a Postcolonial Era* (London: The English Association, 2000), pp. 1–16, p. 5; and 'migrant's art' in Elleke Boehmer, *Colonial & Postcolonial Literature* (Oxford: Oxford University Press, 1995), pp. 205–6.

17 For Rushdie, migrant writing and 'weightlessness', see Boehmer, *Colonial & Postcolonial Literature*, pp. 232–42.

18 On Kipling and his legacy, see Edward Said, *Culture and Imperialism* (New York: Vintage, 1993), pp. 159–96.

9

Postcolonialism and 'The Figure of the Jew': Caryl Phillips and Zadie Smith

Bart Moore-Gilbert

Connections between Jewry and today's postcolonial world can be traced back to the Roman dispersal of the Jews in AD 70. This led, for example, to the establishment of a Jewish community in Cochin within a few decades. Amitav Ghosh's *In an Antique Land* (1992) reminds us that by the Middle Ages there were well-established economic and cultural networks between the Mediterranean, Egypt and India, involving Jews and non-Jews. With successive expulsions from other European regions in later periods, Jewish refugees proliferated in the colonial world. Salman Rushdie's *The Moor's Last Sigh* (1996) addresses the fate of Jews (and others) evicted from Spain in 1492, who found their way to regions as diverse as the Caribbean and India. South Africa received refugees from pogroms in Czarist territories in the late nineteenth century; and, as Caroline Link's film *Nowhere in Africa* (2003) depicts, Kenya provided a haven for some Jews escaping the Nazis in the 1930s.

With the advent of modernity in the late eighteenth century, 'the figure of the Jew' emerges as a trope in the discourses of colonial subjects. A characteristic dichotomy of attitude is established early in this period. Thus the sometimes patronising, even anti-Semitic, register of Ignatio Sancho's *Letters* (1782) contrasts with Olaudah Equiano's enthusiastic ethnographic self-fashioning in the image of the Jew in *The Interesting Narrative* (1785). Whereas the Jamaican-born Mary Seacole's *The Wonderful Adventures* (1857) contains an unflattering portrait of 'Jew Johnny', towards the end of the nineteenth century Zionism emerges as a major inspiration for Black thinkers across the diaspora, from E. W. Blyden in Liberia to W. E. B. Du Bois in the US. Certain twentieth-century anti-colonial nationalists, like Arthur Griffiths and Marcus Garvey, were hostile to Jews. Others, like Frantz Fanon and Aimé Césaire, theorised colonial racism partly by analogy with European anti-Semitism. Such ambivalence of attitude continues to this day, as will be seen.

The cultures born of slavery persistently invoked Jewish history as a model for its own articulation of suffering and displacement. Such standard tropes as 'Zion' and 'Babylon' persist in many postcolonial texts of the Black diaspora, for example Sam Selvon's *The Lonely Londoners* (1956). Here, the central character, significantly named Moses, acts as leader of those newly departed from the Caribbean to the supposedly 'promised land' of London. 'The figure of the Jew' recurs in less obvious contexts, too. Thus Sally Morgan's *My Place* (1988), following Patrick White's *Riders in the Chariot* (1961), compares the fates of Aboriginals and twentieth-century European Jewry. Equally, Salman Rushdie argues that writers like himself, originating from the Indian sub-continent, should draw on the experience of previous migrations to orient themselves within the former colonial centre: 'We can quite legitimately claim as our ancestors the Huguenots, the Irish, the Jews . . . the history of immigrant Britain'.[1] The work of many of his contemporaries, from Hanif Kureishi's *Birds of Passage* (1983) to Atima Srivastava's *Looking for Maya* (1999), suggests that this hint has certainly been profitably heeded in respect of the Anglo-Jewish example.

The focus in this chapter is on two such writers, Caryl Phillips and Zadie Smith. Phillips' engagement with 'the figure of the Jew' is central to several of his novels, from *Higher Ground* (1989) to *The Nature of Blood* (1997). It also inflects his travelogues, especially *The European Tribe* (1987) and *The Atlantic Sound* (2000). Jewish experience is equally prominent in both of Smith's fictions to date, *White Teeth* (2000) and *The Autograph Man* (2002). However, the pair differ in several important ways; their place of birth (Phillips was born in St Kitts, Smith in Britain), their gender, their professional location (Phillips now lives in New York, Smith in London), and the kinds of Jew and Jewish history with which they engage. There is one further distinction. Phillips' maternal grandfather 'was a Portuguese Jew whose ancestry goes back to the island of Madeira. I didn't know him, and I didn't grow up in Leeds with any knowledge of him. My mother never really talked about him, and I was in my twenties when I became aware of his ancestry'.[2] Thus, unlike Smith, Phillips writes partly as an insider to 'Jewishness' (though technically he is not one). If 'the figure of the Jew' is crucial to both writers' exploration of (post)colonial diasporic experience, their contrasting treatment of the trope may owe something to these differences between them.

The contrast might be broached in terms of Edward Said's perception of opposed ways of registering the 'contrapuntal' nature of what he calls the 'overlapping territories, intertwined histories' of the modern world and the communities which form it. Smith's vision is what Said would call 'symphonic', Phillips' that of the 'atonal ensemble'.[3] The difference might be described in shorthand fashion in terms of a desire to emphasise, respectively, similarities and differences between the communities chosen for comparison, and it organises the two authors' analyses at a number of levels, thematic, stylistic and ideological.

The 'symphonic' nature of Smith's representation of contemporary intercultural relations, including those between metropolitan minorities of 'New

Commonwealth' origin and Jews, rests on a model of inter-action which corresponds closely to Rushdie's celebrated account of *The Satanic Verses:*

> [It] celebrates hybridity, impurity, inter-mingling, the transformation that comes of new and unexpected combinations of human beings, cultures, ideas, politics, movies, songs. It rejoices in mongrelisation and fears the absolutism of the Pure. *Mélange*, hotchpotch, a bit of this and a bit of that is *how newness enters the world*. It is the great possibility that mass migration gives the world, and I have tried to embrace it. *The Satanic Verses* is for change-by-fusion, change-by-conjoining. It is a love song to our mongrel selves.[4]

Smith's vision of cultural hybridity is not one of unalloyed celebration. The confused and often angry Millat in *White Teeth* is clearly a casualty of his multiple cultural affiliations. And the description of the security apparatus at Alex's synagogue in *The Autograph Man* is a reminder that anti-Semitism persists today as much as epidermal racism.[5] In general, however, Smith conceives of cultural hybridity like Rushdie, as a desirable dialectical process in which different traditions, cultures and identities merge to create a new, superior, unified third term.

At the stylistic level, such fusions are instantiated by *White Teeth*'s combination of conventions drawn from Bollywood and Western soap opera; in *The Autograph Man* by the juxtaposition of the *Kabbalah* and Zen philosophy as narrative resources. They are embodied thematically in many ways. For instance, Adam conjoins study of the *Torah* with a Rastafarian devotion to *ganja* in constructing a Jewish-Caribbean road to Enlightenment. Most radically, they are signalled in Smith's emphasis on racial mixing. In *White Teeth,* Irie is the product of the Englishman Archie's marriage to the Jamaican-British Clara; in *The Autograph Man*, Alex Li-Tandem is born to a Chinese father and Jewish mother. Such beings attest to the futility of attempting to police desire, ethnicity and identity in the name of Purity and point towards an emergent metropolitan culture which is less divided on racial lines. Smith's vision represents an alternative to assimilationist doctrine, which 'allows' minorities to remain visibly distinct while requiring them to adopt the cultural traditions and values of the dominant ethnicity. Norman Tebbitt's infamous 'cricket test' ('Which side do they cheer for? . . . Are you still looking back to where you came from or where you are?') is invoked in *White Teeth* as an example of this tendency on the part of the dominant society.[6] Magid's slavish mimicry of 'Englishness' represents its internalisation by minorities themselves. Equally, Smith rejects versions of multiculturalism which preserve the authority of the dominant ethnicity as 'first amongst equals' or as the guarantor of cultural diversity within the nation – as the increasingly marginal nature of Archie's role as arbitrator within the text suggests. She also resists those discourses in both 'host' and migrant society which see hybridity as an undesirable dilution of supposedly authentic identities. Poppy's unhealthily exoticising interest in Samad's supposed 'Indianness' embodies the former tendency. However, Hortense objects to Archie as Clara's mate on the grounds of race (absurdly, given that it transpires that she is mixed-race herself) and KEVIN represents an unacceptable purist obsession with Islamic tradition.

In both novels, 'Jewishness' is represented as an integral part of contemporary metropolitan life. This is symbolised in various ways. For example, Malkovitch's Bakery is a familiar landmark within the physical environment of *White Teeth*. The community includes Hasidic Jews as well as the Chalfens, a successful family, whose secularity is balanced by a fierce pride in their Jewish genealogy. Equally, in *The Autograph Man*, the trio of doctrinally differing rabbis are minor characters whose recurrence normalises the community they represent; and Alex and Adam (who is Black) embody further the variety of 'Jewishness' in the modern world. Smith's emphasis on this plurality undermines the idea that there is an essential 'Jewishness', as does Alex's failure to complete his intended book on the distinctions between 'Jewishness' and 'goyishness'. In extending to 'Jewishness' antifoundationalist arguments that have been made about 'Blackness' by critics like Stuart Hall and Paul Gilroy,[7] Smith denies all the communities with which she engages any exceptionalist or essentialist mandate as well as undermining the grounds on which regimes of stereotypes about them rest.[8] Indeed, at times, the positions of Blacks and Jews are not just equivalent but interchangeable in Smith's work. *The Autograph Man* opens with Lenny Bruce's contention that 'Negroes are all Jews' (n.p.) and for Alex, Marvin's class position makes the latter 'a Jew' (p. 54). And the desirably contingent nature of identity which underlies Smith's conception of cultural hybridity is best indicated by the fact that, in both texts, the romantic interest is largely fulfilled by the union of those of Jewish blood and non-Jews. In *The Autograph Man* Alex wins Esther, and in *White Teeth*, more radically still, Irie – pregnant by either Millat or Magid – teams up with Joshua.

The 'symphonic' nature of Smith's vision of contemporary intercultural relations – and those between Jews and 'New Commonwealth' minorities more specifically – is complemented by her style. Smith's brand of comic realism, her predominant narrative mode, belongs to a long-established mode of British fiction, represented pre-eminently, for Smith, by E. M. Forster. She has commented on how Forster's humane liberal vision generates 'the shape' of his fiction, based as it is on 'ideas of human connection' which reach their supreme expression in 'the multiplicity-in-unity that he found in India'.[9] As this implies, Smith's own deployment of the genre stresses integration at both the formal and social/ideological levels. In terms of the former, it is noticeable how often she uses parallelism, and how often minor characters and motifs recur. In *White Teeth*, for example, the Nazi scientist whom Archie spares at the beginning of the text in 1945, reappears at Marcus Chalfen's launch of his research-findings in genetics at its climax, in

1999. Her endings comply with the norms of comedy, with an emphasis on the reaffirmation of community.

More specifically, she conveys the 'multiplicity-in-unity' of multiracial community more confidently than Forster manages in *A Passage to India*, a text which is repeatedly invoked in *White Teeth*.[10] If the conclusion of her mentor's novel is that the realisation of this ideal is some way off, symbolised in the way that Aziz and Fielding veer away from each other on their last ride, *White Teeth*, by contrast, suggests that Forster's vision is now attainable. The relationship between Archie and Samad, which begins in the colonial era, is clearly partly an updating of that between Forster's protagonists. For all its problems, the pair enjoy an enduring friendship based on equality and mutual respect. The cross-ethnic relationships which abound in *The Autograph Man*, notably between Alex and Kitty, reinforce this message.

If Smith's primary genre is 'comic realism', albeit of an often self-reflexively postmodern kind, the optimism of her work perhaps also rests on the fact that her engagement with 'the figure of the Jew' is clearly circumscribed. Certainly, there is reference to the lamentable fate of European Jewry in the mid-twentieth century; in *White Teeth*, the refugee Sol and the former Nazi Perret are chilling reminders of the Holocaust. However, her primary engagement is with young British Jews in the period since 1980. None is a victim of their Jewishness specifically. Smith's sanguine vision is partly grounded in a specific conviction of London's potential to nurture tolerant kinds of hybridity, in contrast to the New York of *The Autograph Man*, which is highly segregated.[11] In this regard, Smith is part of a clear current in contemporary 'Black' British thinking. Gilroy has noted the emergence of new kinds of non-essentialist approaches to the relationship between race and culture in 1980s London.[12] Yasmin Alibhai-Brown also argues that the metropolis now affords unforeseen possibilities for self-identification and community: 'I wish to claim London for us and those who think like us. Here we will preserve that historic fudge – a Britishness which is a civic device to bind people together without recourse to ethnicity'.[13]

Such emphases give Smith's work a redemptive tone, suggesting that while the Holocaust cannot be forgotten, and while the thinking which led to it still offers salutary lessons, a new cultural dispensation has emerged within which that trauma can begin to be healed. Certainly, the Holocaust is not represented as a pressing preoccupation for any of her Jewish characters. In *The Autograph Man* Alex is aware of his maternal relatives' disappearance and has himself visited Auschwitz. But he is unable to connect such events to his own life.[14] In New York, he is dismayed to find that in his hotel room the history channel offers nothing but programmes on Hitler.[15] This parallels Smith's treatment of slavery and colonialism in *White Teeth*. Irie's search for her 'roots' is seen as understandable, though the family history she uncovers proves much more provisional and ambiguous than anticipated. But Samad's obsession with colonial history and its injustices, represented by his devotion to the memory of his ancestor Mangal Pande, is deemed excessive. Symbolic of the increasing irrelevance of this kind of colonial history to contemporary multicultural London is the fact that Pande's portrait is only very reluctantly hung in O'Connell's.

The significantly different nature of Phillips' engagement with 'the figure of the Jew' in the context of diasporic postcolonialism can be immediately detected in his style, which even in his novels is characterised by a naturalism never far removed from the reportage of his travelogues. If Forster is Smith's principal inter-text, perhaps the biggest influence on Phillips' fictional treatment of the trope under discussion is Anne Frank's *The Diary of a Young Girl* (1947), which *The European Tribe* describes as 'one of the most important books of the century'.[16] (It is worth pointing out that Phillips' very first (unpublished) piece of fiction was about a teenage Jewish boy in wartime Amsterdam, inspired by a programme he watched about the Nazi occupation of Holland.) The third part of *Higher Ground* and, more obviously, Eva's first-person narrative in *The Nature of Blood* are modelled to different degrees on Frank's spare, but precise, record of her life in hiding. The self-effacing, seemingly unliterary, style of his novels' treatment of 'the figure of the Jew' implies that even this much further on from Auschwitz than Theodore Adorno, the artistic representation of such events remains highly problematic, bringing to mind the latter's famous claim that the Holocaust rendered poetry, at least, redundant.[17]

As this implies, the tone of Phillips' work is often bleakly tragic, a world away from the sometimes slapstick comedy of Smith. In part this is also because he ranges much more widely over time and space than the latter. *The Nature of Blood*, for example, represents the dismal experience of fifteenth-century Venetian Jewry in counterpoint with the history of the Holocaust and of Israel from its emergence to the present time. This allows Phillips to introduce deeply uncomfortable aspects of Jewish experience that Smith does not touch on in any detail. More fundamentally, there is no sense in Phillips' work that a line can yet be drawn under such events. Not only is Israel clearly represented in his texts as a state still in the making, but the discourses shaping the historical events which led to its foundation continue to cast a dark shadow on the contemporary world. For Phillips, 'forgetting' these aspects of history (for whatever reason) does not promise healing; rather, it threatens their recurrence. In *The European Tribe*, he quotes George Santayana to this effect,[18] and himself relates the ethnic cleansing in Yugoslavia to increasing amnesia about 'the final solution' (p. xiii).

The fact that the Jewish experience in the Second World War is what first prompted Phillips' own reflections on his predicament as a 'stranger' (pp. 66–7) in Europe, perhaps explains his subsequent characteristic juxtaposition of Jews and Blacks as co-sufferers of the dark side of Modernity. Time and again, his Black characters, historical and contemporary, are shown as victims of processes of 'Othering' similar to those suffered by the Jews. Consequently, it is no surprise that Phillips rejects any hostility on the part of Blacks towards Jews – and *vice versa*. In *The Atlantic Sound*, for example, he becomes increasingly uneasy with his Black guide to Liverpool, Stephen, who peddles a 'simplistic' anti-Semitism based on the 'fallacious' supposition that Jews were 'largely responsible for the slave trade'.[19] Such attitudes echo what *The European Tribe* deplores as 'the virulent anti-Semitism' (p. 53) of much African-American discourse. Instead, Phillips insists on the validity of Fanon's insight that anti-Semitism is inseparable from epidermal racism and that attacks on either minority group are implicitly aggressions against the other.

But if slavery, colonialism and the Holocaust all signify the dark side of Modernity, and are unfinished business in terms of their continuing deleterious impact on the modern world, Phillips is keen to respect the differences between these events, and the communities which suffer them. The rationale for this is provided during his visit to Auschwitz in *The European Tribe*, where Phillips comments: 'At least the Atlantic slave trade had some vestige of logic, however unpalatable' (p. 97). As a consequence of this vital difference, Phillips is impatient with those who would make such histories equivalent or interchangeable. In *The Atlantic Sound* he criticises Afrocentrists wishing to commemorate the slaving fort of Abandze as the Black Auschwitz. Even more baffling to him are those African-Americans who insist not just that they are 'the descendants of Hebrew Israelites driven into African exile from Jerusalem in AD 70' (p. 168), but even that they are the 'truest' Jews.

The 'atonal' nature of Phillips' engagement with 'the figure of the Jew' in relationship to postcolonialism also owes something to his scepticism about the possibility or even desirability of cultural hybridity as Smith conceives of it. His characters' experience of displacement instead instantiates Rushdie's perhaps less often remarked warnings against celebrations of diasporic experience as an unproblematic space of inter-cultural 'translation': 'Sometimes we feel . . . that we fall between two stools'.[20] Phillips' own discomfort with his 'in-between' position, belonging fully to neither Europe nor the Caribbean, is a recurrent theme of his travelogues. There is an abundance of Millat-figures in his fiction. A good example is the unnamed narrator of the first section of *Higher Ground* who endures 'the worst tragedy that can befall a man',[21] which is to be marooned between cultures. Caught in a no-man's land between a native African society, which despises him for his presumed treachery, and the white slave-trading culture on the coast, where he acts as an interpreter, and which despises him on account of his colour, the narrator's 'linguistic duplicity' (p. 57) condemns him equally in the eyes of both. But the Jewish Irene-Irina in *Higher Ground* is equally stranded in post-war Britain, her hyphenated name indicative of a radically disabling split in her identity. Indeed, one might argue that for Phillips, the history of

Jewry is the most extreme evidence of the liabilities of 'in-betweenness'. Whether 'Italian' or 'German', the Jews in *The Nature of Blood* are liable to persecution precisely because of their interstitial location.

In Phillips' work, then, there is no question of homogenising or sublating different histories of persecution and displacement into a monolithic 'migrant experience'. This corresponds to Homi Bhabha's conception of intercultural relations in the diaspora. Drawing on the work of Mikhail Bakhtin and Jacques Lacan, in particular, Bhabha advances a model of hybridity in which – as with Smith's work, too – 'the traditional grounds of racial identity are dispersed, whenever they are found to rest in the narcissistic myths of Negritude or White [or Jewish] cultural supremacy'.[22] However, Bhabha proposes that the most productive way to understand the cultural and identificatory interaction between diasporic communities and 'host' societies is not as a synthesis which produces a new whole by dialectical progression. Rather, the communities involved exist in a relationship of productive tension, with traffic across border-lines between them which are troubled but not dissolved. Or, as Stuart Hall puts it, a desirable politics of hybridity involves the attempt 'to build those forms of solidarity and identification which make common struggle and resistance possible but without suppressing the real heterogeneity of interests and identities' involved.[23] Symbolic of Phillips' primary emphasis on difference is that – in contrast to Smith's work – potential affective relationships between Jews and Blacks are never fully realised. Thus in *Higher Ground* the Caribbean Louis is unable to connect properly to Irina-Irene; and in *The Nature of Blood*, Stephen's contact with Malka, the Falasha Jew from Ethiopia, is equally fleeting.

Nor is Phillips convinced that there yet exists a space allowing intercultural negotiation on non-hierarchical terms, which is commensurable with Smith's vision of London. Certainly, the representation of the major cities of Europe, including London, in *The European Tribe* emphasises conflict and segregation between different ethnicities rather than the 'multiplicity-in-unity' of Smith's city. Liverpool, another major city with a long history of migrational influxes, is presented equally sceptically in *The Atlantic Sound*. Phillips draws parallels between the uncomprehending reception he receives on his research visit and that endured more than a century earlier by the West African John Ocansey. More bleakly still, Phillips becomes uncomfortably aware of antagonistic divisions between 'Liverpool-born Blacks' and later waves of migrants from the non-Western world, even those from Africa.

As one might expect from these emphases, by contrast to Smith's 'symphonic' fiction, the structure of Phillips' texts is characteristically 'atonal' or disjunctive. For example, in *Higher Ground*, the three narratives relating to slavery, the position of Blacks in the US in the 1960s and the Holocaust are presented consecutively as self-contained narratives, with no explicit cross-references between them. Conceptual correspondences and affective resonances have to be inferred. In *The Nature of Blood* this technique is modified.

It interweaves three different narratives, and four distinct points of view, in paratactic fashion, with no regard for the conventions of traditional fictional organisation like stability of narrative perspective or temporality, linearity, chapter divisions or unity of genre. The effect is that of a mosaic, or a work of Cubism, with the fictionalised accounts of the experience of a Holocaust victim and survivor, the 'Othello' figure and the essentially documentary history of the Jews of Portobuffole, constantly interpolating each other. The text requires considerable effort to negotiate its steep shifts in temporality and point of view, which effectively make the reader experience the kinds of disorientation and displacement felt by the characters themselves. Thus while important parallels emerge between Jewish experience and that of Blacks in Phillips' narratives, and there is some sense of their inseparability (symbolised, for example, in *The Nature of Blood*, where 'Othello' and Stephen Stern both pass through Cyprus, albeit some centuries apart), they remain clearly demarcated and finally incommensurable.

The contrasting engagements of Phillips and Smith with 'the figure of the Jew' are highly productive for the understanding of postcolonial diasporic identity in different ways. The comparison also suggests that the handling of the trope is by no means homogeneous or uniform in contemporary postcolonial writing. However, if the conjunction has proved enabling in many ways, it is notable how little the two authors engage with the 'problem' of Palestine. Certainly, Smith rejects any kind of racial or cultural exceptionalism including, by implication, Jewish exceptionalism. *The Autograph Man* even at times proposes in postmodern fashion that 'Jewishness' is a matter of position rather than blood or tradition. But such perspectives are not brought to bear explicitly upon the contemporary politics of the Middle East. Israel is mentioned directly only once in either of Smith's novels, when Irie is enigmatically described as being 'stuck between a rock and a hard place, like Ireland, like Israel, like India' (*White Teeth*, pp. 425–6).

By contrast, Phillips addresses Israel extensively and is certainly critical of the nation at moments. His doubts are primarily related to what he represents as its racism, which is seen as part of Israel's European legacy, towards Black Jews. *The Nature of Blood* closes with an account of the later life of Stephen Stern, who left Germany in the 1930s to live as a 'pioneer' in Palestine. Isolated and disillusioned in old age (his predicament is an ironic comment on the failure of the new community he envisaged), he forms a relationship with Malka, who together with many fellow Falashas, has recently been airlifted to Israel. 'Othered' by the dominant groups in Israeli society, as it was in Ethiopia, Malka's community is viewed as an exotic commodity, to be economically exploited: '*The mayor of the town in which we were first placed complained. He had requested that he be sent only those who could sing and dance, so that he might form a folklore group for tourists*' (p. 208). Despite Stephen's own distance from such lamentable attitudes towards 'Third World' Jews, his own relationship with her has uncomfortable connotations of parasitism. In *The Atlantic Sound*, similarly, Phillips explores the predicament of a group of African-American Zionists who have returned 'home' only to be met with bewilderment and hostility. The guards around their Negev desert settlement seem designed to confine them within their 'camp' as much as to protect them.

But even Phillips' work does little to explain why Israel is so widely regarded as a late, albeit peculiar, example of a colonial formation, and one of the most brutal, in its treatment of its indigenous and conquered Arab populations.[24] Farhana Sheikh is a rare exception among contemporary postcolonial writers in raising the question of Israel's victims, even tangentially. *The Red Box* (1991) follows the fortunes of a pair of teenage girls born in Britain of Pakistani parents as they seek to resolve competing cultural affiliations in the metropolis. Muslim identity, in their eyes, necessarily involves solidarity with Palestinians. Conversely, Palestinians offer diasporic Muslims a model of resistance to oppression. Interviewed by a teacher after some graffiti is scrawled on school buildings, Tahira explains their actions thus:

> We wrote PLO 'cos, well, on telly, they're always the bad lot. You know, bombs, terrorism. It's like no one wants to hear them . . . No one wants to hear any of us. The gorrai [whites] want to shut us up like . . . that's why we wrote PLO. It means we ain't going to give up and we ain't just little school-kids being naughty.[25]

By contrast, other contemporary postcolonial diasporic texts, even those which directly address 'Islamic fundamentalism', generally fail to recognise the issue of Palestine as a factor in its emergence. For example, neither Rushdie's *The Satanic Verses* (1988) nor Kureishi's *The Black Album* (1995) acknowledges the role of Zionist state policy in fuelling Islamic discontent. This is surprising, at least to the extent that both these writers have paid homage to the work of Edward Said.[26] The lack of engagement with the question of Palestine in contemporary postcolonial diasporic writing is perhaps the one shadow on its otherwise productive engagement with 'the figure of the Jew'.

FOR FURTHER READING

For a hard copy list of the works of Caryl Phillips up to 2001, see *Contemporary Novelists*, ed. David Madden et al., 7th edn (New York: St James Press, 2001). For a more up-to-date list on the internet of the works of both Phillips and Smith, see the British Council website: <http://www.contemporarywriters.com/authors/>.

Cheyette, Bryan, 'Venetian Spaces: Old-New Literatures and the Ambivalent Uses of Jewish History', in *Reading the 'New Literatures' in a Postcolonial Era*, ed. S. Nasta (Cambridge: Brewer, 2000), pp. 53–72.

Head, Dominic, 'Zadie Smith's *White Teeth*' , in *Contemporary British Fiction*, ed. R. Lane et al. (Cambridge: Polity, 2003), pp. 106–19.

Ledent, Benedicte, *Caryl Phillips* (Manchester: Manchester University Press, 2002).

Smith, Zadie, 'Love, Actually', *Guardian* 'Review', 1 November 2003, 4–6.

Squires, Claire, *Zadie Smith's* White Teeth (London: Continuum, 2002).

NOTES

1　Salman Rushdie, *Imaginary Homelands: Essays and Criticism, 1981–1991* (1991; rpt. Harmondsworth: Penguin, 1992), p. 20.

2　E-mail to Bart Moore-Gilbert, 29 October 2003.

3　Edward Said, *Culture and Imperialism* (London: Chatto and Windus, 1993), p. 386.

4　Rushdie, *Imaginary Homelands*, p. 394.

5　See Zadie Smith, *The Autograph Man* (London: Penguin, 2003), p. 428. All quotations are from this edition; page numbers are given in the text.

6　Zadie Smith, *White Teeth* (Harmondsworth: Penguin, 2001), p. 123. All quotations are from this edition; page numbers are given in the text.

7　Stuart Hall, 'Cultural Identity and Diaspora', in *Colonial Discourse and Post-Colonial Theory: a Reader*, ed. P. Williams and L. Chrisman (Hemel Hempstead: Harvester Wheatsheaf, 1993), pp. 392–403; Paul Gilroy, *Between Camps: Nations, Cultures and the Allure of Race* (Cambridge, MA: Harvard University Press, 2000).

8　See Smith, *The Autograph Man*, p. 305.

9　Zadie Smith, 'Love, Actually', *Guardian* 'Review', 1 November 2003, 6.

10　See, for example, Smith, *White Teeth*, pp. 56, 424.

11　See, for example, Smith, *The Autograph Man*, pp. 266, 323.

12　Paul Gilroy, 'Urban Social Movements, "Race" and Community', in *Colonial Discourse and Post-Colonial Theory*, ed. Patrick Williams and Laura Chrisman (New York: Columbia University Press, 1994), pp. 404–20.

13　Yasmin Alibhai-Brown, 'Nations under a Groove', *Marxism Today* (Nov. /Dec. 1988), 47.

14　See Smith, *The Autograph Man*, pp. 92–3.

15　Ibid., p. 302.

16　Caryl Phillips, *The European Tribe* (London: Faber, 1999), p. 68. All quotations are from this edition.

17　Theodore Adorno, *Prisms*, trans. S. and S. Weber (London: Neville Spearman, 1967), p. 34.

18　See Phillips, *The European Tribe*, p. 85.

19　Caryl Phillips, *The Atlantic Sound* (London: Vintage, 2001), p. 81. All quotations are from this edition; page numbers are given in the text.

20　Rushdie, *Imaginary Homelands*, p. 15.

21　Caryl Phillips, *Higher Ground* (London: Picador, 1993), p. 57. All quotations are from this edition; page numbers are given in the text.

22 Homi Bhabha, 'Remembering Fanon', Foreword to Frantz Fanon, *Black Skin, White Masks* (1952), trans. C. L. Markmann (London: Pluto, 1986), p. ix.

23 Stuart Hall, 'New Ethnicities', in *Stuart Hall: Critical Dialogues in Cultural Studies*, ed. David Morely and Kuan-Hsing Chen (London: Routledge, 1996), p. 444.

24 See, for example, Aijaz Ahmad, *In Theory: Classes, Nations, Literatures* (London: Verso, 1992), pp. 18, 31–2; Neil Lazarus, *Nationalism and Cultural Practice in the Postcolonial World* (Cambridge: Cambridge University Press, 1999), pp. 136–7.

25 Farhana Sheikh, *The Red Box* (London: The Women's Press, 1991), p. 87.

26 Rushdie, *Imaginary Homelands*, pp. 166–84; Hanif Kureishi, 'Introduction' to *My Son the Fanatic* (London: Faber, 1997), pp. vii–xii, p. x.

10

Mingling and Metamorphing: Articulations of Feminism and Postcoloniality in Marina Warner's Fiction

Chantal Zabus

Like two feisty goddesses at an antique repast, Mary Douglas and Marina Warner recalled, over lunch in 2001, Elias Canetti's reason for not liking a book: 'It hasn't any transformations in it'.[1] Our two deities motioned that this rule should prevail in contemporary fiction. Transformation, altered states, metamorphing, shape-shifting loom large in today's scientific developments – from stem cell research to genetic engineering – and in contemporary culture, which has produced mutants, replicants, aliens, cyborgs and clones.[2] Such metamorphic avatars also imbue Warner's novels, which interweave two dominant movements of the twentieth century: postcoloniality and feminism. Both movements question the very concept of history and the way it foregrounds the point of view of the winners and of the male sex.[3] Yet, beyond such redressing of wrongs, Warner further links female oppression and the oppression of the colonised. She also explores the ambiguity of female intercessing, womanly interstices and other chinks, which inevitably weaken 'his story' and enrich her story through fiction and myth.

Marina Warner's engagement with feminism is palpable in her theoretical writings, such as *Alone of All Her Sex* (1976) and *Monuments and Maidens* (1985), and in her fiction, which place her in a sisterly continuum, from Angela Carter and A. S. Byatt to the Canadian Anne Carson and, in a feminine *hauntology* of sorts,[4] from Margaret Atwood to Toni Morrison, who stage poltergeists, duppies, zombies and revenants. Similarly, Warner's concern with postcoloniality is in essence metamorphic. Indeed, like Frantz Fanon, she sees colonisation as the brutish replacement of one species of men by another and as the traumatic transformation of an individual into a colonised subject, let alone its zombification. This is particularly relevant when 'possession' amounts to both 'wealth' and 'haunting'. The imperial enterprise becomes an incubus savagely bent on soul-theft. The loss of soul and, therefore, the dehumanisation of the colonised, are both a precondition and a consequence of slavery.[5]

In shaping her stories and reconfiguring ancient materials, for which she was predisposed as an Oxford-trained historian, Marina Warner looks for 'congeners', that is, 'materials through which one culture interacts with and responds to another, conductors of energies that may themselves not be apparent or directly palpable in the resulting transformations' (M18). Thus, congeners are also activators of change. Throughout her work, Warner refocuses traditional perceptions of history, fiction's supplementary Other, through the binocular lens of allegory and the tale. Such anamorphosis entails, as the name indicates, a distorted or transformed image that appears normal when viewed from another perspective, and for our purpose, involves looking at matriarchal prehistory as well as the colonised or repudiated cultures. Among the most transformative experiences of history, Warner numbers the encounter with the newly discovered *Mundo Otro*, as Columbus first called the Americas. Beyond postcolonial disillusionment and resentment, Warner imagines, in her fiction, the early contacts and exchanges between Europe and the Americas.

Born in London in 1946 of an English father and an Italian mother, and brought up in Brussels and Cairo, with roots going back to Thomas Warner of St Kitts, Marina Warner is herself a migrant between worlds. Borrowing the phrase 'positive shadow' from the historian Peter Lamborn Wilson to characterise the ways vanquished cultures can still exercise a 'perfume of seduction' over their conquerors, Warner explores these moments of 'reciprocal transformations' (M20). Refractions of this cultural hall of mirrors abound in her fiction.

Her first novel, *In a Dark Wood* (1977), features an early congener in the Jesuits' mission in sixteenth- and seventeenth-century China, when a subtle complicity settled in between Confucian philosophers and Christian missionaries. One such missionary is the Portuguese homosexual Jesuit Andrea da Rocha, whose theoretical moorings become the *raison d'être* of the contemporary Catholic priest Gabriel Namier. While faith is haemorrhaging out of him, Gabriel clings to the idea that religion is a matter of intellect rather than feeling. Conversely, his niece Paula connects religion with magic and ritual and puts Catholic priesthood on a par with Papuan shamanism. Through Gabriel's theological musings, Warner seeks to disentangle herself from what she once called 'the Catholic body' (SW125) and, more largely, the power Catholicism wielded over her (body and mind) during her formative years in a Brussels convent.

'The good news of Christ', according to Gabriel, put an end to a barbaric age of human sacrifice and ousted the quintessentially feminine worship of Aphrodite, Athena and Artemis. Warner ventriloquises through Paula that myth has a universal application and stories are traversed by the hatred of women. Mythical, stranded, rock-bound female figures such as the Amazons 'massacred by Hercules in one of his Labours', the Ethiopian princess Andromeda 'left on a wretched rock', and Ariadne, the Cretan maiden who helped Theseus escape the Minotaur's labyrinth and, as a reward, got 'dumped on a rock in mid-ocean',[6] augur the marooned and islanded women of *Indigo* (1992) as well as the diasporic fugitive of *The Leto Bundle* (2002).

In exposing the overthrow of fertility goddesses and earth-mothers of ancient worship by male military paragons, Warner comes across as a maternalist. Maternalists, who postulate an alternative model of human organisation before the advent of patriarchy, hold that powerful goddesses were allegedly dethroned and replaced by a dominant God, and that the Mother Goddess was transformed into his consort. The Judaeo-Christian exalted father figure tellingly connects two vignettes in *In a Dark Wood*, that is, the religious debate in China, which climaxed with the Emperor expelling the Papal Legation, and Gabriel's experience in Sicily, where he has to conduct interviews on order from the Vatican to verify the accuracy of Maria Pia's claim of her vision of the Virgin Mary. Although Maria's exudation causes Gabriel to bristle, he cannot simply dismiss her experiences as psychiatric delusions and wonders why 'a child's dream [shouldn't] be equally powerful?' (*DW*205). In an essay, Warner has recounted how one Fabio Gregori saw in 1995 bloody tears streaking the face of the statue of the Madonnina near Civitavecchia, Italy, on the day of the Feast of the Purification of the Virgin (*SW*189). However, Warner takes care to place this pious fraud alongside alien abductions, the grievous antics of stigmatics and the self-mortifying female body.

'In a Dark Wood' refers to Gabriel's nightmare in which he is pursued by the four querulous hounds of his patron saint, the archangel Gabriel, who comes to reclaim him. This nightmare prefigures Gabriel's end. While he seeks the dark wood of the London Heath to douse his fiery desire for Oliver, he is assaulted by two youths who call him a 'Fucking, filthy fairy' (*DW*237). They leave him, an asthmatic, outside of his puffer's reach so that he dies of suffocation and becomes the subject of libelous speculation for scandalmongers. This reversed Annunciation is, however, tempered by heterosexual romance, as Oliver and Paula kiss and feel secure in their Godless world.

Palimpsestically, painting in Warner's novels often lies in filigree behind the fictional surface, as if art was the key to all mythologies. In this, she differs from English postmodernist writers who often draw on the repertoires of peripheral or sub-literary genres such as gothic horror, pornography and the lower arts. The painting Gabriel Namier sees in the National Gallery, Da Vinci's *The Virgin of the Rocks*, forces this sexually and ontologically bereft priest to contemplate the Virgin Mary's sealed 'cave of the womb', the mother 'who was never a yawning abyss into which a man falls and is swallowed up' (*DW*23). This denied feminine netherworld is also featured, in its most conspiratorial dimension, in Warner's subsequent novel, *The Skating Party* (1982).

The skaters on a frozen river – Viola and Michael Lovage, their son, and Michael's female student lover – are intimately connected to two paintings: Gerard David's diptych in Bruges, *The Judgment of Cambyses*, and the sixteenth-century frescoes on the bathroom walls of Cardinal Birbarotti's Borgia apartment in the Vatican. Like the twofold watchers in *The Judgment* of *Cambyses*, 'those inside the painting and those outside it',[7] Viola comes to understand that the bathroom frescoes tell Homer's tale of sexual revenge – 'Mother, son, father. Concubine' (*SP*173). Her epiphany illuminates the novel's *dénouement* and inspires her entreaty to her son to distract the young student from her husband's andropausal infatuation and seduce her. This romance is underwritten by the College boys' homosociality, which complexifies the interpenetration of sex with monogamous romance.

Beyond the hints dropped in *In a Dark Wood* at a possible homeomorphic alignment or ritual equivalence between the Catholic vocation and shamanism, Michael Lovage's anthropological research investigates the power base of the priesthood as social control in the Western Pacific Ocean. Among the Idia of Palau, babies born with the umbilical cord around their necks are destined, through the removal of their tear ducts, to become forever weeping poets, who take on the world's 'capital of grief' (*SP*34). In one flashback, the curtain lifts on an Idian girl who, because of her love for a boy from a lower caste, is condemned to a slow death if she fails to confess to being a witch. While Michael accepts the girl's sacrificial self-starvation, which warrants the tearful poets' praise of her heroic fortitude, Viola clamours: '"There must be an absolute moral law, there must. Or we're brutes!"' (*SP*102). More largely, this cleavage between universalism and cultural relativism reflects on the necessary grafting of the postcolonial condition onto a brand of feminism, which posits woman as oppressed by all patriarchal cultures in and outside the West.

The racy romance between the bewitching student, who recalls the insolent 'witch' of Palau, and the Lovages' son announces the phenomenon of parentectomy, the strategic severance of the young from their biological or surrogate family, which traverses the fabric of Warner's later novels. Such a shift coincides with the move, in women's fiction of the 1980s, away from biological motherhood for female relationships to metaphors of sisterhood, friendship and of surrogate motherhood.

The Lost Father (1988) and *Indigo* (1992) are twinned family histories, which required Warner 'to sit in judgment on [her]self', as Ibsen once held about the writer's task (*SW*264). Taking this as banner, Warner explores two of her 'imaginary homelands', Puglia, where her mother was raised during the Fascist years, in *The Lost Father*, and, in *Indigo*, the Caribbean, where the Warners, on her father's side, were planters and slave-owners. *The Lost Father* results from 'this migration of race memory, of the spirit of the Southern patriarch into the voice of the English granddaughter',[8] whose fictional *alter-ego* is the narrator Anna, who is writing *The Duel*. This novel-within-the-novel finds all its significance when Anna's grandfather, Davide Pittagora, overhears his friend Tommaso insulting his sisters and by the law of the *mentita*, challenges him to a duel, during which Tommaso's bullet ricochets into Davide's head, causing him to die of a thrombosis much later. Although the duel was never historically attested, the cultural historian at work here gives way to the seer and re-creator of true stories of false memories. Through the name 'Pittagora', after the Greek philosopher Pythagoras, Warner rehabilitates the old lineage of the people of Puglia, thereby hyphenating Greek ancestry and Italian history.

While visiting some excavations in 1909 in Rupe, Davide and his friend see a wall-to-wall frieze of bare-bottomed nymphs in a lewd orgy with animals suckling at their breasts, 'not a single man around' (*LF25*), which harks back to the pre-patriarchal past of Italy. Also, the fall of Addis Ababa in 1936 allows Warner to denounce the Italian colonisation of Ethiopia by 'the bullet and the bed' and Mussolini's dream of claiming it as 'Abyssinia, part of the new empire of Rome' (*LF201*). The Abyssinian Queen of Sheba holds a special appeal for Warner, for she, as an outsider, inspired love in Solomon when visiting him in Jerusalem: 'her manners were foreign, she was black but comely: *Nigra sum sed formosa*' (*LF228*). It is therefore no wonder that Davide's brother composed a music piece in her honour as part of a play. But the performance is interrupted – and so is the disclosure of the Queen of Sheba's supposedly hirsute legs – by an irate Commissioner who, nauseated by the play's female import, laments the loss of manliness in Italy. Yet, that manliness, Warner argues, is compounded by the strength of the women who were left behind after male emigration to America.

The appeal of the Mediterranean is double for Warner, for it is both her mother's birthplace and the cauldron after mingling in the great ports of Venice and Naples. When Davide is sailing to America from the Bay of Naples in 1913, he thinks of Orpheus who turned back to look at Eurydice as they were leaving the underworld and 'the place where this happened lies near Naples, too, of course' (*LF146*). In *Indigo*, Warner focuses on the broader Atlantic, on the smaller but historically dense space of the Caribbean as a fertile 'arena of mutation and change, and a space most propitious to the play of the imagination' (*M20*). This metamorphic and phantasmal zone, notably captured in Shakespeare's *The Tempest* (1611), is also a place of linguistic and discursive transmogrification. History is conveyed through story-telling, pointing to a deficiency in colonial history and providing the reparatory tale. Thus Warner gives voice to the daughterly tales and pays tribute to the story-tellers of the Caribbean as well as the pre-Gutenberg, oral culture of women.

Serafine Killebree, the nanny to the Everard family, whose ancestry can be traced to the Caribbean basin, opens and closes *Indigo* with her alarming stories of the Caribbean past, which she conjures up, as in a Renaissance masque, to the Everard girls, Miranda and her 'sister-aunt', Xanthe. Although her name is Creole patois from the French *coulibri*, she suggests less the humming bird than the Queen of Sheba or the *diablesse* with the cloven hoof of Caribbean lore. With one foot in society and the other outside of it, the story-teller often shows stigmatised characters how they can achieve insider status and be transformed without forfeiting their intrinsic selves. Patterned after Jean Rhys' Christophine in *Wide Sargasso Sea* (1968), itself a prequel to *Jane Eyre* (1847), Serafine emerges as the prototypical female keeper and transmitter, who conveys tales to a female audience. Warner thereby re-establishes the tales as women's stories from domestic milieus, later tapped by male collectors. Woman is here to man what dialect is to language, what myth is to history, what orature is to literature: its prime originator.

In addition to its double temporal perspective (the 'now' plot [London in the 1980s] and the 'then' plot [Liamuiga in the Caribbean in the 1600s]), the book is divided into six parts along colour lines from 'Lilac/Pink' to 'Maroon/Black'. It is rewarding to read *Indigo* chromatopically, across the colour-spectrum, for history, to Warner, results from the mingling of 'strands of different colours'. Besides euphonically conjuring the word 'indigenous', indigo is also 'the original colour used in "blueprints". It's the colour of the ink used for the first pattern' (*SW265*). In peeling off the layered patterns, Warner recovers those deeper blueprints and thus redrafts history from that primordial, feminine perspective.

Xanthe and Miranda access Caribbean history through Serafine's tale of the fisherman Amadou and his wife Amadé and of the phosphorescent, tusky sea-host, Manjiku, whose deepest desire is to procreate, for 'he wants nothing better than to be a woman'.[9] Manjiku's desire to swallow pregnant or menstruating women, like the snake in Apuleius' *The Transformations of Lucius*,[10] arises from 'the thirst for the Other – to elide difference by becoming one, by incorporating'. Manjiku therefore combines both the savage traits of the sea-monster designating *terra incognita* in early cartography and those of the European invader, for he is white and devouring. In a variant of 'Beauty and the Beast', Manjiku becomes Prince Charming once he has swallowed the young woman, Amadé, who drowns out of true love for Amadou, after he has forsaken her for a beautiful mermaid. The seductive death of the 'tiny silver woman' in Warner's subtext foretells Xanthe's death, whereas Amadé's rebirth as the bride to a new Manjiku reserves a happy ending for Miranda. Indeed, Miranda marries George Felix, aka Shaka, after the Zulu leader, who ends up as 'The Unnamable One'. As if to give the lie to *The Tempest*, which *Indigo* rewrites/re-rights, and to the colonial denial of miscegenation, this interracial couple has a girlchild, Feeny, and not, as in the Bardscript, a little Caliban.

Conversely, the flight of Xanthe from her autocratic father is very much akin to the bid for autonomy of fairy-tale female characters, often wronged daughters. She marries Sy, a real estate speculator, who aims to prove V. S. Naipaul wrong, whom he quotes as having once said (in *The Middle Passage*, 1962): 'History's built around achievement, and nothing was ever achieved in the Caribbean' (*I291*). Sy's maritime empire turns out to be a dystopia for tourist consumption and Xanthe drowns while her would-be knight is 'mapping the waters' (after *Indigo*'s subtitle). Deep down at the sea-bottom,

Xanthe's body undergoes a pearly sea change and is enshrined in an oyster-like mollusc's walled chamber. It is only through death that Xanthe becomes 'vulnerable to love' (*I*353).

Like the Cameroonian Werewere Liking, who dreams of a new female race of 'jasper and coral',[11] Warner often speaks of the coral reef as capable of hosting ultimate transformations and deep revolutions. Also, both Miranda and Xanthe are connected with oysters. Miranda smells 'of the sea, like oyster, fresh and salty' (*I*249) and Xanthe's 'salty cyprine' is made all the more slippery by Sy's 'greedy mouthwatering' (*I*299). Besides its poetic assimilation to female genitalia in a state of arousal, the oyster is symbolic of androgynous and hybrid wholeness. Tellingly, the post-independence female Prime Minister of Liamuiga endeavours to revive her country's economy and restore the island's psychic wholeness through the oyster trade and the ancestral worship of the coral reef. She thereby returns the island to female leadership and asserts the novel's gynocentric thrust.

In the 'then' part of *Indigo*, Warner retrieves her forebears' Creole past of exogamy, that is marrying outside a community, and miscegenation, inter-breeding between races, by foregrounding Governor Warner's first wife, the Kalinago (Carib) woman named 'Barbe', and their progeny, 'Indian' Warner, and thus providing the untold story of illicit relationships between bucca-neer and marooned, governor and slave. Warner recreates the troika that used to be Prospero's in *The Tempest* by casting Ariel, the Arawak orphan girl, and Caliban/Dulé, an Igbo survivor, as Sycorax's foundlings. For delivering Dulé with an oyster-shell knife from a drowned, pregnant woman cast off a slave-ship in 1600, Sycorax is accused of witchcraft, or *obeah*, and forced into exile to another part of the island. There, she thrives as a dyer of indigo, one of the most valued staples in the transatlantic trade. Rather sym-bolically, it is after a bitter altercation between Sycorax, the inappropriately lewd (foster-)mother and 'bedisened crone' (*B*44), and Ariel, her pubescent daughter, that Kit, the unlawful British usurper, comes to shore and destroys what Adrienne Rich called 'the organic authority' of women in pre-patriar-chal societies.

As in many such eroticolonial encounters – Barbe and Warner, La Malinche and Cortez, Pocahontas and John Smith (in the nineteenth-century 'romantic' version), Tituba and John Indian, Joanna and Gabriel Stedman[12] – Ariel 'collaborates' with Kit, heals him, and responds to his concupiscence, which is here wrought with ambiguity and interracial curiosity. Warner's prose is tinged with feminist compassion for the woman 'split in two' (*I*152), caught between the (s)mothering of Sycorax and the sexual power she holds over the White man, who will father Roucoubé or 'Red Bear Cub'. By having frank sexual relations with Kit, Ariel incarnates both the sacrosanct Algonquian Princess Pocahontas and the lustful Indian squaw, her darker sister. Like Barbe, the legendary Carib intercessor, who merges with the his-torical Madame Ouverard,[13] Pocahontas reportedly came 'through the forest on a dark night to warn [John Smith] of the attack by her father', Powhatan.[14] Despite the fact that various accounts diverge as to Pocahontas' motivation, all are unanimous in casting her as an insider leaking information to the enemy.

In Warner's apocryphal rendering, Ariel's warning is not duplicitous. She inadvertently 'warns' Kit of Dulé's attack by kissing him more fervently than usual, as if bidding farewell, which raises Kit's suspicions. In *Indigo*, the 'true' story is buried in Ariel's silence and it is the Dominican Père Labat's version, in which she is praised for 'rais[ing] the alarm' (*1220–1*), that Serafine helps pass on to Miranda, who will then pass it on to her daughter, Feeny. As a colonised subject, Serafine is the ironic transmitter of the official story of Ariel's betrayal. Like fiction, history is exposed as a discursive practice that is ideologically conditioned. Warner stresses the prevalence of language, the power of the female memory to transmute stories, over the overweening fabricated discourse of male history.

Indigo reads like a botched fairy-tale, in that 'the golden girl before whom everything lies is not Xanthe but Miranda'.[15] Romance is a *dénouement* that customarily crowns Warner's novels. Her last novel to date, *The Leto Bundle* (2002) is, however, not a romance. It is imbued with a dark pessimism, characteristic of end-of-millennium turmoil and, because it interrogates morality, it may be said to rank with Iris Murdoch's and John Fowles' post-war ethical fiction. *The Leto Bundle* builds on the admittedly narrow 'postcolonial condition' by portraying the new Albion (the UK) with its capital Enoch (London), as a 'postcolonial' country, which is itself part of a Europe that remembers its rape from Zeus.

The Leto Bundle reaffirms Warner's conviction that many episodes of rape and forced insemination lie at the foundation of cultures and nations. Hierogamy or the rape by a god is precisely how Leto's story begins. In a revisitation of 'Leda and the Swan', Leto, born *circa* 325 CE, is raped by a bird-like man-god and delivers her navel-less twins, Phoebius and Phoebe, that is, Apollo the god of the sun and Artemis the goddess of the moon. Hatching is thus confirmed as a fertile mythopoeic figure, along with mutating, splitting and doubling. The Ovidian episode when a group of rushcutters on a lake shore refuse to allow the goddess Latona to bathe and purify herself after giving birth to the divine twins has inspired the chapter in which Leto, after being gang-raped by the rushcutters, inflicts the same punitive metamorphosis and turns the rapists into croaking frogs. 'The witches' duel', which describes female sequences of struggle through successive metamorphoses, as in the sea-nymph Thetis' strategies to escape the protean Peleus, is extended as a metaphor governing the whole novel.

Originally a late Greek mummy, whose tomb was presumably carved a thousand years after the fall of Troy, Leto travels through time. Over the centuries, she is alternatively a cuttlefish squirting ink at her lover, the guest of a talking she-wolf in Lycania, Laetitia in a convent in Cadenas-la-Jolie,

Lettice when aboard a vessel before being delivered to a pirate in the Caravanserai, until Leto and her twins are tipped over into the present. She then becomes a clandestine masseuse in Italy, a prostitute during the siege of Tirzah (Kosovo), where she abandons Phoebius, undamaged, to a better lot in Enoch, and then, an asylum seeker in contemporary Enoch, to climax as 'Ella Outis', a missing person. The goddess of the diaspora is doomed to wander, with her twins, until they find a new United Kingdom, which embraces, after Salman Rushdie, 'chutnification, the blending of spices and herbs and the fruits of the earth'.[16]

Kim McQuy, a dark-hued orphan from Tirzah and a present-day Enochite schoolteacher, champions this kind of multicultural composting which is necessary for all new growth. In a passionate exchange of e-mails, which reveals Warner's technophilia (as opposed to, say, Murdoch's or Fowles' technophobia), Kim challenges the curator at the National Museum of Albion, Dr Hortense Fernly, for whom the past is prologue and who is contemptuous of Kim's belief in Leto's capacity for shape-shifting. The hyper-real permanence of Leto gives new vigour to the political movement Kim spearheads on the web, HSWU, 'History Starts With Us', the 'us' being the 'visible presences', the 'foreigners, outsiders, colonial subjects, or diasporic denisens of our muddled-up world' (L92). It turns out that Kim, after 'KIM' – standing for 'Kale Iere Mnemosyne', as in the opening invocation of the prayer to the goddess Memory – is Leto's long-lost son, Phoebius.

Hortense's realisation that Leto is indeed a perfect unifying symbol for fragmented times comes too late and Kim dies, accidentally stabbed by a child-snatcher. It looks like Kim's death puts an end to the new mongrelised non-native state of Albion, but his message lives on beyond the postcolonial condition and Leto's 'threnody'. This particular kind of Greek lament crowns the history of Leto, which is made of fragments from papyri, annals and archives, of 'fragments' (L181), and other bits, very much like her bundle, which, however, contains the basic, necessarily impure ingredients of great civilisations. Hortense Fernly, however, intuits that a womanly orature lies behind male archives, as 'the author might have dictated to a scribe. In which case, the writer could have been a woman' (L33).

For Warner, narratives of positive transformations progress through 'a series of shed skins . . . to an ultimate perfected outcome, released from disfigurement or transmogrification' (M24). Mutating finds its concrete embodiment in Phoebe's body, glued to the tarmac during the siege of Tirzah and damaged by flying shrapnel lodged in her flesh. At first 'otherworldly in its lambency' (L255), Phoebe's skin gets a new grafting and glows with an Apollonic, new-made radiance. Warner's incursion into body-modification reflects her belief in interspecies translation, based on the unavoidable and enriching impurity of ethnicities and the contemporary fragility of personhood, at a time when DNA has replaced the soul.

Kim's stance in favour of a new secular faith, whereby religion or creed could never be the basis of the identity of a nation, is akin to Warner's meditations on the metempsychosis or soul migration, which deals a cruel blow to the Judaeo-Christian idea of individual uniqueness, already under attack in her early novels. Warner enlarges Edward Said's 'voyage in' to refer to the movement and integration of Third World thinkers into the metropolitan First World,[17] to all outsiders. Beyond the patchwork, the mosaic and the melting pot, Warner posits the 'bundle' as a migrant metaphor for the mongrelised identities of our soul-searching times. The container of that bundle is the story, which shape-shifts according to the teller.

Two movements – postcoloniality and feminism – inhere in Warner's fiction. In so far as they both rewrite history, they offer 'alter-native' reinscriptions of woman and the colonised. Not only does Warner envisage the female and hence doubly colonised subject under the yoke of both colonialism and patriarchy (as in *Indigo*), she also shows that history is in essence myth-making (*The Lost Father*) and that religion is a suspension of disbelief (*In a Dark Wood*, *The Skating Party*). Any entity thus far considered as stable such as 'Man', 'body', 'identity' becomes unstable, metamorphic, mutable and endlessly transformable (as in *The Leto Bundle*) once it is (re)visited by the feminine. Future states (both as nations and physical conditions) are therefore bound to be altered states.

FOR FURTHER READING

For a hard copy list of Marina Warner's work up to 2001, see *Contemporary Novelists*, ed. David Madden et al., 7th edn (New York: St James Press, 2001). For a more up-to-date list on the internet, see the British Council website: <http://www.contemporarywriters.com/authors/>.

Bush, Barbara, *Slave Women in Caribbean Society 1650–1838* (London: James Currey, 1990).

Hester, Marianne, *Lewd Women and Wicked Witches: a Study of the Dynamics of Male Domination* (London: Routledge, 1992).

Hulme, Peter, *Colonial Encounters: Europe and the Native Caribbean, 1492–1797* (London: Methuen, 1986).

Gilroy, Paul, *The Black Atlantic: Modernity and Double Consciousness* (London: Verso, 1993).

Minh-ha, Trinh, *Woman, Native, Other: Writing Postcoloniality and Feminism* (Bloomington and Indianapolis: Indiana University Press, 1989).

Zabus, Chantal, *Tempests after Shakespeare* (New York: St. Martin's Press/London: Palgrave, 2002).

NOTES

1 Elias Canetti, *Fantastic Metamorphoses* (Oxford: Oxford University Press, 2002), p. 211. Hereafter cited as *M*; page numbers are given in the text.

2 See Marina Warner, *Signs and Wonders: Essays on Literature and Culture* (London: Chatto & Windus, 2003), p. 341. Hereafter cited as *SW*; page numbers are given in the text.

3 Günter Grass and Stanley Elkin, quoted in Brian McHale, *Postmodernist Fiction* (New York: Methuen, 1987), p. 91.

4 I owe this term to Jacques Derrida in *Specters of Marx*, trans. Peggy Kamuf (New York and London: Routledge, 1994), p. 4. Originally *Spectres de Marx* (Paris: Galilée, 1993).

5 See Marina Warner, 'Introduction' to Samuel Taylor Coleridge, *The Rime of the Ancient Mariner* (London: Vintage, 2004), p. ix.

6 Marina Warner, *In a Dark Wood* (London: Vintage, 1977), p. 25. Hereafter cited as *DW*; page numbers are given in the text.

7 Marina Warner, *The Skating Party* (London: Vintage, 1982), p. 86. Hereafter cited as *SP*; page numbers are given in the text.

8 Marina Warner, *The Lost Father* (London: Picador, 1988), p. 192. Hereafter cited as *LF*; page numbers are given in the text.

9 Marina Warner, *Indigo: or Mapping the Waters* (New York: Simon & Schuster, 1992), p. 216. Hereafter cited as *I*; page numbers are given in the text.

10 Marina Warner, *From the Beast to the Blonde: on Fairy Tales and Their Tellers* (London: Chatto & Windus, 1994), p. 259. Hereafter cited as *B*; page numbers are given in the text.

11 Werewere Liking, *Elle sera de jaspe et de corail* (Paris: L'Harmattan, 1983), Marjolijn de Jager, trans. as *It Shall be of Jasper and Coral* (Charlottesville and London: University of Virginia, 2000).

12 John Gabriel Stedman's *Narrative of a Five Years' Expedition Against the Revolted Negroes of Suriname* (1796), quoted in George Lang, 'In Every Clime: Literary Notes Around the Discovery of Srana-Tongo Creole', *Dutch Crossing*, 44 (Summer 1991), 60–76.

13 See Jean-Baptiste Labat, 'Voyage aux Isles. Chronique aventureuse des Caraïbes 1693–1705', ed. Michel Le Bris (Paris: Editions Phébus, 1993).

14 Quoted in Philip Young, *Three Bags Full. Essays in American Fiction* (New York: Harcourt Brace Jovanovich, 1972), p. 177.

15 Quoted by Nicolas Tredell in 'Marina Warner in Conversation', in *London*, 19 March 1992. Published in *Poetry Nation Review* (July/August 1992), 36.

16 Marina Warner, *The Leto Bundle* (London: Vintage, 2002). Hereafter cited as *L*; page numbers are given in the text.

17 See Edward W. Said, 'The Voyage in and the Emergence of Opposition', in *Culture and Imperialism* (1993; rpt. London: Vintage, 1994), pp. 288–316.

PART III

Feminism and other -isms

11

Regeneration, Redemption, Resurrection: Pat Barker and the Problem of Evil

Sarah C. E. Ross

Whoever fights monsters should see to it that in the process he does not become a monster. And when you look long into an abyss, the abyss also looks into you.

Pat Barker's epigraph to *Blow Your House Down*, from Friedrich Nietzsche, *Beyond Good and Evil*

Is Pat Barker a feminist or a realist novelist? Barker's early novels, *Union Street* (1982), *Blow Your House Down* (1984) and *Liza's England* (1986), all focus on working-class women, victims of poverty and violence, factory workers and prostitutes: 'women who have got short shrift both in literature and in life'.[1] But her great success, particularly in the 1990s (the first novel in her acclaimed *Regeneration* trilogy was published in 1991), has to a large extent been associated with a move away from feminism, 'to male protagonists, a favouring of the masculinised spheres of pub, battlefield, hospital or government, and a leaning towards the epic rather than domestic scale'.[2] *The Man Who Wasn't There* (1988), the *Regeneration* trilogy (1991–5) and Barker's subsequent three novels, *Another World* (1998), *Border Crossing* (2001) and *Double Vision* (2003), all focus primarily on male protagonists, and it has become something of a commonplace to say that Barker has become no longer (just) a feminist, that she has achieved 'double status as [a] feminist and mainstream writer'.[3] Barker has been hailed for her exploration of manhood and masculinity, and her ability to 'write outside her experience'.[4] As Maya Jaggi writes, 'By the late 1980s Barker had published three highly praised novels, but she was pigeonholed as northern, working-class, feminist and gritty'; in 1999, Michael Thorpe wrote that 'If any contemporary English novelist has made redundant that male reviewer's discriminatory phrase woman novelist, it is Pat Barker'.[5]

Replacing 'feminist' as the most common categorisation of Barker's work in recent years is 'realist': reviewers have referred to her as a 'conscientious realist' and to 'social realism at its purest' in her novels, and numerous critical studies have focused on her as a realist writer.[6] In this chapter, I wish to explore the interaction between feminism and realism in Barker's work, defining her as 'at first' a feminist, but investigating the ways in which the concerns of her early novels – identifiably feminist, although also a great deal more – inform her later ones. The feminist standpoint is a political one, aiming at the most basic level to expose and/or redress imbalances in power based on gender, primarily deprivations and injustices experienced by women. Barker's early novels exemplify the way in which gritty, realistic exposure of the details of impoverished women's lives can serve this aim; in doing so they also meet the primary criteria of social realism, which delineates interactions, lives and power relations within our everyday society. As Lyn Pykett comments, 'Like the nineteenth-century social novelists Barker uses realism to confront and explore the individual's experience of family, the local community and the wider society', and she describes *Liza's England* (formerly *The Century's Daughter*) as 'among other things, a "condition of England" novel'.[7] John Kirk, defining Barker as a working-class novelist, makes the important qualification that, unlike nineteenth-century realist novelists, Barker imposes 'no hierarchy of discourses'; she 'erode[s] the distance between "outside" observer and observed', giving voice to the classes who are traditionally observed.[8] Even in her early focus on women as victims of social ills and violence, Barker in fact explores gender, class, society and history in complex, multiple interactions. Women are not the only victims of social evils; nor are they only victims.

It is this wide-ranging engagement with social ills on which I wish to focus, exploring in this essay Barker's unflinching interrogation of the nature of evil in several social, political and historical forms. *Union Street, Blow Your House Down* and *Liza's England* all explore the gritty lives of women in deprived industrial northern England, but in each novel, an empathy, if not a sympathy, for male victims and perpetrators of violence runs alongside her feminist concerns. Male characters, often drunks and wife-beaters, are frequently as trapped as their beaten wives – or scarred by two world wars. War casts long shadows over *Liza's England*, as it does over the psyche of the teenage Colin in *The Man Who Wasn't There*, and with her *Regeneration* trilogy, Barker moves to explore in detail the devastation of war: the ultimate male experience of violence and evil. The *Regeneration* trilogy also introduces the paradigm of the psychologist and patient, a mutually invasive relationship which runs through Barker's three most recent novels, *Another World, Border Crossing* and *Double Vision*, alongside an exploration of a new exemplum of social evil: the child killer or would-be killer. The settings of these novels are, once more, predominantly domestic, but the domestic is impinged upon by violence, both that of war, past and present, and of violence closer to home. It is increasingly the problem of evil that has become Barker's defining preoccupation, and with it, the tricky, flawed notion of its solution. Barker's latest social realism, like her early feminism, is characterised by her robust refusal to rest in one-sided ascriptions of blame or in easy fictional solutions. Conscientious realism defines her early exploration of women in relation to evil, and it continues to define her exploration of evil in the most troubling violent phenomena in modern-day Britain, as she examines the question of whether redemption from violence is possible in individual psychology, history or art.

Pat Barker does not reject the label 'feminist' – and she cannot. The central characters of her first two novels are working-class women, victims of poverty and violence, factory workers and prostitutes. *Union Street*'s milieu is a deprived, desperate quarter of an industrial northern town in Thatcherite Britain, and each of the novel's seven vignettes focuses on a girl or a woman, from pre-adolescent rape victim Kelly Brown to the dying Alice Bell, who is crushed by the conditions of her life. Kelly Brown's parental neglect culminates in her rape; Joanne Wilson is trapped by premarital pre-ganancy, Alice Bell by the nexus of age and poverty. Each is trapped most profoundly by socio-economic geography: by an upbringing in Union Street or, worse still, Wharfe Street, 'the worst street in the town' (*US*72), where 'career options' consist of the production line at the cake factory or domestic drudgery. *Blow Your House Down* focuses on the most female of occupations: prostitution. Brenda, the character focused on initially, wants to look after her children, but conditions of work at the chicken factory make combining the two impossible. Women in this novel pluck and are plucked, they fuck and are fucked: through Barker's imagery, the two alternatives become one and the same, equally violent, equally destructive. *Union Street* and *Blow Your House Down* articulate, as Margaretta Jolly has noted, a 'socialist-feminist' vision, one which 'ultimately sees women's suffering as rooted in the effects of their relation to production'. As Jolly observes, socialist feminism, rare in recent British women's fiction, harnesses the political agenda of the largely middle-class feminist movement to an awareness of the functions of class as an element fracturing any supposed 'sisterhood'.[9]

The unflinching and sometimes shocking depiction of women's physicality in these novels is defined as feminist by Barker herself. '"It's Virginia Woolf's 'truth of the body'"', says Barker. "As a woman, you have to tell that truth"'.[10] In the world of backstreet abortion and prostitution, Barker's 'truth of the body' is far from poetic or genteel. Liza's female predecessors and contemporaries 'wore out by the time they were thirty', devastated by childbearing; they are epitomised by Liza's middle-aged mother whose womb is falling out, held in place by an unreliable rubber ring.[11] Childbirth, abortionists' grubby fingernails, live-born foetuses are all described in detail. Kath's brutal rape-murder in *Blow Your House Down* is described particularly graphically; in this case, shocking detail serves to highlight the horror at the centre of the characters' grainy lives, as well as creating a vivid parallel with the brutality of the chicken slaughterhouse.

Barker admiringly cites another definition of feminism, proffered by Carol Shields: '"the belief that women are people"; it shouldn't have to be asserted, but it does'.[12] Barker's desire to reinsert women into stories and recent histories is a driving force in *Liza's England*, whose eponymous heroine was born as the clock strikes midnight at the turn of the twentieth century. Twentieth-century British history is told primarily from Liza's point of view: she sees her brother off to the First World War and receives notification of his death; she loses her son in the Second World War; she struggles to feed her family, and raises the granddaughter born of her daughter's liaison with a soldier. Watching her daughter labour in the same room in which she had laboured a generation earlier, Liza 'turned to the fire, only to feel it strip the flesh from her face and reveal her mother's bones. Eileen was not Eileen, Liza was not Liza, but both were links in a chain of women stretching back through the centuries, into the wombs of women whose names they didn't know' (*LE*211). Alice Bell in *Union Street* reflects similarly on the fragments of her life that pass through her head on her final walk: 'Were they the debris of her own or other lives? She had been so many women in her time' (*US*239). Barker's vision is of individual female humanity – entrapment and suffering – but also of the likeness of female suffering in impoverished communities. *Union Street*'s vignettes are separate, but overlapping details and interweaving stories insist on the likeness of women and girls, 'the women of Union Street' (*US*219), who struggle to make ends meet, to bring up families, to be individuals in bleak social and economic circumstances.

Barker's second articulated view of the feminist enterprise – the assertion that 'women are people' – deserves further attention, as it ramifies in at least two ways in the development of her fiction. Even in her early novels, the assertion that 'women are people' does not preclude a related sympathy for male characters who, like the female (although in different ways), are also frequently crushed by life circumstances or trapped in roles that they cannot escape. George Harrison, in effect the focus of the 'Blonde Dinah' vignette in *Union Street*, seeks sexual union of a kind that he has been unable to experience within the strictures of married life; his experience reveals to him that his views of women are primitive, that there are not in fact 'two sorts of women: the decent ones and the rest' (*US*210). More fundamentally, unemployment traps and corrodes men such as George, as well as Liza's husband Frank (in the 1920s) and Stephen's father Walter (in the 1980s) in *Liza's England*. Liza's England is a society that wears down working-class men and women alike, as the youth club over which Stephen presides in the 1980s illustrates. Thatcherite Britain has created a breed not just of women, but of '*people* without hope' (*LE*219; my italics). It is in aspects such as this that Barker's early novels can be identified not just as feminist, but as 'condition of England' novels, contributing to 'debates in the 1980s concerning the condition of the English working class'.[13]

And just as Barker's early novels demonstrate an empathy for male as well as female characters, so her depiction of female victimhood is always an uneasy or, at least, a complicated one. The women of *Union Street* and *Blow*

Your House Down are not straightforward victims, or even clearly 'the oppressed': they are very frequently complicit in the social evils of which they are also victims. Kelly Brown's mother is 'On [her back] for any bugger what fancied a poke, and the kids left to God and Providence' (*US*176). We fear that Brenda, departing for her night's work at the opening of *Blow Your House Down*, is turning a wilful blind eye to her daughter's fear of 'Uncle Norman'. Iris King, who is kindest to the young and the weak (Kelly Brown, Alice Bell) in *Union Street*, also presides over the novel's most shocking scene, the induction of her daughter's late-term abortion and the disposal of the live-born foetus. *Blow Your House Down*, most explicitly, explores the complex interrelationship of women's victimhood and ill-doing, implicitly condemning the actions of streetworker Jean who, devastated by the murder of her friend Kath, kills her client in the – likely mistaken – belief that he is the culprit. Switching to first-person narration from Jean's point of view, Part Three of the novel reveals Jean's own uncertainties, her own doubts about the validity of her actions, as well as the fact that her actions have not put Kath to rest. She dreams of the serial killer, who 'turned around . . . *and I was looking into my own face*' (*BYHD*381). As the novel's epigraph, quoted at the beginning of this essay, insists, in fighting monsters, Jean has herself become one; she has looked into the abyss, and the abyss has looked into her.

Of these two wider ramifications in Barker's early novels of her insistence that 'women are people' – a recognition of oppression of people other than women, and a complex sense of the nature of evil – the first has been most frequently cited as defining Barker's novelistic trajectory in the 1990s. Margaretta Jolly correctly identifies 'a maturing, rather than rejection, of the political vision of earlier "second wave" women novelists' in the expansion of Barker's concerns out of a single gender category, and she identifies Barker's wider protest as one against 'the exploitations of class and gender'.[14] Stephen, the gay youth worker in *Liza's England*, is the first of her male characters who battles perceptions of male sexuality, and *The Man Who Wasn't There* explores the clashes of class, sex and fatherlessness in the identity of adolescent Colin. Such a wider exploration of the frequently debilitating effects of class and gender is vital to the remarkable vision of the *Regeneration* trilogy, in which the 'ruthless' yet compelling Billy Prior (*ED*76) is the focus for Barker's extended exploration of the functions of class, gender and male sexuality. Prior is fractured not just by his experience of extreme violence in France, but by the divisions of class and constrictions of sexuality in late-war England, in a paranoid atmosphere of 'constant surveillance' (*ED*75) and the crushing of anyone who assails the 'established order' (*ED*9). Aggressively bisexual and 'equally *not* at home' (*ED*110) with either his 'own' people or those of his 'toffee-nosed' (*ED*15) lover Charles Manning, Prior splits into Jekyll and Hyde personalities, one of which tries to assist the pacifist acquaintances of his youth, the other of which betrays them.

But while an ongoing and expanding concern with 'the exploitations of class and gender' is a defining and compelling feature of the *Regeneration* trilogy, I would like to suggest that a more fundamental strand linking Barker's early novels with the trilogy, and with her most recent three novels, is her preoccupation with the nature of evil itself. Her early novels move rapidly from exploring social ills – the social and political exploitations of (predominantly) women – to considering evil in more fundamental forms: evil that is not simple, that does not take 'a single, recognizable shape' (*BYHD*401–2). Barker's evil or, more accurately, evils are social phenomena, and as such their manifestations and ramifications are invariably marked by gender and class; but the evil that she explores, and people's experiences of evil, both as victims and as perpetrators, while coloured by gender and class, are ultimately more fundamental than those. So it is that she moves from the exploration in her early novels of social ills experienced primarily by women to the *Regeneration* trilogy, which is defined by the horror of twentieth-century war – an historical experience so powerful that it serves as an archetype of evil, with its complex interrelation of perpetrator and victims.

Siegfried Sassoon and his fellow soldiers in the *Regeneration* trilogy have seen 'Armageddon, Golgotha, there were no words, a place of desolation so complete no imagination could have invented it' (*R*44). Sassoon's poetry tells Rivers and us that they have looked into the abyss:

To the Warmongers

I'm back again from hell
With loathsome thoughts to sell;
Secrets of death to tell;
And horrors from the abyss.
Young faces bleared with blood,
Sucked down into the mud,
You shall hear things like this,
Till the tormented slain
Crawl round and once again,
With limbs that twist awry
Moan out their brutish pain,
As the fighters pass them by. (*R*25)

Sassoon's 'loathsome thoughts' are actualised in the horrors experienced by his fellow patients at Craiglockhart war hospital. Billy Prior's breakdown is precipitated by discovering the eyeball of his recently blown-up private: 'What am I supposed to do with this gob-stopper?' (*R*103). And David Burns' own private horror – being blown head-first into the stomach of a decomposing German soldier, whose liquefying organs filled his mouth and nose – are beyond even the ability of W. H. R. Rivers, the renowned Craiglockhart psychologist, to redeem. While war also undeniably affects women, such as Liza or Sarah Lumb, whose loss of her first fiancé has left her face 'scoured out by grief' (*GR*76), this particular experience of evil – at the Front – is uniquely male. Men in this society have to fight and face violence: this is the reality that causes Charles Dodgson to prefer little girls to boys, and that precipitates Rivers' own stutter as a newly breeched four-year-old, looking at the portrait of his namesake's leg being amputated, cauterising tar at the ready, during the Napoleonic Wars. War, in the *Regeneration* trilogy, is the archetypal male experience of evil.

The historical paradigm of war also allows Barker to extend her exploration of victimhood's complexity, as she confronts a particularly fraught, and historically insoluble, blurring of victim and perpetrator. Sassoon writes of the soldier as a Christ-figure, 'The Redeemer', 'reeling in his weariness, / Shouldering his load of planks, so hard to bear' – and yet, as he reflects ironically, 'Christ isn't on record as having lobbed many Mills bombs' (*R*82). Rivers, contemplating a stained-glass church window at a post-Somme church service, reflects that the Crucifixion and Abraham's sacrifice of his son Isaac are 'the two bloody bargains on which a civilization claims to be based. *The* bargain, Rivers thought, looking at Abraham and Isaac' (*R*149; see also *GR*104).[15] An irreconcilable tension between perpetration and victimhood is concentrated in the figure of Rivers, who is Abraham, a father figure to the young men he treats, Sassoon's 'father confessor', yet complicit in their sacrifice, (re)fitting young men for active service. Rivers' business is *restoration*, 'the restoration of [patients'] mental health' (*R*238), a task that parallels his pre-war work with Henry Head on the regeneration of physical nerves (*R*46–7). Treating his patients involves pain, the insistence that they remember and confront their traumatic memories from the Front, that they do not repress them: with his patients, Rivers looks into the abyss. Of David Burns, Rivers believes that '*Nothing can justify this* . . . . *Nothing nothing nothing*' (*R*180–1; italics original), and the friendship he develops with Sassoon increases his doubts about the validity of the First World War in its later stages. Yet his job remains 'fitt[ing] young men back into the role of warrior' (*R*238). Far from becoming a monster himself, Rivers is deeply humane; influenced by Sassoon's arguments and the suffering of his patients, he is more than the empathetic strip of wallpaper Billy Prior accuses him of being. In Rivers, we see 'a conflict between his belief that the war must be fought to a finish, for the sake of the succeeding generations, and his horror that such events as those which had led to Burns' breakdown should be allowed to continue' (*R*47). Pacifism is not depicted as a solution in the *Regeneration* trilogy, yet a profound conflict between the necessity for participating in a particular form of evil (war) and horror at its consequences remains.

'I am in hell' (*AW*250): these are the final words of Geordie, the centenarian and First World War veteran in *Another World*, spoken at his death in the 1980s. *Another World* distances the horror of war temporally, but insists that time does not necessarily heal trauma. Helen, an academic psychologist, has tape-recorded Geordie's recollections of the war, theorising that his memories are malleable as they are distanced by time; however, Geordie's grandson Nick comes to recognise that time, for one who has confronted hell, may not be 'an ever rolling stream, but something altogether more viscous and unpredictable, like blood. Suppose it coagulates around terrible events, clots over them, stops the flow' (AW270–1). Nick recognises that 'Recovery, rehabilitation, regeneration, redemption, resurrection, remembrance itself . . . depend on that constantly flowing stream' (AW270–1). Just as Henry Head's nerves will never recover fully from his own and Rivers' experimentation, so in *Another World* 'old wounds . . . leak into the present' (AW75). The experiences of war are so hellish that full recovery, regeneration is never possible.

Another World's title refers less to Geordie's past than to an 'other world' of violence that is altogether more domestic than war. Nick and his composite family – his daughter Miranda, wife Fran, her son Gareth, and Nick and Fran's baby son Jasper – uncover on the wall of their run-down mansion a portrait of the house's Victorian family. The portrait reveals deep dysfunction, with a 'golden-haired toddler at its dark centre' (AW40); Nick comes to learn that the two-year-old, James was found murdered under a bonfire heap on 5 November 1904, the prime suspects (although acquitted) his half-brother Robert and half-sister Muriel, themselves aged eleven and thirteen. Nick's daughter Miranda recognises, at the portrait's inadvertent unveiling, 'It's us' (AW41), and so a Victorian equivalent of the James Bulger murder plays itself out, although with less tragic consequences, in Nick's modern-day family. Gareth injures Jasper with a stone to the head on a beach trip gone wrong, a sleep-walking Miranda later protesting 'I didn't do it. . . . I wasn't there' (AW220). The uncomfortable configuration of violence and culpability in children is Barker's central theme: Gareth is a misfit, a child on the brink of adolescence wrenched into a new environment, but he is not a product of the violent estate on which their neighbourhood borders. 'Another world' is less the historical world or even the deprived world which surrounds the family's 'good' neighbourhood than another world present in the domestic, middle-class everyday, the 'other side' of inexplicable childhood violence, committed 'not for any reason' (AW52). Violent potentiality always shadows the potential for good; it is 'the skull beneath the skin, or the anger that's always on the outside, trying to get in' (AW235).

Another World, Border Crossing, and Barker's latest novel, *Double Vision*, have been called 'an unofficial trilogy' of sorts:[16] uniting them is a focus on a new archetype of pure evil, the child-killer (or would-be killer), as well as an interest, extending the character of Rivers, in the psychologist. Nick's occupation as a psychologist is a relative sideline in *Another World*, but *Border Crossing* explores in depth the mutually invasive relationship between child criminal Danny Miller, now a young man, and his psychologist, Tom. As a ten-year-old boy, neglected in ways that Gareth is not (and thus more classically a victim-villain), Danny murdered a pensioner when she surprised him in her home. Confronted by Danny thirteen years later, Tom is faced with a manipulative personality that seeks to define itself by insinuating itself into others, by crossing borders; as the novel explores, 'the real question is: can people change?' (*BC*52) Danny Miller's 'redemption' (*BC*53, 154) would be too pure, too complete a solution in this novel, which never eschews the full social and psychological complexities of ill-doing and its ramifications; rather, Tom assists in creating a young man who functions, but who remains sinister, lurking in the shadows of others' worlds, 'wrapp[ing] himself round other people' (*BC*132). In Danny's case, Tom concludes, this is success – success that is 'Precarious, shadowed, ambiguous, but worth having nevertheless' (*BC*216).

Danny Miller re-emerges, as Peter Wingrave, in *Double Vision*, still sinister, still insinuating himself. Echoing his actions as a ten-year-old, he breaks into sculptor Kate Frobisher's isolated house at night, dressing in her clothes and going over the lineaments of her emergent sculpture of the resurrected Christ. It is not until this ultimately benign scene, late in the novel, and the revelation of his past, that we understand his eerie presence at Kate's road accident at the novel's opening, when he has stood over her semiconscious body but failed to act, for fear of alerting the authorities to himself. Danny does not, in the end, incarnate evil action in *Double Vision* – his precarious new state holds, if precariously – but evil and the potential for violence none the less impinge on the domestic world of northern England. The vicar's eighteen-year-old daughter, Justine, suffers a home invasion that parallels the actions of Danny Miller when he was ten: surprising burglars in her employer's home, she is lucky enough to suffer only the burglar's terrified beating. The attack on middle-class Maggie in *Blow Your House Down* is a forerunner to this incident, and the physical and psychological effects of Maggie's attack are far more significant than those of Justine's. Yet *Double Vision* remains – for this reader at least – a more ominous novel, emphasising in its very lack of actual horror the doubleness of middle-class English domesticity: good is always shadowed by the potential for evil.

Justine's lover, war correspondent Stephen Sharkey, and his recently dead photographer colleague, Kate's husband Ben, are the links in this novel between the domestic world of the northern English countryside and foreign arenas of war – and yet the two worlds are one:

> A man gets off a train, looks at the sky and the surrounding fields, then shoulders his kitbag and sets off from the station, trudging up half-known roads, unloading hell behind him, step by step:
>
> It's part of English mythology, that image of the soldier returning, but it depends for its power on the existence of an unchanging countryside. (*DV*201)

Double Vision is set against the aftermath of Sarajevo and 9/11, and in the pall of black smoke from the pyres of the British foot-and-mouth crisis of

2001–2, all events which, ideologically as well as literally, have scarred the English countryside and its inhabitants. War is present in the quiet English countryside of here and now – and yet the ominous *Double Vision* is also Barker's most positive of novels in its conclusion in relation to evil. For widowed Kate, in particular, the creation of the risen Christ *is* a resurrection; the 15-metre figure also implicates, symbolically, Peter Wingrave, and the war-ravaged, love-healed Stephen Sharkey. In traumatised or profoundly damaged people, in history and across time, full regeneration may not be possible, but precarious redemptions, resurrections of the human spirit, are possible in individuals and communities, and are representable in art.

Socialist feminism and conscientious realism are, in Pat Barker's case, aligned in one novelistic trajectory. Rather than a shift in focus, an unflinching view, ever broadening, is discernible in her fiction, on social ills, violence and downright evil. Feminism is a political stance, seeking to expose and address particular, gender-based, forms of social ill, and Barker's own version of feminism was always peculiarly sensitive to the operation of class as well as gender, in male as well as female identities. Barker's early sensitivity to male entrapment and to female complicity in social problems is indicative of a concern that is broader than straightforward feminism: a concern with evil itself. The *Regeneration* trilogy sees her confront, head-on, an historical, and therefore unmalleable, archetype of evil, in which the male experience of perpetration and victimhood are inextricably bound together. *Another World*, *Border Crossing* and *Double Vision* relocate evil in modern, middle-class, domestic Britain, exploring the figure of the child criminal, and the ever-insoluble problem of the child-killer's redemption. 'Recovery, rehabilitation, regeneration, redemption, resurrection, remembrance itself' (*AW*271): these terms are recited through the perspective of Nick in *Another World*, but they are also Barker's mantra, the redemptive possibilities to which she returns again and again. From feminism to her more recent, broader, social realism, Pat Barker combines a conscientious, unflinching approach to the problem of evil with a measured consideration of possibilities – always tempered – for regeneration, redemption, resurrection.

FOR FURTHER READING

For a hard copy list of Pat Barker's work up to 2001, see *Contemporary Novelists*, ed. David Madden et al., 7th edn (New York: St James Press, 2001). For a more up-to-date list on the internet, see the British Council website: <http://www.contemporarywriters.com/authors/>.

Critical Perspectives on Pat Barker, ed. Margaretta Jolly, Sharon Monteith, Ron Paul and Naheem Yousaf (Columbia, SC: University of South Carolina Press, 2005).
Sharon Monteith, *Pat Barker* (Plymouth: Northcote House Publishers, 2004).

NOTES

1 Katha Pollitt, quoted on the cover of *Union Street and Blow Your House Down* (New York: Picador, 1999). All quotations from these novels (*US, BYHD*) are from this edition; page numbers will be given in the text. For Barker's other novels, the following editions have been used, and quotations will appear with abbreviations in the text: *The Century's Daughter* (London: Virago, 1986). Republished as *Liza's England (LE)* (New York: Picador, 1996). *Regeneration (R)* (London: Penguin, 1991). *The Eye in the Door (ED)* (London: Penguin, 1993). *The Ghost Road (GR)* (London: Penguin, 1995). *Another World (AW)* (London: Penguin, 1999). *Border Crossing (BC)* (London: Penguin, 2001). *Double Vision (DV)* (London: Hamish Hamilton / Penguin, 2003).

2 Margaretta Jolly, 'After Feminism: Pat Barker, Penelope Lively and the Contemporary Novel', in *British Culture of the Postwar: an Introduction to Literature and Society 1945–1999*, ed. Alistair Davies and Alan Sinfield (London and New York, Routledge, 2000), pp. 58–82, p. 59.

3 Jolly, 'After Feminism', p. 60.

4 Michèle Roberts, quoted in Maya Jaggi, 'Dispatches from the Front', *The Guardian* (16 August 2003), 8 pages. Available online at: <http://books.guardian.co.uk/departments/generalfiction/story/0,6000,1019519,00.html>, 6 (retrieved 30 June 2004).

5 Jaggi, 'Dispatches', p. 5; Michael Thorpe, 'The Walking Wounded', *The World and I*, 14, 10 (October 1999), p. 258.

6 Michael Caines, 'News from the Burning City', *TLS*, 5293 (31 August 2003), 19; David Dalgleish, 'From the Mouths of Babes', May 2001, 3 pages. Available online at: <http://www.januarymagazine.com/fiction/bordercrossing.html> , 3 (retrieved 10 March 2004).

7 Lyn Pykett, 'The Century's Daughters: Recent Women's Fiction and History', *Critical Quarterly* 29, 3 (1987), 71–7, 73.

8 John Kirk, 'Recovered Perspectives: Gender, Class, and Memory in Pat Barker's Writing', *Contemporary Literature*, 40, 4 (1999), 603–26, 612.

9 Jolly, 'After Feminism', pp. 63–4.

10 Quoted in Jaggi, 'Dispatches', p. 5.

11 See *Liza's England*, pp. 218, 252 and 137.

12 Quoted in Jaggi, 'Dispatches', p. 5.

13 Kirk, 'Recovered Perspectives', p. 604.

14 Jolly, 'After Feminism', p. 67.

15 The significance of Abraham's sacrifice of Isaac is perhaps suggested to Barker by Wilfred Owen's poem, 'Parable of the Old Men and the Young'.

16 Caines, 'News from the Burning City', p. 19.

12

'Partial to Intensity': The Novels of A. L. Kennedy

Glenda Norquay

A. L. Kennedy is a writer repeatedly identified as one of the brightest hopes of contemporary British fiction. With the distinction of being described by the literary magazine *Granta* as one of the 'Best Young British Novelists' in both 1993 and 2003, and a number of significant literary prizes to her name, she has also contributed to the development of other new writing careers, in her editing of *New Writing Scotland* between 1993 and 1995.[1] Through detailed dissection of sexual passion, familial relationships and dysfunctional individuals, Kennedy deploys the short-story form to startling effect in *Night Geometry and the Garscadden Trains* (1990); *Now That You're Back* (1994); *Original Bliss* (1997) and *Indelible Acts* (2002). Unafraid to tackle sexual violence, emotional pain, abuse and loneliness, she writes in a style that is laconic and often darkly humorous. To address such stark issues in longer fiction, with its emphasis on sustained narrative rather than the shock of a brief encounter, Kennedy might have been expected to moderate her forceful style; instead she has created three powerful and demanding novels which compel the reader into confrontation with extremes: *Looking for the Possible Dance* (1993), *So I Am Glad* (1995) and *Everything You Need* (1999).[2] As Kennedy herself acknowledges, she is 'partial to intensity', and her fiction is resolutely uncompromising in its exploration of dark and difficult issues.[3]

She is also uncompromising in her resistance to categorisation, dismissive of 'literary theorists who want everything neat and under the author's thumb'.[4] Her suspicion of being placed within a grouping headed 'feminism', 'realism' or 'postcolonialism' can therefore be imagined, although her work can be understood through several of these perspectives. Although she claims 'I never got the feminist thing',[5] the location of her interests in the private and emotional – the domain of relationships and desires, the body and its boundaries – has led to her being identified with the concerns of feminism, while her status as part of a new group of exciting and experimental Scottish voices emerging in the early 1990s has meant she is also viewed as a writer challenging the conventions of realism in a postcolonial context. The dislocations in her narrative, always defamiliarising for the reader, are increasingly directed towards reflections on the writing process itself, creating a self-reflexivity shared by other contemporary British novelists. Yet although she engages with both the politics of gender and the dynamics of national identity, her strong views on the role of the writer and the responsibilities of writing have meant that she has publicly disavowed easy connections with feminism or a new Scottish consciousness or British postmodernism. As Sarah Dunnigan has commented in a fine essay on Kennedy, the writer is characterised by her 'refusal to be pinned down to any literary "philosophy" or credo of gender or nationalism'.[6] Before locating Kennedy in a wider context, then, it is important to identify the central concerns of her fiction.

A. L. Kennedy is a writer consistently interested in the 'big' questions around love, life and death, but these abstractions are presented through detailed realisation. Although clearly addressing specific social and political issues, her fiction does not explore these directly through the broad representation of a social world conventionally associated with realism. When editing a *New Writing Scotland* volume subtitled 'Last Things First', Kennedy commented on the extent to which contributors appeared drawn to 'the four last things': death, judgement, heaven or hell. Framing these concerns, she suggests, there may be notions of 'personal loss or gain' but they also emerge out of 'a sharpening sense of political endings and beginnings, an increasing insecurity at local and international level'.[7] The apparently intense focus on the personal which dominates Kennedy's work can be understood in similar terms: from the finely detailed dilemmas of her characters' thoughts and experiences emerges an engagement with much larger social and philosophical issues. It is from this dynamic, rather than any specific examination of issues related to feminism or postcolonialism, that Kennedy gains her strong sense of the morality of the writer's role. Writing itself becomes a kind of resistance, an articulation of belief: 'I am saying that any author, writing any kind of fiction on any topic, resists the forces which deny our communal humanity. They cannot do anything else – that is the nature of their work'.[8] Difficult or playful or painful as Kennedy's work may seem at times it is underpinned by this conviction of the redemptive power of creativity. It is the same adamantine sense of the pleasure and power of language in the making of fiction, which has shaped her highly crafted challenges to its conventions.

The characteristic seriousness and ambition of Kennedy's writing is evident from her first novel, *Looking for the Possible Dance*, in which a dialogue between the central character, Margaret, and a disabled boy she meets on the train taking her away from Scotland, becomes a small but significant structuring device for the novel's narrative. As Margaret asks 'James Watt', symbolically named after the Scottish inventor of the steam engine, questions about his life and he replies with scrawled notes, she enquires whether he is on medication. Denying any use of drugs, the boy replies triumphantly that he is 'FUC WON HUNNER PERCEN MEEEEEE' (p. 191). Kennedy's fiction consistently engages with the question of what this triumphant claim might mean: the possibility of becoming 'one hundred per cent' a self within the complicated dynamics of subjectivity. It is in within these parameters that her fiction might be related to both feminism and postcolonialism. Feminism is impelled by a concern with challenging and transforming structures of exclusion, with the exploration of marginalised subjectivities and attention to voices. Postcolonialism can be seen as an expansion of possible subject positions. Kennedy's fascination with the politics and contradictions of the self emerges out of similar concerns. Her forceful and innovative transcription of the words of a boy who is excluded from the conventions of communication and social interaction points to an interest in the breaking down and reassembling of conventional categories of language and fictional form, to the extent that typography becomes part of the challenge to contemplate what it might mean to be 'one hundred percent me'.

A. L. Kennedy is clearly writing in a context that is informed by feminism. In her work there is recognition of the social constructions of femininity which have held women in particular roles and positions of powerlessness, and her frequent interest in themes of domestic violence and child abuse show her alertness to the inequalities classically associated with such structures of power. Her central female characters could, however, be described as post-feminist, working with an explicit recognition of the ways in which their own lives might be mapped out very differently from women of a previous generation. (Kennedy views herself as less preoccupied with feminist issues than Janice Galloway, another Scottish novelist with whom she is often compared, because Galloway had to operate within an environment dominated by male writers.[9]) In each of Kennedy's novels the central women – Margaret, Jennifer and Mary – see themselves as autonomous, both in their sexuality and their choice of lifestyle. While often confused about the direction in which they wish their lives to go, they rarely doubt that they have an element of control. As the critic Alison Smith comments: 'She explores [gender] and is not dictated to by it'.[10] So, while Kennedy maintains an interest in the power relations in systems of difference generated by biological characteristics, her concern is more evidently with the ways in which the structuring of human subjectivity through love and pain, loss and presence, need and separation, shapes relations between men and women, between the self and the social. In this respect, her work moves further away from realist concerns with the determinations of identity in a specific social context, towards a greater emphasis on interiority and the kinds of game-playing and fragmented narratives associated with a different, but equally important form of feminism, which emerges out of poststructuralist thinking and is often referred to as French feminism.[11] As the writing of Jeanette Winterson also demonstrates, such undermining of conventions of voice and form can offer an equally convincing challenge to the discourses of authority.

A similar relationship obtains between Kennedy's writing and postcolonialism. As her fiction shows, her understanding of self is very much shaped by the Scottish context in which she grew up, in a culture that was on the margins of colonial power. Questions around the discourses of national identity, the notions of 'home' and 'belonging' explored by postcolonialism, are present in her writing but always with an awareness of their complicating effects. 'The problem' as she identifies it, is, 'I am a woman, I am heterosexual, I am more Scottish than anything else and I write. But I don't know how these things interrelate'.[12] Keen to point out Scotland's own role in colonial rule – 'I was also unaware that centuries of cultural oppression and manipulation, along with campaigns of militarisation and armed occupation, had made it very likely that I would connect feelings of Scottishness almost solely with military display'[13] – her suspicion of nationalistic feeling is also evident in her unease with being glibly and unhelpfully labelled as a 'Scottish writer'. 'I react with boredom, if not alarm and downright nausea, every time the Scottish or British media wallow out into another sterile and shallow dissection of Scottish culture . . . Today I would like to be international'.[14]

Kennedy's concern with the possibilities and problematic of being 'one hundred percent me', while touching on specific social and political practices, is therefore more relevantly situated within larger ontological concerns identified with psychoanalysis and philosophy. Her explorations of the psyche appear to operate with a Lacanian refinement of Freud's understanding that from the moment of birth our sense of self is predicated upon lack, by the child's separation from the mother; driven by loss and isolation we are always searching for the (illusory) possibility of wholeness.[15] Language itself emerges from and is predicated upon lack, upon absence. Exploration of what it means to be 'me' therefore takes Kennedy into the darkest of areas, examining boundaries of the self and how these are structured. So she is fascinated by the relationship between subjectivity and the body, as pain and pleasure define identity, and interested in the self as constructed through social and cultural contexts and through emotional relationships. Living with the recognition of death becomes another key theme – 'Why else do you write? If you could live forever why would you bother?' – as does the linguistic structuring of consciousness.[16] But for Kennedy these questions are rarely gender or culture specific.

Driven by her desire to confront the largest questions of existence, Kennedy's fiction becomes progressively more experimental in the means chosen to meet her aims – the juxtapositions of different forms of narrative, typographical experimentation, shifts in temporal perspective, increasingly abstract character representation and less 'realist' plots – and increasingly explicit about its own agenda. Her most revealing expression of the writer's business is in her essay, *On Bullfighting*.[17] In this brave confrontation with a defiantly difficult subject, Kennedy traces a journey through Spanish history, the landscape of Spain and the experiences of the bullring, overlaying it with her own physically painful and psychologically fragile progress as a writer unable to write. Forcing herself both to watch and write about what she has seen in the ring of a *corrida,* and searching out equally agonising

memories of the last days of the poet Lorca, she enacts the conviction under-
lying all her fiction, that it is the writer's responsibility to confront the
extreme, the painful, the unthinkable. For Kennedy the technical and ethical
problematics of writing are intertwined. Puzzling over her position as
observer taking photographs of a gored matador, for example, she writes:

> should I have photographed him, because he was bleeding for me to see,
> because to waste this insanity would be to make it even less eloquent, to make
> his best efforts pass without trace? Or should I have let him be, while my
> hands began to sweat against the camera casing and I used its magnifying eye
> to help me pay too much attention, to try to know, to understand?

Meanwhile, the woman beside her looks at this observer as if she were 'a
slightly alien thing' (p. 135).

Kennedy's sense of herself as an 'alien thing', a spectator whose responsibility is to confront pain and destruction with a certain dispassion in order
to understand it, is characteristic of all her fiction, shaping her tone, structuring her narrative strategies, dictating her material. As in *On Bullfighting*,
in which the detailed and detached analysis of the taurine world is contextualised by a highly personalised account of the writer's own attempted
suicide, physical pain and psychic distress, Kennedy's novels present an intimacy, an exposure of experience, but in a succinct, dryly humorous tone that
belies the emotional intensity present. Through this combination the writer
can offer 'the full realisation of a unique presence, a voice other than our
own: the viewpoints of human beings beyond ourselves: the precision of
experiences we cannot have'.[18]

Looking for the Possible Dance, Kennedy's first novel, deals – as the title
suggests – with the pleasures and pains of partnership, explored through the
sexual and emotional dynamics between two characters, Margaret and
Colin, and through Margaret's relationship to her dead father. In this, the
most Scottish of Kennedy's novels, personal relationships are placed within
a specific social and political context. Tackling the abrasive individualism of
Thatcherite Britain and the determining effects of Scottish culture also makes
this her most 'realist' text, in its direct engagement with a material world.
The theme of memory – a central concern of all Kennedy's fiction and one
with clear stylistic implications, evident in her deliberate play with tenses –
is also present in this first novel, but emerges as an assessment of personal
and social pasts which shape the individual's consciousness. Surrounding all
these themes is an engagement with what is described as 'the biggest, easiest
secret in the world': 'We're going to die' (p. 131). Facing this great unspoken, the fact of death, the novel suggests we can find a starting point from
which to live.

So I Am Glad is, as the title suggests, a much more joyful novel, although
it too is interested in the redemptive power of pain. As in her first novel
Kennedy presents a central female character dehumanised by her life, but in

this more extreme version the narrator, Jennifer, is set apart from human relations. Using violent sex as a means of avoiding communication, she relies on her job as a 'voice' in radio and advertising to avoid interactive human contexts. The novel, moving away from realism, takes as its plot the intrusion of Savinien, the ghost of Cyrano de Bergerac, into the narrator's life, tracing his blossoming relationship with Jennifer and his need to return to his own time. The fantasy of longing embodied in such a story brings Kennedy's fascination with the intersections of past and present and the shaping force of loss into sharper evidence.

If her previous two novels trace a movement away from the social and naturalistic into more abstract concerns, *Everything You Need* occupies a world almost unshaped by normal determinants of the environment, with action taking place in a writer's colony on an island. In this novel the intensity of an enclosed world means that wider social concerns impinge only tangentially. The sexual killing of a local child, for example, which would occupy a major plot device in a more conventionally realist text, features only as an uneasy, peripheral motif. Again concerned with a father–daughter relationship, Kennedy presents this novel primarily from the father's point of view, but the narrative moves between father's and daughter's thoughts, conversations and their written texts. This world of isolated individuals seeking to find contact through recovering the past and negotiating painful/pleasurable relationships with each other is familiar territory for Kennedy. Longer and more ambitious than her previous novels in its complicated juxtaposition of voices, thoughts and kinds of text, *Everything You Need* offers the least by way of conventional narrative rewards, but constitutes a significant advance in the intellectual and metaphysical demands made upon the reader.

Different as the novels are, Kennedy's concerns remain insistently with the question of being in the world. Rather than taking her only into abstractions, her interest in the structures and contradictions of the self produces subtle and detailed explorations of its manifestations. So the boundaries of the physical body, interpersonal relationships (particularly those in which emotional and sexual desire meet), temporal intersections and the dynamics of language emerge as dominant preoccupations of her fiction.

Although 'writing the body', a term referring to women's gendered relationship to the word, has become a commonplace within feminist criticism, Kennedy's interest in the body is fuelled as much by metaphysical speculation as it is by gender politics.[19] What it means to be 'one hundred percent me' leads into explorations of the relationship between interior and exterior bodily selves. In many ways the body seems to represent the most essential model of selfhood – one that can be identified in biological terms if nothing else – but even that apparently fixed definition raises questions about demarcations of internal and external selves, the relationship between mental and physical senses, the dynamics of emotional and physical pain. The place where the body and emotions are closest – the arena of sexual desire – therefore occupies a key space in Kennedy's writing. If her fiction appears particularly concerned with the erotics of violence, it is because the clearest challenge in defining these boundaries is when physical pain is related to, prompts or is prompted by desire. The startling obsession with pain evident in all her writing emerges from this recognition that: 'Pain makes the individual whole . . . it unites body and soul in something beyond the body/soul dichotomy.'[20] Again and again in Kennedy's fiction physical pain, often brought about through acts of violence, becomes a means of making characters feel that they are 'themselves', offering an affirmation of their senses.

Its most striking enactment is in the crucifixion scene that falls like a shadow across the apparent realism and everyday social interest of *Looking for the Possible Dance*. When Colin inadvertently crosses the sinister loan shark, Mr Webster, and is nailed to the floor by his hands and feet as a warning, Webster tells him that the pain he is inflicting is a gift because it will subsequently allow him to 'be alive'. This shocking moment also serves as a defining context for every other kind of being alive that is addressed in the novel. Just as Kennedy describes bullfighting as ritual of dark extremes from which comes art, so the concept of '*duende*' – Lorca's term for the transcendent but melancholy moment which inspires – dominates this and subsequent novels.[21] In *So I Am Glad* Jennifer's inability to communicate leads her into extreme sadomasochistic relationships as a means of connecting with herself and with others through physical pain. With Savinien, who both does and does not occupy a bodily space, there is a liberating tenderness in blurring the boundaries between their bodies. And in *Everything You Need* the confrontation with pain is made explicit by the credo of the writer's colony: they must encounter seven moments of extremity and danger before they can be true writers. Nathan Staples, novelist and agonised father, experiences this fragility of subjectivity when his attempted suicide is accompanied by Glenn Gould playing Bach, an effect which 'squeezed at his sum, at his still breathing total, at his only way of being Nathan Staples' (p. 22).

Although the sense of 'being' ourselves is structured through consciousness of bodily boundaries, it is also shaped by our difference from, and desire for, others. Emotional relationships are another part of the spectrum of existence Kennedy explores. While her interest in the dynamics of sexual interactions and frequently abusive exploitations of power in domestic and sexual abuse is clearly informed by perspectives established through feminism, her fiction is often equally sympathetic to the thraldom of men by their own insecurities and desires. In *Everything You Need* Nathan is dominated by a longing for his ex-wife, which shapes and threatens to destroy the fragile relationship he is attempting to develop with his daughter. As their differing needs clash, characters in all her novels struggle towards an articulation of 'want' which does not in itself invalidate their sense of completion. In *So I Am Glad*, Jennifer, emotionally destroyed by parents who forced her into collusion with their own needs, is offered redemption by Savinien. In the fluidity of both his bodily and temporal boundaries he offers a possibility of 'completion' which is comforting and terrifying. The unique dynamic of their exchange functions as symbolic intensification of all powerful human relationships in which, as Jennifer notes 'I love you' (the affirmation of presence and completion) is inextricably linked to 'I miss you' (p. 203), the recognition of absence and separateness. In *Looking for the Possible Dance* it is Margaret's relationship with her father which serves as a model of fulfilment: 'Her father and her pleasure have always been close. As if one could not be there without the other' (p. 6). After his death her changing view of their life together and apart holds her to the past and constrains her present relationship with Colin until she can move on into that precarious combination of separation and symbiosis represented in the image of the dance.

These intersections of past and present, presence and absence, intrinsic to Kennedy's thematic exploration of selfhood, also shape her narrative strategies. As various critics have noted, not only is her writing characterised by fragmented narratives, with episodic and chronological disjunction, but the movement between past and present tenses dominates even her sentence structures.[22] In *Looking for the Possible Dance* this narratological complexity is indicative of Margaret's adherence to the past and its shaping power on her understanding, 'Every year, in November, her father died' (p. 86); 'He died tomorrow' (p. 88). This play with tense also serves as an ironic reminder of authorial presence and its atemporal omniscience, 'It was close to the end of February, just over a year before she would lose her job' (p. 115), reinforcing the reader's understanding of each moment as always contextualised within a range of other narratives.

Kennedy's deliberations in *On Bullfighting* about whether a scene of high drama in the bullring is filmic or photogenic – 'The spectacle appears to be photogenic, but not filmic – to show best in frozen moments of poise, set aside from the vagaries of the bull, the slips and fumbles of the man . . .' (p. 137) – point to a tension in her longer fiction, between the desire to focus on the intensity of the moment and the need to construct longer narrative patterns. While *Everything You Need* does not offer glimpses of the future, it too renegotiates a past, established in Nathan's reflections and writerly reconstructions over a seven-year period. *So I Am Glad*, while offering intermittent glimpses of Jennifer's past which allow the reader to construct an evolutionary narrative for her, also provides an ironic distance through Jennifer's commentary as 'novelist' and our increasing consciousness of the textuality of her tale. Linguistic play with tense offers a solution to the competing demands of film and photography, narrative patterning against symbolic cameo, but in most instances Kennedy is drawn to the intensity of the moment, even if this makes her fiction appear fragmented and, at times, difficult.

For Kennedy to present comforting patterns of seamless narrative would, in any case, be philosophically antithetic to her recognition that subjectivity is structured through lack, absence and dislocation. Instead, her fiction exposes the powerful desires shaping communication. In *Everything You Need* Nathan tells his young daughter a story: 'In the beginning there . . . was no Africa, no America, no Scotland: there was only one great, big island with everything in. All very cosy. It was wonderful. Then things broke apart' (p. 143). He concludes: 'because we're all parted . . . the words . . . I mean, now we're separate, we need something to speak and something to write and read . . . and it's . . .' (p. 145). In this myth of lost unity the novel presents an image of communication very closely aligned to psychoanalytic models of speech acquisition, identifying language as predicated upon lack, loss, absence. Out of that sense of separateness, that need to bridge a gap, comes both speech and narrative. In Kennedy's fiction this understanding is manifested in its deployment of 'speaking' voices, either through specific narrative personae or in direct address to the reader, and in the increasingly explicit attention given to writing itself. While *Looking for the Possible Dance* draws attention to its own textuality through experiments with typography and defamiliarising narrative dislocations, *So I Am Glad* marks its own status as text in direct addresses to the reader and the narrator's emerging role as 'novelist'.

Writing is, for Kennedy, a dialogue structured by presence and absence; as Mary, the embryonic novelist in *Everything You Need*, acknowledges, writing fiction is simply 'making paper speak to someone who isn't there' (p. 158). While putting pen to paper draws the self together in an affirmation of presence, it also recognises an implied other and the future absence of the writer. *So I Am Glad* concludes with Jennifer enacting this perception: 'So now there's no one here but me and you and this. I will miss this and I will miss Savinien and I will be glad' (p. 280). Nathan's last act in *Everything You Need* is to close his novel and leave it for his daughter to read: 'You know now as well as I do how this works. You understand what happens here. This is where I'm in your hands completely. Please, my darling, have need of me' (p. 567).

In this way Kennedy imbricates fiction itself in the ontological complexity she explores. The increasingly self-referential quality of her writing, which might appear playfully postmodernist in nature, emerges from much darker existential questions. That acknowledgement of a textual dynamics of need between writer and reader serves in itself as a metaphor for being, for the ways in which our sense of self requires completion through interaction with an other. It is only in the act of communication, as James Watt discovers, that we can be: 'FUC WON HUNNER PERCEN MEEEEEE.'

Kennedy's fiction recognises that we are impelled by a myth of unity, a desire for completion, which may fuel the politics of gender or nation but which also structures much deeper physical and psychic frameworks. Rather than attaching herself to any particular cause or identity grouping, Kennedy addresses the construction of identity as manifested in the body, in familial and social relationships, and through writing itself. In order to do so she has to fragment the flow of her narratives and detach herself from simple character identifications. Kennedy's freedom to write in this way emerges from the social and political gains of feminism and postcolonialism which raised the consciousness of speaking subjects. From that base, however, she can then move towards more experimental forms of fiction which both examine and question the construction of subjectivity itself. It is testament to the achievements of feminism, postcolonialist thinking and earlier challenges to realism that she can find the voice and form in which to tackle such large questions with conviction, mastery and, of course, intensity.

FOR FURTHER READING

For a hard copy list of A. L. Kennedy's work up to 2001, see *Contemporary Novelists*, ed. David Madden et al., 7th edn (New York: St James Press, 2001). For a more up-to-date list on the internet, see the British Council website: <http://www.contemporarywriters.com/authors/>.

Bell, Eleanor Stewart, 'Scotland and Ethics in the Work of A. L. Kennedy', *Scotlands*, 5, 1 (1998), 105–13.

Craig, Cairns, *The Modern Scottish Novel: Narrative and the National Imagination* (Edinburgh: Edinburgh University Press, 1999).

Dunnigan, Sarah M., 'A. L. Kennedy's Longer Fiction: Articulate Grace', in *Contemporary Scottish Women Writers*, ed. Aileen Christianson and Alison Lumsden (Edinburgh: Edinburgh University Press, 2000), pp. 144–55.

March, Christie Leigh, 'A. L. Kennedy's Introspections', in *Rewriting Scotland* (Manchester: Manchester University Press, 2002), pp. 134–60.

McMillan, Dorothy, 'Constructed out of Bewilderment', in *Peripheral Vision: Images of Nationhood in Contemporary British Fiction*, ed. Ian A. Bell (Cardiff: University of Wales Press, 1995), pp. 80–99.

Smith, Alison, 'Four Success Stories', *Chapman*, 74–5 (Autumn/Winter, 1993), 177–92.

NOTES

1 See <http://www.a-l-kennedy.co.uk> and <http://www.contemporarywriters.com>.

2 All quotations are from *Looking for the Possible Dance* (London: Minerva, 1994), *So I Am Glad* (London: Jonathan Cape, 1995), and *Everything You Need* (London: Jonathan Cape, 1999). Page numbers are given in the text.

3 'On Being a Writer', PEN Lecture, Edinburgh Book Festival, 2001, <http://www.a-l-kennedy.co.uk/PEN.htm>.

4 <http://www.a-l-kennedy.co.uk/faq.htm>. See also, 'If I respect my reader

and am willing to enter into a relationship of trust, if not love, with them, I would prefer not to be labelled and categorised in return' ('Not Changing the World', *Peripheral Vision: Images of Nationhood in Contemporary British Fiction*, ed. Ian A. Bell [Cardiff: University of Wales, 1995], pp. 100–2, 102); and 'schools and histories and academic literary theories are of no relevance. It's not to do with writing' (C. L. March, 'Interview with A. L. Kennedy', *Edinburgh Review*, 101 [1999], 99–107, 106).

5 *Edinburgh Review*, 101 (1999), 107.
6 Sarah M. Dunnigan, 'A. L. Kennedy's Longer Fiction: Articulate Grace', in *Contemporary Scottish Women Writers*, ed. Aileen Christianson and Alison Lumsden (Edinburgh: Edinburgh University Press, 2000), p. 145.
7 Introduction, *Last Things First (New Writing Scotland 13)*, ed. A. L. Kennedy and James McGonigal (Aberdeen: Association for Scottish Literary Studies, 1995), n.p.
8 PEN Lecture, Edinburgh, 2001, <http://www.a-l-kennedy.co.uk/PEN.htm>.
9 Christie Leigh March, *Rewriting Scotland* (Manchester: Manchester University Press, 2002), p. 134; *Edinburgh Review*, 101 (1999), 108–9.
10 A. Smith 'Four Success Stories', *Chapman*, 74–5 (Autumn/Winter, 1993), 177–92, 192.
11 See Toril Moi, *Sexual/Textual Politics* (London: Methuen, 1985); and E. Marks and I. de Courtivron, *New French Feminisms* (Brighton: Harvester, 1980).
12 'Not Changing the World', in *Peripheral Vision: Images of Nationhood in Contemporary British Fiction*, ed. Ian A. Bell (Cardiff: University of Wales Press), pp. 100–2, 100.
13 *The Life and Death of Colonel Blimp* (London: British Film Institute, 1997), p. 21.
14 PEN Lecture, Edinburgh 2001.
15 See Darian Leader and Judy Groves, *Introducing Lacan* (Duxford: Icon Books, 2000); and Elizabeth Wright, *Lacan and Postfeminism* (Cambridge: Icon Books, 2000).
16 *Edinburgh Review*, 101 (1999), 118. Of *Everything You Need*: 'It's basically all about language', *Edinburgh Review*, 101 (1999), 117.
17 *On Bullfighting* (London: Yellow Jersey Press, 1999).
18 'On Being a Writer', Edinburgh Book Festival Lecture, 2003, <http://www.a-l-kennedy.co.uk/writer.htm>.
19 See 'Introduction: The Story So Far', in *The Feminist Reader: Essays in Gender and the Politics of Literary Criticism*, ed. Catherine Belsey and Jane Moore (London: Macmillan, 1989).
20 Jonas Frykman, *Identities in Pain* (Lund: Nordic Academic Press, 1998), p. 13. For an excellent discussion of Kennedy's work in relation to pain and violence, see L. Stark, 'Beyond Skin: The Exposed Body and Modern Scottish Fiction', unpublished PhD thesis, University of Edinburgh, 2001.
21 *On Bullfighting*, pp. 38–9.

22 See Sarah M. Dunnigan, 'A. L. Kennedy's Longer Fiction: Articulate Grace',
   pp. 144–5; and Christie Leigh, March, 'A. L. Kennedy's Introspections', in
   Rewriting Scotland, pp. 134–60.

13

Gender and Creativity in the Fictions of Janice Galloway

Dorothy McMillan

Janice Galloway has become something of an all-rounder: her repertoire includes short stories, poems, theatrical, operatic and sculptural collaborations, and music reviews as well as her three novels, *The Trick is to Keep Breathing* (1989), *Foreign Parts* (1994) and *Clara* (2002).[1] The novels are my concern, but Janice Galloway's other literary, visual and musical experiments inform the techniques of the three long fictions. In these Galloway often presents women's lives as following the pattern of short stories or vignettes with numerous repeated epiphanies or clarifications, sometimes negative, sometimes positive, rather than driving towards definitive or climactic closure. She is well known for her exploitation of the visual possibilities of the page, and she structures *Clara* in sections which roughly follow Robert Schumann's song cycle, *Frauen Liebe und Leben* (Women's Life and Love). It is perhaps the voracity of Galloway's formal experimentation that constitutes her feminism as much as her actual subject matter.

The Trick is to Keep Breathing deals with the breakdown, hospitalisation and possible recovery of schoolteacher Joy Stone, following the death by drowning of her married lover and colleague, Michael Fisher, in a hotel pool during their holiday in a foreign resort; the death gradually clarifies itself in a series of narrative retrospects. Joy teaches in a secondary school, and having abandoned her cottage to dry rot, now lives in a depressed outlying council estate in a town like Kilmarnock. *Foreign Parts* covers the driving holiday in northern and central France of Cassie and Rona, two single women in their late thirties, friends and colleagues, working in Welfare Rights in Glasgow. Cassie's life from her teens with Chris, her partner of thirteen years, and her not very successful flings with other men, are invoked by means of holiday snapshots, the more distant past of the First World War by a visit to a war cemetery and by two letters home written by Rona's grandfather from the trenches where he died before he was thirty, and the distant past of Europe by the tourist sights that the friends visit. *Clara* is the story of the nineteenth-century pianist and composer, Clara Wieck Schumann, from her childhood, dominated by her music-teacher father who had decided that he would make her famous, to the premature death in a lunatic asylum of her husband Robert, the now-celebrated composer. Clara Schumann lived for a further forty years after the death of her husband but Galloway chooses to focus on the bitter struggle of Robert and her father to possess her, and thus to write about how Clara negotiated the often conflicting demands of music and love, work and motherhood.

All three novels centre on women, the two first on Scottish women. All of the women are in different ways trying to find a way to live, a way to *be* in more or less adverse circumstances. It is probably impossible, then, to write about Galloway's novels without invoking gender or identity or nation. And given the obsessive invocation of making and unmaking which attends these issues, with this triplet goes an equally inevitable retinue of fragmentation, construction and deconstruction. Of course, Galloway's case is not particular and it has become difficult to determine whether these terms and issues reflect the conditions of our existence or the clichés of academic fashion, or both. And Galloway has herself invited her critics to harp on these strings. *The Trick is to Keep Breathing* asks repeatedly about the nature of identity – the school, says Joy ironically, 'tells me what I am' (p. 11). *Foreign Parts* as early as its thirteenth page knowingly invokes the structuralist shibboleth BRICOLAGE, the French term for odd-jobbery, made modish by Lévi-Strauss' definition of mythical thought as a 'kind of intellectual bricolage' in which something new is shaped out of bits and pieces of existing systems.[2] And finally *Clara* has a focus on a woman's life and work that engages variously with making and unmaking, with the constitution of identity through life and work, especially work, and with the incipient disintegration of identity in emotional, professional and political turmoil.

And so why not embrace, rather than worry about the accepted terms for describing all this? One reason for wishing at least to use the terms gingerly is that critical shibboleths have a way of making everything the same rather than drawing out distinctive qualities, and Galloway is a most original artist, even in her use of conventional material and method. On the one hand, she falls within recognisable traditions of writing, yet on the other is upsettingly off-the-wall, seeming to need to reinvent the wheel every time. It is this formal innovation, this refusal to be told what she cannot do, that I believe constitutes her feminism. It is a personal rather than a theoretical position.

On the face of it, her typographical tricks place her in a tradition that has been mostly male and goes back at least to Sterne. The *New York Review of Books* is quoted on the cover of the paperback edition of *The Trick*: 'Resembles *Tristram Shandy* as rewritten by Sylvia Plath'. This invokes an icon of the carnivalesque and an icon of feminism but Galloway's take on both remakes tradition. Sterne's typographical tricks are a response to the new amazing truth that black marks on a page can tell the story of a man's inner as well as outer life. But Galloway is writing well after the normalisation of the novel and *her* 'tricks' are ways of keeping her narrative alive, parallel tricks to the one demanded of Michael Fisher, who would not have drowned had he found the way to keep breathing. This trick eludes Joy's lover but the trick of keeping the novel above the water of normalisation is one function of Galloway's typographical experiments.

Cairns Craig has remarked that Galloway's technique mimics the way that Joy is being written into roles she cannot inhabit, while her sense of self slips into the marginal fragments which function as a form of self-assertion as well as representing self-loss: 'the marginal material of the text becomes the site of the author's insistence on the fact that her character is not simply contained within her novel but challenges the boundaries by which she is contained'.[3] Yet a great deal of the narrative and visual experimentation of the novel takes place in the centre not in the margins of the text, and functions satirically to clarify the terrible comedies that Joy plays out as she tries to survive. Joy speaking silently to her friend Marianne, now in America, says, 'What will I do while I'm lasting, Marianne?' (p. 15). One of the things she does is to put up with the visits of a health visitor sent by her ineffectual doctor. These visits attempt to coerce Joy into 'normality' defined by the lowest common denominator of daily existence – their oppressiveness is signalled by visual disruptions of narrative convention. The refusal of textual normalisation wittily conveys Joy's stubbornness in the face of the coercion of social normalisation. Joy has already fanatically cleaned the nasty council house for which she has had to haggle with 'tiny-minded Mr Dick from the Housing Authority' because the tenancy was in dead Michael's name. As she assembles the tea things her emotional strain is figured in the page layout, with the nearly forgotten but indispensable biscuits (p. 20) tucked in at the end of a sloping list. And then there is the health visitor's speech-bubble comment:

The health visitor becomes a cartoon character and Joy has to function on the same plane as a series of similarly not fully human characters. The process of becoming normal may involve dehumanising oneself, but as long as the text refuses to give in and become like any other text, there is some hope that Joy will do the same. As long as the text resists normalisation, refuses to behave itself, there is some hope that healing will not mean giving in. Unfortunately, there is a kind of not giving in which is damaging since it is the product of impotent frustration. This kind is emblematised by Norah, another patient in the mental hospital: 'Norah kicks the wall and presses all the buttons in the lift till they jam' (p. 121). The trick is to find the space between one kind of dehumanisation and another.

If the typographical tricks of *The Trick* have the function of defying coercion, the visuals of *Foreign Parts* have a more positive force. *Foreign Parts* is a road novel in the way that *Thelma and Louise* is a road movie; unlike the film it is life- rather than death-oriented and, while claiming less significance than the film, has a good deal more. It explores the friendship of two women within the context of the wider, often hostile, world and celebrates the possibility of friendship in spite of the insecurity of the self. The form of *Foreign Parts* is disconcertingly disrupted. Galloway exploits the irony of a road novel which refuses to proceed in a linear manner – if a road novel can't drive forward, what can? The typography of the fiction is used in the first place to signal different narrative kinds, asking different questions, all of which impede or impel progress. Rona's grandfather's letters and the spoof guidebook entries ask how things got to be like this; the snapshot commentaries ask how I, Cassie, got to be like this and the whole asks why, in the light of this, we go on, why we do things and what the doing means.

The guidebook entries framed with funereal black borders are very funny, yet they dangerously kill the life they try to evoke:

> Possible trips from ARRAS could include that to the Vimy Ridge and to Notre-Dame-de Lorette's national cemetery with its 20,000 tombs where eight ossuaries contain the remains of 26,000 unidentified soldiers. There is also a small museum. Not far is a museum-diorama of the battle fields for those who wish to relive the great campaigns.

Cassie keeps pointing this out; Rona, who does not expect guidebooks to contain the meaning of life, is less critical. Other tricks are sometimes a little *voulu* as, for example, the visual figuring of a shopping trolley (p. 120); or the interior of Chartres cathedral with its 16×6 repeats of the word glass (p. 99). Yet, they are all the consequence of an exuberant perception of the world that will not veto any possible way of conveying itself. And they are supported by linguistic invention of an unusually high order which enables clarifications of experience, Virginia Woolf's 'moments of being', female versions of epiphanies. Typically with Galloway such moments permit profundity while avoiding portentousness.

In *The Trick* epiphanic moments are more often negative than positive, their clarifications occurring on the edge of despair. Sometimes the defamiliarised ordinary becomes monstrous – as when Joy plunges her hand in a can of vegetable soup, deriving the message, 'I didn't have to eat' (p. 38), which preludes her self-emptying bulimia. Elsewhere a sandwich on a psychiatrist's desk, 'pink stuff spilling out the inside' (p. 105), provokes disgust, or a reflection in a shopping-mall mirror makes the observing self unrecognisable: 'The hair needed washed and combed and my eyes were purple' (p. 191). Immediately after this vision Joy buys 'the biggest bottle of paracetemol I could find' (p. 192). But negativity, breakdown, dissolution and disintegration are challenged by opposing forces of constructive self-exploration. The writing process is kaleidoscopic (the kaleidoscope is a favourite metaphor of Galloway's) – these moments of clarification are repeatedly shaken to yield new patterns. A new pattern is emerging at the end of the novel, but it is provisional. Galloway refuses the cliché of a happy ending – happy endings are, after all, narrative coercion, trying to ignore 'the arbitrariness of things' against which Joy realises 'there is no armour' (p. 77).

This seems a bleak lesson and some critics have found *The Trick* a bitter, if brilliant, novel. Douglas Gifford speaks of 'the slightly unattractive quality of *The Trick*, embodied in Joy's caricaturing of health visitors, doctors, teachers, ministers – virtually everybody in any kind of authority, accurate yet somehow over-the-top unkind'.[4] Yet Joy's tart, sometimes contemptuous manner goes along with peculiar generosities which give voice to the downtrodden and not very bright. And this generosity is given depth by the clear-sighted recognition that loving others is not an insurance policy. Joy has accepted her kinship with her fellow patients, has not used her education as a separator. During the ghastly evening out arranged for them by the hospital, she joins in: 'Over dessert we talk sex, money, religion, family. There need be no taboos. We are all beyond the pale' (p. 168). But kinship does not help in the end. Here is Joy's reward as the patients discuss going home for Christmas:

> We coo like pigeons and Isa hands round Black Magic. I hover over the box knowing not to take one would be bad form. I steel myself for the dipped brazil. Without warning, Janey wheels, pushing her face too close.
> You don't like us do you?
> I just look. I don't know what else to do.
> Think you're better than this place, don't you. Think you're better than me. Eh? Well fuck you teacher. Fuck you. (p. 220)

Being a teacher has failed to provide Joy with meaning and now it isolates her in non-meaning, exposed and unprotected. This is alarmingly near the novel's end; it is daring of Galloway to flirt with the abyss till the last.

The novel ends with Joy alone with her Christmas fairy-lights, her whisky and her Débussy tapes. She imagines learning to swim, imagines at least into the next week and the next – far enough for survival: 'I listen watching the coloured lights, fanning like sea anemones over the ceiling, till the music stops'. And as she listens she hears her own voice saying, 'I forgive you' (p. 235). The trick, then, learned as the fairy-lights metamorphose into the basic and beautiful life-form of the sea anemone, is to go on without armour, even without love, to forgive the world for being what it is, and to forgive people for letting one down, by meanness, by incomprehension or, like Michael, simply by dying, and to let one's self off the hook. This moment of clarification is, however, provisional. There is no such thing as safety and the novel ends with the injunction, 'Watch the lights' (p. 236).

As in *The Trick*, moments of clarification in *Foreign Parts* work both positively and negatively, proceeding in an apparently haphazard way towards a tentative destination. The vignettes, which focus on the snapshots of Cassie's previous holidays with Chris, illuminate an increasingly dysfunctional relationship from the inappropriate snap outside Victoria Coach Station when the seventeen-year-old couple, 'Hicks from the Sticks', flounder in the rush of the capital, to the moment in a happy, crowded bus in Antalya when Cassie realises that she no longer wants to be with 'Chris, scowling and clutching his beach bag' (p. 189). They are characterised by a terrible honesty of looking which justifies Cassie's sniping, bitchy voice by providing a balancing vision of surprising beauty. Cassie has just fled from a cockroach in a shower, pretending generously to let Chris go first. She peeps into the shower room:

> [It] was Chris: one hand cupped under his scrotum and the other scratching a lather into the pubic hair. Just Chris. A second of confusion and something that might have been anger only then he knew it was me. I said everything ok and he just smiled.
> Chris in the shower.
> His penis drips soap. (73–4)

Cassie and Rona more or less reject men but moments like this make the rejection regretful.

How far do they embrace each other? Lavinia Greenlaw describes Cassie and Rona as 'inextricably and irritably bound together'.[5] Most of the irritation comes from Cassie, but then so does most of everything since she is the narrative filter, even when an impersonal voice takes over. Cassie, Galloway cleverly insinuates, never quite does Rona justice, even as she loves her. In Cassie's version Rona is boringly methodical and stolid, persistently refusing the nagging questions about being that Cassie equally persistently picks at like scabs. But the clarifications of life that from time to time explode upon Cassie usually come through Rona. Cassie's unsparing or jaundiced eye sees Rona drinking her nasty shipboard tea, 'sooking' and sniffing (p. 6), or eating a plum: 'a single bead of juice fattened on the underside of the plum then dropped, melting into the breastbone area of her T-shirt' (p. 60). But Cassie also hears Rona's delightfully dirty laugh, sees her beautiful feet and relaxes into her loving attentiveness when she is ill. Although she is exasperated by Rona's refusal to 'disturb the universe', or to worry about growing old and dying, the expansion of Cassie's perceptions always owes something to Rona whose calm acceptance of the here and now – 'We're on Holiday' (p. 63) – gets Cassie as close as she can get to transcendent experience. It is Rona who, driving in the dark, half-intuits a field of yellow roses, the sight of which provides another clarification of their relationship to each other and to all things. The novel leaves Cassie and Rona at the edge of the sea and perhaps at the edge of a closer life together, skiffing stones, 'defying gravity' (262). Cassie has for the moment stopped fretting – she has decided to wait and see. Again Galloway refuses to coerce her characters into reformation or definitive change, allows them the freedom to be inconsistent and incoherent.

In these 'moments of being' Galloway places her individual stamp on modernist methods; her narrative voices are even more startlingly original. Lavinia Greenlaw remarks on her 'rare gift for peeling back the skin of language to expose its anatomy, its rhythm and flow, without draining the life from every sentence'.[6] Galloway clears the decks by unpicking various coercive, normalising discourses. In *The Trick* there is the language of women's magazines which tries to assure women that happiness can be secured in a few easy steps: 'Present suggestions for the man in my life, games the children will love, recipes for my BEST EVER CAKE' (p. 221) and the equally vacuous language of psychotherapy: '*Courage and bereavement*: coming to terms with death. **Chapter 1:** I will be shocked and angry. I am not to worry. It is normal to be shocked and angry' (p. 171). Most devastating for Joy is the unctuous language of the funeral sermon, the clichés of which airbrush out the awkward truths of Michael Fisher's life, extending conventional sympathy and love to the legitimised wife and children, while wiping out the lover he was with when he died. In *Foreign Parts* Cassie irritably attacks the normalising language of the travel book and she gives all male language a fairly hard time for trying to place and coerce women – reserving, however, some sympathy for the inarticulate promises of Rona's young grandfather's letters, for after all these young soldiers were more surely silenced than contemporary women ever can be, for they can fight back. And the fighting-back woman's voice of both novels is Galloway's finest contribution to the contemporary novel. She simply does what she likes with an astonishing assurance that seems quite effortless but must have been hard won. In and out of first, second and third person she goes, and each time the choice seems just right, the words work so hard yet seem so much at ease and this is oddly the case even when Joy is at her most neurotic or Cassie's fuse at its shortest.

Two facets of the narrative voices might be felt to be particularly Scottish achievements – the gallows humour and the deployment of ordinary speech to ask the big questions. In neither case has the tradition been particularly female, deriving perhaps from Hogg and working its way through to Kelman, whom Galloway admires. But Galloway goes her own way – women are not really supposed to make jokes, but for Joy it becomes a way of assuring herself that she is alive and, if she makes male doctors uncomfortable in the process, so much the better. Joy does ask the big questions from time to time, but Cassie never stops. She asks them, however, with a colloquial levity that might paradoxically be described as intense. Contemplating candles that have gone out prematurely in Chartres Cathedral, she reflects that 'the whole thing was unfair, somehow . . . Only a coil of black smoke by the time you'd got to the end of the street and you oblivious, whistling tunes as you walked back home thinking things were fine fine fine while behind your back, God had stopped listening' (p. 101). Cassie herself refuses to dignify her questions or her activity as a traveller.

She describes herself and Rona as 'fraudulent moochers in other people's territory, getting by on the cheap' (p. 150). Glenda Norquay neatly takes this as a defining figure for a whole way of being.[7] And it is precisely this self-deprecation coupled with a refusal, nevertheless, to shut up that makes Galloway's woman's voice so light yet profound.

These, then, are the techniques that Galloway refines to answer her own question 'How does an intelligent woman cope with now?'[8] But what use are these achievements when Galloway comes to *Clara*? For Clara Schumann is not coping with 'now' but with 'then'. On the face of it, *Clara* is the most obviously feminist of all Galloway's novels: the reclamation of women's voices has been one of *the* feminist aims. But the great nineteenth-century virtuosa, Clara Wieck Schumann, was hardly in need of such recovery when Galloway began her six years of research into her life and times. Galloway points out, however, that although she had been told about Schumann at school, it came with the rider that, while she was a great pianist, performer and interpreter, as a composer she wasn't much good. And the father of Galloway's son, a pianist, referred to Clara as Robert Schumann's 'bitch of a wife'. The problem, then, was *how* Clara was known.

Clara Schumann has been the subject of many biographies in German, French, English and Japanese. Some biographies deal with significant parts of her life – her girlhood, her marriage, her relationship with Brahms in the later part of her life – while others attempt to cover all of it. Her letters have been published in German and translated into French and English, again in various groupings designed to make at least some episodes in her life tell coherent stories. These versions of Clara offer experience organised and subdued. She has also been the subject of films and television dramatisations. Galloway's *Clara*, then, works to fragment and shake up much that had seemed fixed and secure, since attempts to fix a woman's life, to make consistent and coherent sense of it may tell falsifying and coercive stories. Galloway found that it was biography and history that fictionalised Clara. Galloway's fiction purports to tell a 'truth'. But it certainly 'tell[s] it slant'.[9]

The voice of *Clara* is as unsettled and unsettling as anything Galloway has written and it's hard to give a sense of it without extensive quotation – there are lots of short sentences, but to quote a few of them will not give the sense of how the narrative rushes about. The busyness of the narrative is one consequence of its even-handedness, for Galloway tries to give the perspective of Clara's father and her husband, even though the chief filter is Clara herself. This is generous of Galloway, for both men tried to appropriate Clara's person and her voice. Wieck, training her for virtuosity from very early childhood (her first public performance was given when she was nine) began her diary, initially writing it for her and always reading and commenting on it. When she married Robert Schumann, against her father's will and after a successful court action against Wieck for defamation, Wieck kept her diaries and did not relinquish them until she was a forty-year-old widow with seven children. Robert insisted on their keeping together a marriage diary until his institutionalisation at his own request following his suicide attempt in the Rhine at Dusseldorf. Clara Schumann had to deal with controlling individuals who were repeatedly themselves out of control. But Galloway is scrupulously fair – the most telling feminism, of course, gives men their due. She tries to get under the skin of both Wieck and Robert, and has a good deal of sympathy for Robert, who is presented as a prisoner of his own creative drives and who was in many ways as generous-hearted as he was tormented.

Galloway has her work cut out for her. And the prose is under great strain as it copes with Wieck's obsessions, Robert's wilder visions and frantic composing and writing, as well as trying to convey how Clara felt about her work, her father, her husband, her children, her tours, her fame and the troubled, revolutionary times she lived through. Thus the woman's story, which seems to be the obvious project of the fiction, turns out to be only one of the novel's aims, for her story is always inextricable from his stories and history. Galloway is not intimidated by this task: the larger-than-life quality of all the novel's figures, the persistent excess of their actions is tamed by the opposed attention to minutiae be they boiled fish and sickness, or the children's things Clara fortuitously finds in her pocket – a ribbon of Eugenie's, a button of Felix's – and presses into the dead hands of her husband.

Galloway also manages to convey something of Clara as mother. Mothers are always a problem for women – we have to embrace them and reject them simultaneously. Galloway is throughout concerned with women's relationships with their mothers: Joy's mother walked into the sea, failing to drown herself, where Michael accidentally succeeds and her surrogate stepmother/sister, Myra, terrorises her with her heavy hand, literal and metaphorical. Cassie's story begins in 'Chapter None' when she is a wee girl running away from her single-parent mother, who catches her and roughly tells her 'You've no daddy any more' (0). It's always the mother's fault – a truth that lurks in wait for most of us – and poor Clara, who was deprived of her own mother after she was divorced by her father, not only had to provide for her family, but also suffer their pain while she was absent on tour earning the necessary money, as well as the opprobrium of Robert's doctor for failing to find 'the simplest or most obvious means of avoiding her remorseless pregnancies' (p. 356), as if the leaking breasts and the pregnant belly between her and the piano were wholly her choice.

Clara is a *tour-de-force* about which, nevertheless, I have some misgivings. Partly they are inevitable misgivings about any fiction which is not freestanding. Joy and Cassie and Rona yield more of themselves in re-reading but they are also perfectly themselves at every point of their fictions. Clara's articulations sometimes seem not quite right and Robert and Wieck and Clara are sometimes indistinguishable. Would Clara and her father both have thought, 'You'll do?' Did Clara really occasionally sound like Cassie with her 'Lordknew wheres' and 'Lordknew whats'? The past is perhaps not a foreign enough country in *Clara*. Gregory Dart's rather sour review in the *TLS* accuses Galloway of an excess of 'somehows', a 'very modern impatience with nineteenth-century formality' which shows that her 'historical sympathy is growing thin'.[10] This seems too dismissive, for Galloway is trying for a voice simultaneously modern and alien and more often than not she gets it right.

In the end, however, I feel that it is in the first two novels that Galloway does most for the female perspective and is best able to deploy what I have identified as her fighting-back female voice. I admit, however, to a general feeling that writers should engage with 'now' rather than 'then' and that is perhaps coercive of me. Galloway avoids pastiche, which is the pitfall of most novelists who go to the past, but she cannot avoid the constraints that the known past inescapably puts on any representation of it, however formally inventive that representation may be. Janice Galloway's method in *Clara* seeks fluidity, yet at the end of the novel Clara does not have an open future like Joy and Cassie and Rona. The novel's last message is 'work alone endures' and its last words are 'She has nothing to do but wait' (p. 423). This seems unsatisfying as a homage to the nearly forty years of Clara's life that followed Robert's death. Forms of creativity are fighting each other here, since we have such a strong sense that Galloway's need for an effective culmination to her novel denies real significance to so much of Clara's life.

And so, in providing creative female perspectives, the 'moments' of the earlier novels seem more liberating than the planned disruptions of *Clara*; and when the past speaks to Cassie Burns, Galloway finds permanence in contingency more satisfyingly than she does in the historical excursions of the later novel:

> Corroded by the wind and the rain, eyeless and nose-free, most of the hair chipped off, yet the tracery of a half-smile was still there, radiating nine-hundred years across the road to Cassie Burns, spinster of some other parish entirely, hemmed in at this table with the plastic cover held on with clothes pegs, surrounded by second coffee cups and flakes of bread, a bottle of cheap plonk entirely finished and a bit of cheese Rona had left on her plate. (p. 107)

We must be able to access the past if we are to understand ourselves but the past is slippery and treacherous and sometimes will only give itself equivocally – we catch it out of the corner of our eye.

FOR FURTHER READING

The best source for Janice Galloway's work is her own website, <http://www.galloway.1to1.org>, which has biographical information, interviews, reviews and essays.

Craig, Cairns, *The Modern Scottish Novel Narrative and the National Imagination* (Edinburgh: Edinburgh University Press, 1999).

Norquay, Glenda, 'Janice Galloway's Novels: Fraudulent Mooching', in *Contemporary Scottish Women Writers*, ed. Aileen Christianson and Alison Lumsden (Edinburgh: Edinburgh University Press, 2000), pp. 131–43.

NOTES

1 *The Trick is to Keep Breathing* (Edinburgh: Polygon, 1989); *Foreign Parts* (London: Cape, 1994); *Clara* (London: Cape, 2002). All quotations are from these editions; page numbers are given in the text.

2 Claude Lévi-Strauss, *The Savage Mind* (London: Weidenfeld and Nicolson, 1966), p. 21. Galloway's invocation of 'bricolage' is, however, playful and returns the term to its origins since it appears at the roadside simply as an advertisement for odd-job work. Thus she is able simultaneously to validate her eclectic method, yet light-heartedly deny the heavy theoretical weight that has accrued to the term.

3 Cairns Craig, *The Modern Scottish Novel Narrative and the National Imagination* (Edinburgh: Edinburgh University Press, 1999), p. 195.

4 Douglas Gifford, 'Renaissance and Revival', *Books in Scotland*, 50 (Summer, 1994), 1–7, 4.

5 Lavinia Greenlaw, 'Holiday Reading', *TLS*, 6 May 1994, 20.

6 Ibid.

7 Glenda Norquay, 'Janice Galloway's Novels: Fraudulent Mooching', in *Contemporary Scottish Women Writers*, ed. Aileen Christianson and Alison Lumsden (Edinburgh: Edinburgh University Press, 2000), pp. 131–43.

8 Janice Galloway in interview with Christie Leigh March, 1999, <http://www.galloway.1to1.org/>.

9 Emily Dickinson, 'Tell All the Truth but Tell it Slant', *The Complete Poems of Emily Dickinson*, ed. Thomas H. Johnson (Boston: Little, Brown, 1960), Poem 1129.

10 Gregory Dart, 'The Domestic Muse', *TLS*, 21 June 2002, 25.

14

Appetite, Desire and Belonging in the Novels of Rose Tremain

Sarah Sceats

Is Rose Tremain a feminist writer? In many ways her novels are reminiscent of mainstream nineteenth-century fiction: realist, with narrative drive and satisfying resolutions, handling major themes and moral issues, and emphasising the transformative power of love. Yet if these characteristics suggest a traditional *oeuvre*, it would be a mistake to conclude that Tremain's fiction upholds the status quo. There is, to begin with, a concern with the position of women in society at various points in history. She explores the ways in which women are constrained, their opportunities for choice and action and how they oppose or accommodate themselves to constraints. Less obviously feminist is her use of oblique perspectives, points of view that are frankly marginal to the society depicted. These marginalised protagonists include, among others, an ageing homosexual butler, a dull-seeming housewife, a teenage boy in love with a woman of forty, a young female transsexual, an elderly forgotten novelist, a socially aspiring seventeenth-century physician, an English lutenist at the Danish Court, the wife of a gold prospector . . . Around such diverse figures are woven further perspectives that explore the difficult business of living in often less than ideal circumstances. Many of Tremain's characters are unhappy; most are spurred by the sharp and unforgiving nature of appetite. If her fiction is feminist, it is certainly not so in any male-baiting, politically correct or instrumental way. It is not didactic or polemical but rather displays the limitations, misery and gloriousness of individual human lives. Tremain celebrates small acts of courage. For some this involves resistance, for others enduring; 'you can make decisions to change your external landscape and I think you can make decisions to change your internal landscape as well', she says.[1] Above all, her novels depict the insistent pursuit of what promises self-knowledge, existential confirmation or some significant sense of belonging.

Even within the loose definition I am proposing, Tremain's fiction might be considered less than feminist, given the prevalence of male protagonists in her novels. In at least three cases these male protagonists are given first-person perspectives, a narrative strategy which suggests that these characters themselves are the central focus of interest. Does this mean Tremain is not concerned with individual women's lives? It would, I think, be a mistake to believe so. Tremain's fiction is marked by its richness and subtlety, and her peculiar brand of feminism is, likewise, comprehensive in its focus; women's lives, in her novels, are lived in heterosocial contexts. Understanding women, their problems, traumas, desires and aspirations, of necessity involves understanding men and the cultures in which they operate. Tremain may seem less feminist than liberal humanist, yet I believe that throughout her novels, with their insistence on the variety and multiplicity of life, there runs a thread of concern with the perpetually problematic nature of being female. Existential confirmation and belonging are, it seems, no more important for women than for men, but they are shown to be both problematic and difficult to achieve in what are essentially patriarchal societies.

While she is most celebrated for her historical fiction, the majority of Tremain's earlier novels have recent settings. They are all imaginative works, however, with little 'reportage' or autobiographical writing; Tremain imagines herself into other people's skins. In a statement published on the British Council's *Contemporary Writers* website, she writes:

> I suspect that many writers deceive themselves about why they write. My self-deception is that I create in order to understand and that the final end of it all might be wisdom. This means that I deliberately seek out the strange, the unfamiliar, even the unknowable . . .[2]

In other words, she seeks understanding of precisely what she has *not* experienced. Elsewhere on the same website, critic Jules Smith writes of Tremain's 'inclusive sympathy'. This apt phrase captures exactly the flavour of her work. While social attitudes, systems and politics (in the broadest sense) are treated critically, individuals are rarely if ever pilloried. People – even when they behave reprehensibly – are to be understood, and readers are drawn to inhabit and identify with unlikely subjects for empathy. Tremain's first novel, for example, narrated by a seventy-nine-year-old man, transgresses numerous boundaries: writerly, social and moral. It centres upon the adult Sadler's love for an eleven-year-old boy.

The essence of *Sadler's Birthday* is that Sadler's present life, as a solitary, cantankerous ex-butler in the house of his former employers, is illuminated by his reminiscences. The novel is concerned with loneliness, and implies the need to make the most of love, wherever it occurs. Love and its absence occur in many forms: mother/child relationships, sexual desire, simple friendship and solace. Sadler inherits the house because he offers quiet support and sympathy to the isolated and uncertain Madam, unwittingly nourishing in her a lasting affection. As an old man, Sadler finds a gentle companionship with the 'lonely unlovable Vera', who stays on in the house after their employers' deaths.[3] As the illegitimate child of an abandoned, hungry innocent, the infant Jack Sadler is adored by his mother, who keeps him close despite the stringencies of punishing work in domestic service. His memories of her are highly physical, evoking the smell and warmth of her body. Her care contrasts sharply with that of the evacuee Tom's mother, who reappears after four years' silence only when he reaches employable age.

Sadler's relationship with Tom is initially one of protective identification. He sees himself in Tom. He provides unintrusive, careful affection and security for the boy, a devotion that in turn awakens love and, ultimately, sexual desire. Through kindness Sadler falls victim to a passionate attachment. While Tom discovers his own sexuality with a wry, half-amused lack of emotion, Sadler, 'tremblingly awake' (p. 134), holds the sleeping boy in his arms, and continues to hold him in the tender regard of a lover. When Tom eventually leaves with his mother, giving 'the merest of smiles' (p. 147), Sadler has to push his fist in his mouth to prevent himself screaming. His attachment remains constant to the end of the book. The relationship between Sadler and Tom is never represented as abusive, and Tom simply later rejects 'all that pansy stuff', because it was part of growing up, and no longer appropriate (p. 154). It is Sadler who is damaged, stuck in an emotional state symbolised by a maggoty dead rat under the bed. Tremain says she simply did not consider the relationship as abusive at the time the book was written, although she can see that it may seem so now.[4] The change of climate concerning 'consensual' relationships between adults and minors over the last few decades has been considerable; current thinking about paedophilia has by no means always been the case.[5] Tremain's construction of the relationship here focuses on protective affection and love, what she calls the 'kinship' between the two characters. Indeed, it is possible to read this kinship as paternal – or even maternal – attachment, a re-enactment of Annie's love for the infant Sadler, his love for a substitute son or perhaps even that of the adult Sadler for his immature self.

This novel establishes three factors that continue to resonate through Tremain's fiction. It focuses on a marginal or outsider figure, which is partly what manifests her particular feminism. All the significant relationships in Sadler's life – apart from his fixation on Tom – are with neglected, abused or abandoned women, equally marginal figures with whom he is able in some degree to empathise. The suggestion is of a psychological rather than political feminism: what might be considered 'female' characteristics (empathy, intuition, nurturing) are what define the focus of interest in a character who happens to be male. It raises the possibility of obsession, of being driven by desire or appetite, whether for food, sex, a person, a landscape, a thing. This drive in turn is related, directly, obliquely or even inversely, to feelings of belonging, the desire to locate oneself in relation to whatever it is that confers a fulfilling self-identity, that allows the feeling of being 'right in one's skin'.

Tremain's second and third novels have more obviously feminist themes. In *Letter to Sister Benedicta*, fat, fifty-year-old Ruby Constad evolves from being a sad, helpless and abused wife into somebody more aware, humorous, empowered and self-respecting, who ventures into a wider world. *The Cupboard* features an inherently more gutsy and independent woman, eighty-seven-year-old former novelist and suffragist Erica March, a person of appetite and courage, true to herself and her ideals, but unable to locate herself comfortably in any pre-existing landscape (metaphorical or literal). The next two novels, *The Swimming Pool Season* and *Sacred Country*, are structurally more ambitious. Both evoke fragmentation or instability of belonging, but within a polyphonic or multi-voiced narration, where the narrative point of view is passed between different characters. Such a narrative strategy, with its multiple viewpoints, confounds any straightforward feminist interpretation, but the effect is quite different in each novel. While *Sacred Country* retains a claustrophobic local focus, *The Swimming Pool Season* encompasses two disparate societies, one a village in the Dordogne, the other a group of people revolving around Leni, a dying but powerful woman in Oxford. The link is Leni's daughter and her husband, who have bought a house in Pomerac after the failure of his business. The point of view shifts to encompass in turn more or less all the characters, with varying degrees of sympathy. This includes a rural *ménage à trois*, a Polish woman whose husband is mad, a gay poet, at least two misogynists and the sexually and emotionally yearning of various complexions.

Appetite is frequently on display in *The Swimming Pool Season*, especially in the forms of obsession, compulsion and betrayal. Larry, the bank-rupted creator of swimming pools, becomes obsessed with the prim niece of the local doctor but spends his time with Nadia, a wise Polish busybody who doubles as a sort of Greek chorus commenting on the action. In thoughts, Larry is intertwined with his wife Miriam who has gone to Oxford to care for her dying, antipathetic mother and to spend time by herself. In this quest she is a version of the female figure that recurs again and again in Tremain's fiction, craving independence from given roles. These given roles usually constitute a relentless and invasive obstruction to self-realisation, both in their external manifestations and inasmuch as 'feminine' behaviour patterns are internalised (or inscribed, as Foucault would have it). Miriam's appetite for solitude is difficult to realise, for it is constantly intruded upon, by her mother's manipulation and by the doggy devotion of an old family friend, Dr O, who falls for Miriam when she cries in his presence (a gendered power relation Tremain sketches pointedly but without comment). Pursuing Miriam, Dr O does violence to his own relationship with a plain but devoted young woman who cannot understand why she is set aside just when (unknown to Dr O) she has become pregnant. Miriam's mother's appetite is that of the puppet-mistress, the beautiful, selfish, sometimes spiteful centre of attention, deploying all the manipulative weapons of the unemancipated woman.

Further appetites are displayed, involving the *ménage à trois* and an errant son, who falls into a tumultuous adoration doomed to disappointment.

However, it is clear that appetites, however strong, relentlessly pursued or laudable, are never *necessarily* satisfied. Larry's grand project for a cathedral-influenced swimming pool is unceremoniously aborted and even Miriam's powerful need to return 'home' gives way to longing for her husband. Miriam's earlier rejection of him, the realisation of her desire to go alone to Oxford and her prolonged stay there are largely to do with self-location, for belonging is not so much a question of place, important though that is, as of reaffirming her sense of self. Though she takes time out from married life, moving into her childhood bedroom, it is not until her mother dies that she feels released, 'at home'. Miriam's relationship to herself is something she only discovers through extraordinary circumstances.

It is the quality of needing to feel right in one's skin that permeates *Sacred Country*. This novel spans some thirty years (1952–80) in the life, chiefly, of Mary, a girl who decides that she is really a boy, and pursues a painful journey to masculine adulthood. Clearly, her sense of belonging (or not) is inseparable from her gender. Once again, this is a marginal figure driven by powerful compulsion. At the age of six Mary has little autonomy, so her sense of being an outsider is particularly powerful, the more so because she feels displaced by a baby brother. The situation is exacerbated by the fact that her war-disabled father is rigid, inarticulate and prone to violence, and her mother, who has a very fragile psyche, takes the world as given and never intervenes. No one in this family is 'right in their skin'.

Escape – from place, home, gender, employment, the present, sanity – looms large in all strands of this novel. It is figured in Mary's idealisation of her grandmother's death in a gliding accident, in her mother's covering her eyes when she cannot bear pain, in her father's ultimate suicide. More positively, it is evident in neighbour Edward Harker's belief that in a former life he was a nun, in brother Timmy's flight into the priesthood, in the butcher Walter Loomis' espousal of country music. Walter, another marginalised figure, is also an obsessive. As a young man he tries to yodel for so long that he has to be hospitalised; later, he falls hopelessly in love with a vapid and uninterested girl, remaining so until seduced by the local dentist, whom he again falls in love with (unrequitedly). He is repeatedly ground down by loss and disappointment. Finally, he leaps, pursuing a career in country music in America, where for the first time he feels good: in the right place, physically, emotionally and artistically.

Walter's story is a companion to Mary's, though his transformation is bolder, less traumatic and more rewarding, for he gains physical strength, friendship and a lover to sing duets with. Mary is neither free nor powered by obsession; she is just certain who she is not. She feels herself to be an outsider: to her family, in her school, as a female. Even the kind-hearted treat her as a girl, and professionals (vicar, doctor) simply do not hear. She is able to confide only in Edward Harker, who, believing in the transmigration of souls, takes her seriously. Nevertheless, Mary is driven out of the village by her father's unpredictability and violence. Like Walter, she finds that geographical and cultural relocation offers possibilities for reconstruction of self, both socially and physically. After living in London, she goes to America where she finally becomes Martin and begins to live in the first person. When her doctor writes to summon her back to England for reconstructive surgery she realises that she already has a life, that she has inhabited herself, become present: 'Age isn't the only thing to creep up on us', she tells her fellow worker. 'Sometimes it's happiness'.[6] The exact delimitations of her – or his – body now no longer matter so desperately: he is who she has become.

The notion of belonging to oneself, bodily and psychically, resonates throughout Tremain's narratives, although she does her best to muddy the gendered waters and will espouse no easy feminism. Her remaining novels, with the exception of *The Way I Found Her*, are historical, attempting a wider scope and a more layered and contextualised way of writing individual and social concerns. The first, *Restoration*, draws parallels between the 1660s and Thatcher's Britain, in terms of material excess and competition.[7] Appetite is rampant. The protagonist, Merivel, describes himself as a man of 'brimming appetites' and he has a keen desire to indulge them all.[8] His experiences at Court, and subsequently as husband of convenience to the King's mistress Celia, allow him to do so flamboyantly, for a while, growing fat, libidinous and indolent in the process. Counterpoised to appetite is the theme of exile, for Merivel is cast out from the King's favour when he transgresses the rules of the King's seduction game. At Court, Merivel loses himself in frivolity; in exile he rediscovers his seriousness, or rather has it forced upon him, learning what it is to be removed from privilege, especially for the persecuted, the poor, the sick, the mad. Like a good postcolonial, he discovers the lack of love the periphery holds for the centre.[9] Yet he still feels he belongs to the centre, and when his divided self is eventually rebalanced he is rewarded by partial restoration. As well as a fable for the 1980s, it may be read as a cautionary tale about unreflecting masculinity.

Belonging resonates in this novel in relation to the King, the source of all wealth and privilege. But it also connects with other factors both internal and external. Merivel knows and feels at home in the bustle of London, especially Cheapside, where he returns to live, works and redeems himself. He is much less comfortable at Whittlesea (Bedlam in the Fens) where he goes when rejected by the King. Here he reconnects with his Quaker friend Pearce, who acts as his soul-doctor. Here too his qualities are tested; his appetites for food and luxury are denied and his unsuccessfully contained, abusive sexual appetite is rewarded with further exile and enforced responsibility for the woman he has impregnated. Whittlesea may thus be seen as Merivel's necessary 'dark place'. He feels the most profound sense of belonging, however, at Bidnold, in Norfolk, the estate the King gives to him as husband of Celia. His initial response is an exercise of egotistical sublime. He adores the house and park, decorating and furnishing the house with loving, tasteless extravagance. It stands in his memory as a place of intense, dreamy satisfaction, and it is to a single room in the soberly redecorated house that he is ultimately restored, a reward for his personal evolution. He is, however, reduced, restrained and enhanced with a daughter. His restoration to the house is a (re)discovery of belonging, but in a clearly feminised mode.

Set some decades earlier, *Music and Silence* sees a return to a more refracted story and polyphonic mode, interweaving multiple narratives through omniscient narration and from various perspectives, including letters, notebooks, 'private papers' and thoughts 'plucked from the air'. It is an ambitious novel, structurally, in its dense and interleaved narratives, and thematically inasmuch as it complicates questions of appetite, the body, exile and belonging. The form encourages a multiplicity of points of view and broadens and contextualises concerns that are particularly, though not exclusively, pertinent to women and their lives. Lutenist Peter Claire goes to play at the Court of Danish King Christian IV. An exile of sorts from his native Norfolk, Claire falls in love with Emilia, a lady-in-waiting to the King's consort but his quest is powered by a sense of his own absence, that there is someone, something or somewhere to which he has yet to belong, for which he must relinquish old dreams and longings. The plot is one of postponement, placing repeated barriers between him and Emilia, their two narratives barely intersecting until the end.

Exile though he is, Peter is not exactly a marginal figure, except in his sensitivity. Like the other musicians he is a servant, subject to King Christian's whim, but he is also singled out to be Christian's moral support and confidant. What is significant to twenty-first-century readers is his powerlessness: he is free to leave the King's service and return to England only when the King trades him for a loan. Power and its lack are central to the novel, in both manifest and covert forms, though exercised most effectively within a domestic compass. In this sense the novel is deeply political, indeed feminist, though as always Tremain's focus is subtle. Ostensible power is compromised. King Christian is an absolute monarch but his power is circumscribed in all sorts of ways: by the loss of his dearest childhood friend (and his part in that loss); by the removal of his wife's affection; by the country's economic plight; by the collapse of the grand silver-mining project; and by his own troubled spirit and digestive upsets. He is driven by a perfectionism that is confounded by imperfect reality. His disappointments result in humiliation, loss of purpose, illness, despair; a conviction that everything is 'unravelling towards catastrophe'.[10] It is from this existentially marginal position that he begins to reframe his erstwhile grand visions and violent longings, to discover small perfections (such as exquisitely-made paper), regain a balanced appetite and respond to the devotion of made-over servant, Vibeke. In some sense he is like Merivel: his downfall is public and catastrophic; his redemption lies in relinquishing the brasher aspects of masculinity and the adoption of what might be seen as a more 'female' lifestyle.

For the women in the novel there is rather less room for manoeuvre. If
Peter is bound to the King, Emilia is wholly powerless: as grieving daughter
bullied by father and stepmother; as handmaid to the capricious Kirsten; and
as marriageable daughter being pressed to accept an ageing vicar. Her only
route to autonomy (until rescued by Peter) is death. Other women are similarly hampered by social expectation: Emilia's stepmother can wield power
only through her sexuality; Peter's sister Charlotte, besotted and indulged as
she may be by father and prospective husband, nevertheless has no real alternative to marriage; Vibeke's social rise is carefully engineered by Kirsten's
scheming mother, and involves bullying, bribery and painful dentistry. Even
Christian's mother, Queen Sofie, retains a sense of independence only
through hoarding gold, an obsession that gradually takes her over. These
women's lives are precarious, each one constrained by dependence on men
who have publicly sanctioned power.

Women are by definition marginal within a patriarchal social structure.
All of these women can only pursue self-fulfilment within such a structure,
but all, one way or another, attempt to do so with courage. Most courageous
of all, perhaps, is the egregious Kirsten, Christian's estranged wife, whose
uncensored thoughts and desires are presented through her 'private papers'.
Kirsten is splendidly larger-than-life, immediately recognisable as vain and
self-referential when she claims that her mirror is faulty. She appears to have
no sense of belonging, not to Christian, not to her family, not geographically,
nor even, really, to herself, except in the most physical way. She constrains
her serving women out of resentment, recoils from her children, focuses
entirely upon her lover, Count Otto Ludwig. She becomes enslaved to her
orgasm, turning the Count's complaints into an excuse for flagellation, esca-
lating their sexual pleasures and the intensity of the relationship that even
she recognises as 'derangement' and 'abuse' (p. 86). Pleasure becomes a compulsion.

Kirsten is redeemed only by passing affections, occasional contrition and
not inconsiderable wit. Almost everything is subsumed to her sexual desire;
only her greater need for Emilia prevents her seducing Peter Claire. Her pos-
sessiveness towards Emilia, exacerbated by isolation, loneliness and frustration, finally bursts out into a 'longed for' but self-defeating rage, banishing
her only ally. Though she continues to scheme for the return of her exiled
lover, she turns to her two 'black slaves' for sexual satisfaction. What
Tremain appears to be doing with this character is a *reductio ad absurdum*.
While Peter Claire is constrained he is able, ultimately, to pursue both his
love and his career; Kirsten, by contrast, has authority only so long as she is
Christian's wife. The only power she has is that of her sexuality, for she is
without social position or worldly currency, and is too impulsive to be truly
manipulative. So Tremain makes her wholly passionate: a creature of appetite. Interestingly, Tremain reports positive reader responses to Kirsten who,
she believes, 'strike[s] a chord with very many women of many ages' not just

on account of sexual daring but for her overall courage.[11] Defiance by a woman of this period of her husband (let alone King), mother and neighbours, preferring isolation to capitulation, does suggest strength of character. And Tremain gives her the last word in the novel. Relating a dream that confounds husband and lover, she concludes that the coexistence of opposing feelings proves that nothing is certain. In this conclusion she even achieves a sort of liberation, an acceptance of un-belonging.

The problematic nature of belonging, especially for women, the potent pull of landscape, the sharp drive of appetite and its associated obsessions, along with the relentless pursuit of self-identity are all foregrounded in Tremain's 2003 novel, *The Colour*. Set in 1860s New Zealand, the novel inevitably concerns the marginalised: immigrants to the most distant of the British colonies. Furthermore, it focuses on the gold rush and its effects, both social and individual, on those trying to make good in an alien and seemingly hostile landscape (not for nothing is a big find known as a 'homeward bounder'). Tremain explores the excitement, promise and unpredictable threat of the unknown, while delineating the loss of love in a marriage framed by conventional expectations but subject to immense internal and external stresses.

Joseph Blackstone, his wife Harriet and mother Lilian attempt to carve out a farming life on a bleak piece of land in New Zealand's South Island. Joseph is trying to flee a guilty past, Harriet to avoid a staid life as an English spinster governess, and Lilian – though she wants nothing so much as to remain in England – has no choice, since she is widowed and dependent on her son. Joseph hopes that with Harriet's help he will be able to provide for his mother and make up to her for past failures. He is, however, unable to share himself or engage with the reality of another person (symbolised in his obliterating sexual practices) and he becomes progressively estranged, from Harriet, his mother, the farm: everything but the desire to find gold. 'Without desire, nothing is made' might be his motto, and he is single-minded in his desire (p. 138).[12] Harriet, by contrast, is excited by the challenge of a pioneering life: she is drawn by the idea of self-sufficiency; she longs to be tested, and finds a thrill in the space and the sublimity of the mountains.

The marginal nature of these three people's life together is thrown into relief by that of their nearest neighbours, Dorothy and Toby Orchard, who have made a success of farming and created 'a comfortable little piece of England' (p. 46) in their homestead. They are a well-to-do, energetic couple, with an expectation of success and conventionally gendered spheres of activity. Toby is a large, outdoor, meaty man with noisy clothes and a 'triumphant' appetite (p. 43). Indeed he creates a veritable 'euphoria . . . of eating' pigeon pie (p. 44), though leaving to his wife the more 'feminine' blancmange, which he barely tastes. Toby is undoubtedly becoming a successful settler. Dorothy's role is traditionally domesticated, her main concession to the pioneer life being short hair. Though she rides out onto the property for picnics, it is for maternal and hospitable reasons, and she counsels Harriet that nature is 'too grand', the mountains 'fearful', that women are 'not strong enough for rivers and stars' (p. 46).

From the beginning Joseph's dreams have an English flavour, the yearning of an exile for what has been left behind. Though he wishes to love Harriet, his 'drift towards gold' (p. 121) somehow opens a door to the past, to which Joseph comes to realise he is still profoundly attached. In gold he sees the promise of redemption: it will allow him to put right the harm he did, and *then* he will be free to love his wife. In the interim, however, his soul is shrivelled. He becomes enslaved. The possibility of not having gold on his claim gives him 'a dread so absolute it made his skin crawl' (p. 206) and at one point, exhausted, he almost gets up to continue prospecting in the middle of the rainy night, so relentless is his appetite. By the time Harriet arrives at the claim he is wholly displaced, wild and scrawny, even slightly mad.

Harriet demonstrates the strongest non-specific yearning of all Tremain's characters. She craves belonging in a passionate present tense: in her connection with the land, spiritually, in the wealth of her experiences, in the love of another. Early on, when she is struggling to make something of the farm in the face of Joseph's emotional absence, it is emptiness that dominates her attempts at self-location: 'She longed to confide in somebody. She thought that perhaps what she longed to hear was that almost every life was arranged like this, around a void where love should have been and was not, and that her predicament was therefore an ordinary one' (p. 105). But when Joseph leaves for the goldfields and buys her a horse, she rides astride, indicating a changing relationship to herself and the farm. She and Lilian find that life is easier in Joseph's absence. As with so many of Tremain's women, Harriet is oppressed and constrained by the conventions that frame her expectations. Like Mary in *Sacred Country* she finds that her role, in this case as Joseph's wife, simply does not fit.

Later, during her solitary search for Joseph at the goldfields after Lilian's death, Harriet is overcome by yearning, for something she cannot identify. As a woman on the diggings she is, of course, anomalous. Tremain, it seems, wants to allow her a possibility of belonging not entirely defined by gender. Harriet experiences the thrill of prospecting, alone, upriver away from the main diggings, in 'a slow feast of solitary days' (p. 278). She grows to understand the fascination of gold and its powerful effect on the imagination. In concentrated solitary activity she feels she may be able to formulate the central question of her life (p. 278). What she experiences, after being rescued from a flash flood by the Chinese vegetable-grower Pao Yi, is spiritual ease, 'a perfect sensation of *being*' (p. 321). Then she discovers desire and falls into a relationship that, albeit unconventional, nevertheless reinforces her femaleness and female sexuality. For a while this unlikely couple dwell in a hermetic, dreamlike world, and it is this intimate connection, though it ends in parting, that changes Harriet's being.

As with all Tremain's novels, *The Colour* provides a clear resolution to most of the narrative threads. She tends to resist closures that imply a happy ever after, however, and here the various endings are sadder and more open than in much of her work. There are losses, deaths and partings, and outcomes that do not indicate personal growth. The drive of appetite, the irresistible pursuit of a dream, she suggests, may result in unlooked-for confirmations. The fiercest desires may not, even when realised, yield a sense of belonging, an enhanced self-identity or existential confirmation. For, of course, all these are shifting perceptions, part of the process of living, not a destination to be reached or goal to be achieved. Yet there is also another kind of openness at work, and that has to do with what I have described as Tremain's oblique perspectives. If her writing may be described as feminist it is not because she focuses on women. It is rather that her writing is imbued with a strong suggestion that patriarchal society and fixed gender relations might be otherwise. Many of her characters are thus marginal or undefined in some way. Others undergo radical, depolarising change: her most heartily 'masculine' characters are feminised by experience; her women take on roles or assume characteristics associated normatively with men, and one even adopts male gender. The point is that Tremain appears to deplore the polarisation of male and female essential to patriarchal societies and which, it must be said, is perpetuated by certain strands of feminist theory. There is clearly no woman-centred polemical agenda. In its engagement with issues of desire and belonging in individual lives, however, Tremain's fiction makes inescapable points about the implications of living in patriarchal society. It is one of the strengths of her writing that she maintains a page-turning narrative drive without closing off the uncertainties and slipperiness of the lived life. The lives that she chooses to write about demonstrate slipperiness and uncertainty with an empathetic breadth of vision, psychically, morally and politically. It is this vision that defines Tremain's peculiar brand of feminism.

FOR FURTHER READING

For a hard copy list of Rose Tremain's work up to 2001, see *Contemporary Novelists*, ed. David Madden et al., 7th edn (New York: St James Press, 2001). For a more up-to-date list on the internet, see the British Council website: <http://www.contemporarywriters.com/authors/>.

Bigsby, C. W. E., *Rose Tremain*, Contemporary Writers Series (London: British Council, 1992).
Giddens, Anthony, *Modernity and Self Identity: Self and Society in the Late Modern Age* (Cambridge: Polity, 1991).
Probyn, Elspeth, *Outside Belongings* (New York and London: Routledge, 1996).

NOTES

1 'Costume Dramatist', Interview with Susanna Rustin, *The Guardian*, Saturday, 10 May 2003, G2, 20–3, p. 20.

2 <http://www.contemporarywriters.com>.

3 Rose Tremain, *Sadler's Birthday* (London: Macdonald and Jane's, 1976), p. 167. All quotations are from this edition; page numbers are given in the text.

4 Gilles Menegaldo, 'On Art and Life: an Interview with Rose Tremain', *Revue d'études Anglophones*, 4, Spring, 1998 (Université d'Orléans), 101–19, 104.

5 Tremain's fifth novel, *The Way I Found Her,* features a sexual act between a forty-one–year-old woman and a thirteen-year-old boy that bears more relation to erstwhile notions of benign sexual education than any suggestion of abuse. It is a novel irradiated by adolescent appetite and dwells on belonging both in the problematic self-locations of this stage in life and in terms of place and culture.

6 Rose Tremain, *Sacred Country* (London: Vintage, 2002), p. 353.

7 'That's what *Restoration* was about, though probably nobody realised'. Rose Tremain, quoted in Rustin, 'Costume Dramatist', 23.

8 Rose Tremain, *Restoration* (London: Sceptre, 1990), p. 27.

9 See Bill Ashcroft, Gareth Griffiths and Helen Tiffin, eds, *The Empire Writes Back: Theory and Practice in Post-colonial Literatures* (London: Routledge, 1989).

10 Rose Tremain, *Music and Silence* (London: Vintage, 2000), p. 244.

11 '*Music and Silence*', edited transcript of a 'live chat' on *Book Club,* BBC Radio 4, March 2002.

12 Rose Tremain, *The Colour* (London: Chatto & Windus, 2003), p. 138.

15

Desire for Syzygy in the Novels of A. S. Byatt

Katherine Tarbox

In her tetralogy that comprises *The Virgin in the Garden, Still Life, Babel Tower* and *A Whistling Woman*, A. S. Byatt meditates upon the destiny of irrational desire as it comes into conflict with rational culture. The novels dwell on the failure of scholarship to contain and express the voice of passion, which seeks equal status with the voice of reason. *The Biographer's Tale* and *The Shadow of the Sun* show characters hovering on the edge of transformation as they attempt to evolve beyond Enlightenment consciousness. Byatt finds, in evolutionary psychology and neurobiology, new slants on being, and her novels work towards an articulation of the possibility of *syzygy*. Syzygy is an existential condition symbolised by the hermaphrodite – one who transcends gender by conjoining reason and passion (traditionally associated with maleness and femaleness, respectively) into fully realised humanness that is different from and greater than the sum of those parts.

It is helpful to look at Byatt's exploration of syzygy in the context of gender feminism, a discrete discipline that arose in the 1970s from the more generalised discourse of feminism. Gender feminism centres on the belief that '[g]ender is socially constructed and it becomes an independent and determining factor in the organisation of society'.[1] Psychoanalytic writers sought to understand women's devalued position within patriarchy as an effect of early childhood, when we unconsciously internalise the 'law of the father'. To become men, boys must reject maternal, affiliative values and do the work of history-making, while to become women, girls must do the 'lesser' work of relating and nurturing. Other writers trace the ways in which this self-replicating system saturates all thinking and all forms of expression, from the way we think of ourselves, to the way we construct, conduct, and value all social formations and disciplines. Byatt assumes these truths in her work, but she takes the discussion of gender further, to name the hermaphrodite as the only being who can be fully human and who can create a fully human culture. To elucidate this idea, I will undertake an intensive reading of Byatt's Booker Prize-winning novel, *Possession*.[2]

I begin, as Byatt's 'hero' Roland Michell begins, with Randolph Ash, whose desire catalysed a plot that took over a century to play out. He imagines in his poem 'Ragnarok' the birth of our 'primitive parents' (p. 181), Ask and Embla, to whom the gods give, equally to each, the powers that will make them human. Loki gives 'hot blood . . . red with a human fire, / A stream of vital sparks' ; Honir gives 'sense and understanding and the power / To stand and move' (p. 262); Odin gives the human soul. The couple wakes to life and sees their wholeness mirrored in each other. Loki warns that their wholeness must be 'preserved', because a 'split' would be 'mortal ruin till the end of Time' (p. 262). Ask and Embla have been split, within themselves and from each other, and it is 'ruin' that Byatt anatomises.

The characters in this novel grope through a fog of gender confusion to link, as Christabel says, the 'modern mind to those of ancient days / To the dark dreaming Origins of our race' (p. 318). Byatt seeks to 'connect a bygone time with the very present', as the first epigraph describes, just as Roland finds that 'everything connects and connects . . . as though we held a clue to the true nature of things' (p. 276). Analytical psychology, which studies the coexistence of the modern and the archaic psyche within us, affirms and rewrites Ash's poem for our time by giving us the concept of psychic syzygy: a 'dynamic field' where 'the concept of gender is not very useful',[3] a 'hermaphroditic'[4] field where 'one is always never-only-one, but bound in a syzygy, a tandem'.[5]

The syzygetic psyches of our first parents evolved for survival in a harsh world, and each sex owned a full palette of always available 'agonic' and hedonic' energies which have now, as then, the status of instinct.[6] Agonic instinct drives us to compete, achieve status, reason, follow goals and manage conflict; this instinct Byatt names 'force' (p. 51). Hedonic instinct compels us to bond, care, feel, nurture, imagine, intuit and sense – an instinct Byatt symbolises through blood and sparks. In effect, all children are born as Ask and Embla, each of whom is psychically hermaphroditic, but culture splits them into boys and girls, who must repress entire sectors of their birthright energies, provoking the devastating consequences of denying instinct's insistence that it be somehow lived in the world.

If Ash imagines primordial unity, Christabel looks to 'true pre-history' (p. 190) to lament its split in 'the City of Is', where with 'the coming of warriors and priests' (p. 379), women were drowned. The Church Fathers transformed the hedonic Pan into Satan and projected his qualities onto women, whom they could then subdue. Dahud, Queen of Is, represents man's 'terror of pagan cults and the terror of the passion of the senses' (p. 378); she is 'man's fear of woman . . . of the sleep of reason under the rule of . . . desire, intuition, imagination' (p. 384). Priests and warriors *created* gender, as well as Par-is, which rises into air, while Is sinks into water and becomes Other (p. 178). Loki's gift is named woman, and both she and that gift are derogated and drowned, 'stored / Inside a glassy box' (p. 149). Man dismembers his own psyche and entombs hedonic instinct in oceanic unconsciousness, where it takes on the lineaments of that underworld, making all things 'feminine' appear ichthyian, saurian, demonic. Woman's entire instinctual field sleeps, her agonic power now impotent, her hedonic power made frightening, even to herself. Maimed beyond recognition, she sees herself as Dahud and all things 'masculine' as lupine, werewolfish.

What Dahud *was*, and how her alchemical marriage to the agon might have mitigated social formations, remains unknown. She is recognised only in the forlorn and unintelligible desire for *something* that erupts when we stumble upon a marker for her grave. She can only be a 'vestigial memory' (p. 379), as Christabel reveals when she asks, 'Who knows what Melusina was in her freedom with no eyes on her?' (p. 404).

Christabel mourns the effect of this split in 'The Fairy Melusina', whom she finds to be *something* 'beautiful and terrible, and tragic . . . inhuman in the last resort' (p. 135), something 'without human soul' (p. 189). Raimondin, depleted by his agonic struggles, is a 'draggled knight', with . . . blood grief and extreme fatigue' (p. 318). Unknowingly having lost his female twin, he stumbles onto the fairy's safe space and 'stare[s] at a mystery' (p. 320). The dessicated knight takes a 'long look which consumed his soul into desire' and asks her for water, for, he says, 'I choke on dust' (p. 322). Even as 'her face forbade' (p. 321), he persists, attains his water of life, whereupon she smiles because '[n]ow he was hers' (p. 323).

She tells the story of man, who, finally compelled by desire to exhume his own unlived life, seeks it not in himself but in the woman. She, intuiting his unempathic wolfishness, responds with the only power he gives her, the only power she knows herself to possess – witchcraft. The tragedy of this kind of relationship is that the wolf and the witch are mutually constellating. One who peeks through keyholes, assaults towers, smashes eggs, batters at doors, will call to being either the witch, the sleeping beauty, or the suicidal Sibyl. Each gender perceives the other as, in Ash's words, 'a mythic beast . . . [a] creature from the caverns of men's minds' (p. 504). Relationship between dismembered selves is generated by these unconscious dynamics, and culture remains mired in magical thinking. At this level, relationship becomes a psychotic power struggle.

Jonathan Lear affirms that self-realisation cannot occur except by one's encountering one's Otherness through relationship, where 'I incorporate . . . other-mindedness as part of myself'.[7] The problem becomes, how can one locate one's Otherness when the human other is disfigured? Byatt's second epigraph has told us that it will take her 'many lies' to tell a 'portly truth'. The many lies are the swirling tales, legends, myths that tell a cultural same-story (rendered through the obsessive image of retracing footsteps), and suggest that the split has become a seemingly unstoppable meltdown, a self-perpetuating story, a 'plot of fate' (p. 456) that puts man and woman in the no-win situation of Merlin and Vivien. They duel with magic, she turns him into a senseless stump, but finds that 'magic served only to enslave *him*, – and then where was she?' (p. 384).

We find Ash out in his early letters to Ellen, where, blinded by his own courtly rhetoric, he is unconscious of the wolf clumsily hidden in his words.

She gives him white roses, and he writes, 'I push my enquiring nose in amongst them – not to hurt . . . [O]ne day I will bury my face in their white warmth' (p. 500); he tells her how he once played with poppies and adds, '[I] would fold back the calyx and the tightly packed silk skirts . . . and the poor flaunting scarlet thing would droop and die' (p. 500). She unconsciously recognises this aggression and implodes in terror, to a life of 'silence' and 'avoidance' (p. 494). Her soul goes to sleep and she 'lay suspended . . . as Snow White lay' (p. 252). Lacking 'force' (p. 248) and disowning passion, she becomes like the frozen white roses on her jet brooch. Her dream of the chess game reveals the state of her psyche: her King is incapacitated and her Queen can move only one square at a time.

Christabel, like her leaden lady in 'The Threshold', wishes 'not to be seen', not to live in a world of 'flesh' or 'action', but to retire to a world of 'soft dust' (p. 172). Self-fearing and self-derogating like Ellen, she names herself 'Arachne' (p. 97). But in her poetry we find markers for a voice of desire that undermines conscious beliefs and fears. Though her women of Is are drowned, they have blood pulsing beneath their transparent skin. Her little tailor does wake the sleeping princess, and her Psyche does pine after her missing Eros. Even as the leaden lady draws her lover into suicidal oblivion, she feels 'from deep within, some glimmer, some promise' (p. 172).

The upstanding Ash is one whose life 'seemed to be all in his mind, who lived a quiet and exemplary married life, whose correspondence . . . was guarded, courteous and not the most lively' (p. 10). But his poetry too is haunted by desire, by a 'ferocious vitality' (p. 10) and by characters who live 'at or over the edge of madness' (p. 9). 'Ragnarok' itself reveals his desperation for passionate new life, for great gulps of 'new air' and 'green . . . living sap' (p. 260).

Long before Ash and Christabel actually meet, they have communicated through the 'nocturnal movement of the illegible'[8] in their poetry. He rushes headlong towards her saying, 'I felt you call me . . . and I had to answer' (p. 210); she is for him 'a messenger from some urgent place in the spirit' (p. 211), the bringer of 'some revelation . . . of some unguessed-at other world' (147). Their mutual seduction blooms textually, on the page, the only safe space in culture where one might explore the hypothetical facts of one's being and bring unlived life to presence. While Ash wants to jump into the 'flame which in every way obeys the laws that pertain to fire' (p. 12), Christabel rightly fears the witch's fate: 'I cannot let you burn me up . . . [T]here will be conflagration' (p. 213). He brings her to a threshold crowded with her twin fears, 'agoraphobia' and 'claustrophobia' (p. 61). Ash insists that avoidance 'goes against nature' (p. 211) and that they should rather regret 'the deed than the hesitation, true life and not mere sickly potentialities' (p. 214). She imagines transgression as an exploding house, while he sees it as a bursting chrysalis that births new winged life. They are on the knife point of a choice, at a defining moment. Roland speaks the truth of this novel when he says, 'We are defined by the lines we choose to cross or to be confined by' (467). At such moments one decides either to submit to the self-despoiling law of the father or obey nature's higher law and begin the perilous task of self-reclamation.

In Yorkshire Ash is as 'violently confused by her real presence' (p. 301) as she is by his. Having learned something from his failure with Ellen, he actively seeks the real Christabel, to find what she 'really was – or in her freedom might have been' (p. 308). But Christabel knows the woman is lost, even to herself, and answers, 'You say "I love you" – but who is she, who is "you"?' (p. 218). She sees him as the thirsty knight whose 'soul is . . . lost' (p. 305). She knows he is, despite his protestations, the philandering husband stalking his female 'Anima' (p. 16), without ethical consideration for those whom his adventure will hurt. Aware only of his noble conscious intentions, he brings his wolf to the relationship and will 'know what may be known *by any means*' (p. 218; my italics).

All is lost when, upon taking possession of Christabel's body, he can find only 'my selkie, my whitelady' (p. 301): 'She was liquid moving through his grasping fingers' (p. 308). Hoping to retrace the footsteps of Ask and Embla, who leave on their shore 'a line of darkening prints . . . first traces in the world . . . of love' (p. 263), they accomplish only a vertiginous parody: 'He watched their footprints . . . hers snaking away and back, meeting his, wandering' (p. 304).

Ruin swiftly follows as their relationship collapses into the Raimondin–Melusina plot. Ash is unwilling to dissolve completely through this encounter and needs to return to a status quo that heaps rewards on the Great Poet. Like Merlin, he is doomed to 'suffer a sort of madness. A possession as by demons' (p. 492), and sees Christabel as the 'ruthless woman' (p. 99), a 'demon . . . tormentor' (p. 496). Christabel loses everything she had, and in an agony of pain becomes an 'old witch' (p. 489), saying at the end of her life, '*I have been Melusina*' (p. 544). Theirs has been a relationship between inhuman beings who failed to humanise themselves, an encounter between the 'dragon' and 'tame villatic fowl' (pp. 545–6). However, unable to give birth to themselves in the world, they give birth to Maia.

The contemporary plot offers the Victorian plot its second chance, and the academy replaces Victorian culture as the power field within which individuals must enact the strivings of desire. Woman's putative new freedom notwithstanding, we find in the academy the same split syzygy that drives history's master plot. At the mention of women's writing, Blackadder sounds a 'snarling note', like 'hounds baying' (p. 36). Fergus Wolff first appears to us with his 'voracious smile' (p. 37), standing in the Egyptian room, a phallus between two towering stone legs. He sees Maud as a dangerous witch who 'thicks men's blood with cold' (p. 39). Beatrice is called a 'puffed white spider' (p. 126), and is exiled to a dark crypt, where she smoulders, seeing 'all male members of her quondam department as persecutors' (p. 131).

Maud's female colleagues have 'hissed' (p. 295) at her hair. Women's writing is kept in dusty boxes on dark shelves; Christabel's home in our world, and Maud's niche in the father's house, is the glass-walled Tennyson Tower, a 'skeletal affair in a glass box' (p. 49). Cropper has access to endless funds when it comes to buying material related to Ash; however, 'there isn't much money in women's studies yet' (p. 471).

Blackadder and Cropper are the new warriors and priests who keep the witch-wolf battle alive, and in addition to keeping the departmental women in line, they exert their power to encoffin the hedonic aspects *of writing itself*: those aspects of text that afflict us with passionate desire, disturb and unhinge us, make us crazy so we can become sane. To subdue the hedonic vector of art is to depotentiate its violently radical questioning. Scholars profess to compile 'Complete Works', yet they cut them 'down to size' (p. 272) by excising desire's irrational subtext, with which critical discourse has not evolved to cope. Because she does not deal in 'proof' and 'truth' (p. 36), Beatrice is 'bricked in' (p. 32) and can only stand guard over the 'flittering and flickering' (p. 240) life in Ellen's work.

Blackadder is a 'stringent scholar' (p. 13) who devours the roots of the tree that feeds his life; his 'footnotes engulfed and swallowed the text' (p. 33). His empire is the Ash Factory, a place of 'insufficient oxygen' (p. 30) that will support neither blood nor flame. With his index cards and bulging files, he is the vulture Ellen feared, a carrion creature devoted to the 'pickings . . . and leavings' (p. 33) of Ash. Byatt constructs him as a ghoul, an undead thing that feeds on corpses.

Cropper is the vampire of the piece, adept at 'acquiring invitations' (p. 105) across thresholds where might hide bits of Ashiana, for which he felt 'real pangs, a kind of famishing' (p. 415). He maintains the traces of Ash's life in glass cells and uses them to feed his holographic self. Ash's watch 'ticked near his heart' (p. 418), like a mechanical heart that serves in the absence of his own.

Byatt is constructing an angry argument: scholars are to art what Raimondin is to Melusina; he feeds on her body without ever knowing her soul. Female persons are now invited to this game, but only if they play within the man's rules. Female/hedonic ways of knowing and being are excluded, and without a scrying eye, art remains a mineral thing, a stone without life, an object under glass.

Maud is a literary soldier, armed with index cards and interested not in Christabel's '*life*', but in 'what went on in her mind' (p. 62). 'Icily regular and splendidly null' (p. 343), she is the Lady of Shalott who lives a vicarious life in her tower, the Rapunzel who fears to let down her hair, the sleeping beauty whose flat is a 'bright, safe box' (p. 151). After having been 'battered' (p. 294) in her tryst with Fergus, she flees that 'empty battlefield' (p. 63) to build her bailey higher. Yet her white flat is splashed with vibrant colour. She has been haunted by the questions in Christabel's poem of the sibyl:

Who are you?
Here on a high shelf . . .
Who were you? (pp. 60, 61)

She devotes her energy to the study of liminal poetry. These psychic expressions and investments mark the warm underground spring that flows beneath her glacial surface.

Roland is a pauper, a lowly drudge in the Ash Factory, not a 'full-blooded department male' (p. 131), but a 'failure' (p. 14) with a paper-thin identity: 'He thought of himself as an application form, for a job, a degree, a life' (p. 14). He lives a colourless life with Val in a crypt, and excites 'no emotion more passionate than approbation' (p. 18). A frozen captive of his education, he ignores Ash's 'vanished body' (p. 24) and works, with Ash's death mask on his desk, on Ash's intellect. It is precisely his marginal status that predicts his heroic potential, because in fairy-tales it is always the spurned son who takes a dangerous journey to overthrow the despotic old king. The bumbling son has no stake in the old order, and he has emotional affinity with the captive maidens he will likely meet.

Like the women we have met, he seems barren of all instinctual energy, yet he feels that something is vaguely 'alive' (p. 14) in the library's books. When he exhumes Ash's letters he feels an 'urgency . . . energy . . . violent movement . . . flickers' (p. 21). Like Frankenstein's monster, he is the corpse jolted to life. Our unlikely hero crosses the line that has defined him, and knowing that the letters are 'his' (p. 55), he steals them; he commits the first insurrection, capitulates to instinct's law and begins the journey that will take him into the wilderness of his own lost life.

The quest brings him to Maud, who receives him in her wary, hawk-like mode, but when she asks him why he stole the letters, he answers, 'Because they were alive' (p. 56). He is an unofficial male without wolf energy, and because he finds life in the letters and not in her, Maud drops her defences and reveals her warm blood: 'She blushed. Red stained the ivory' (p. 57). Confident that he will not vampirise her, she invites him over the threshold into her flat.

There he enters Christabel's world as well, when he reads 'The Glass Coffin', a tale she left for those with ears to hear its secret about how men and women might be released from mutual possession. Because it is an important blueprint, it needs retelling at some length. It begins with a humble, out-of-work tailor with no place in the world order. When his strange host offers him a choice of gifts as recompense for his kindness to the animals, he chooses not worldly wealth, but the glass key. The host says, 'You have chosen not with prudence, but with daring' (p. 67). The tailor must allow himself to be borne on the wind, without struggle or fear, to a wild place where he must descend . . . and descend further' (p. 68). The tunnel into the earth is like a birth canal from which he is born into the encoffined princess' presence.

'[T]he true adventure was the release of the sleeper' (p. 71). But when he awakens her, the Black Artist appears to claim her. The tailor runs him through with a shard of the glass coffin, the princess is reunited with her lost twin brother, and they all live happily ever after.

Like all fairy-tales, this tale describes the psychological transformation of the hero. His ability to awaken the sleeper, who is both woman-as-thou and the 'woman' in himself (his hedonic instinct), will depend upon his taking a fearsome journey into his own depths. If he takes an aleatory flight away from the world held in thrall by the patriarchal Black Artist, he may find the princess; but it is at the moment of her awakening that Christabel revises this old tale. She knows that when the princess wakes, she is, in the absence of her lost twin brother – her 'force', her agonic instinct – a vulnerable target, and that vulnerability conjures the Black Artist. This figure is a psychological possibility that lives inside every little tailor, and it is this impulse towards Black Artistry in himself that he must see, recognise and kill. He must *himself* awaken, become conscious of what monster the force-less woman might invoke in him. He may then live in the world with his princess, but only if he allows her to conjoin with her lost brother. The tailor rediscovers a male identity that is not built upon peeking through the keyhole with a killing gaze, but upon earning the key through humility, compassion, and intense self-examination.

The rest of the contemporary plot is deeply connected to this tale through narrative and semantic links and shows Roland's submission to the vagaries of a quest. The tale appears as a shadow of the winter garden scene, where Maud kneels to seek fish under the ice, but sees her own glassy reflection instead. Roland appears behind her and his face joins hers in this mirror, an image of the syzygy, a possibility as yet quiescent in ice. She feels an unexpected 'electric shock' (p. 157).

In a parallel scene Roland peeks through the keyhole when he hears Maud splashing about. She emerges in a dragon-emblazoned kimono, and he fumblingly grabs her thigh and feels his own 'kick galvanic' (p. 162). At this moment he has the opportunity to fall into possession, to become the violating Raimondin constellated by the vulnerable *melusine*. He sidesteps that trap and goes into the bathroom to imagine Maud's face in the mirror next to his. That night he begins his descent, dreams that he is in a bathroom, mummified in cloth and must release 'something' (p. 165) that is also wrapped in wet cloth and 'wringing its veiled hands as it struggles with its wrappings' (p. 165). The bathroom, he knows, invokes his fear of '*something* coming up out of the lavatory bend and striking at him' (p. 165). The something that both he and his culture have flushed returns, like a woman plucked from the drowned depths of Is.

When they allow the wind to take them to Yorkshire, they abandon scholarship and begin to dissolve. Out of her safe box, Maud wonders, 'Who am I?' and in the jet shop removes her turban:

Roland looked at Maud. The pale, pale hair in fine braids was wound round and round her head . . . She looked . . . naked . . . and then, . . . she turned her supercilious face to him and he saw it changed, simply fragile and even vulnerable. He wanted to loosen the tightness and let the hair go. He felt a kind of sympathetic pain on his own skull-skin . . . Both put their hands to their temple, as though he was her mirror. (p. 282)

The old woman puts the mermaid brooch on the counter 'to illuminate its darkness' (p. 282). The mermaid is a cautionary image, and in a moment of superb clarity, Roland lives the text of his dream. He unwinds his own coiled shroud to feel the pain of the other's coiled shroudedness.

In Yorkshire they see what Ash and Christabel saw, a *trompe l'oeil* of flames amidst falling water, a 'fire [that] / Burnt on the cold stones not to be consumed / And not consuming' (p. 289). This seemingly unattainable ideal of relationship causes them to consider an Ellen-like flight. Roland wants to be 'without desire . . . to have nothing' (p. 290). Yet to be without desire is to be like 'whole flocks of exhausted scholars and theorists' who make of love 'a suspect ideological construct' (p. 290). Compulsive desire works underground, however, to stay them from flight, and they decide to abandon for one day all books, all stories, all worlds, to try to find 'something new' (p. 295).

At the Edenic Boggle Hole Maud serves apples and allows Roland to witness the loosing of all her hair. The dormant hedonic-feminine appears, is the something new, and Roland feels 'as though something has been loosed in himself' (p. 296). He says, as though it were his own hair, 'that feels better'; 'it has a right to breathe' (p. 295).

They are exquisitely careful with each other, determined to stay in this *terra nova* that lies between possession and autism. Maud now turns thief, steals Sabine's journal, and they flee to escape the Keystone-Cop pursuit of the professors, who lust to draw their findings back into the academic machinery. They both feel 'mad' (p. 360), but they are far from mad. Not drowning, they are in a ship's cabin under the sea, metaphorically courting a collapse into Queen Dahud's story. They are feeling the inevitable pain of the Phoenix's fire, the exploding house, the boggled confusion of the winged thing newly burst from its chrysalis. Roland says, 'I've just lost everything I've ever had', and the cerebral Maud is 'talking wildly of madness and bliss' (p. 360).

When they are discovered, they must confront the prodigious task of keeping their dialogue alive in inimical Par-is. They face Maud's question: 'Can we survive our education?' (p. 62). The assembled cast reads the letters from Ash's grave, and the interrelated themes of reclaiming life and reviving reading fuse. When Maud learns that she has the blood of both Ash and Christabel, she moves seismically from thinking 'I read the story' to knowing 'I am the story'. If Byatt figures Cropperistic, Par-is-itic reading as vampirism, she figures right reading as transubstantiation. If Maud and Roland may succeed where Ash and Christabel failed, it is because they have submitted to 'epistemophilia': a quasi-sexual desire to be 'implicate[d] . . . in the thrust of a desire that can never quite speak its name . . . but insists on speaking over and over again its movement toward that name'.[9] What Maud calls her 'narrative greed' (p. 363) is the hunger to have 'a transferential relationship with what [one] may not want to see or hear',[10] and to plunge into the *'mise-en-abime'* that keeps reading 'violently yet steadily alive' (p. 511).

Roland describes his movement from academic reading to embodied reading:

> There are readings . . . that map and dissect . . . that count grey little pronouns . . . Now and then there are readings which make the hairs on the neck, the non-existent pelt, stand on end and tremble, when every word burns and shines hard and clear, and infinite and exact. (pp. 511–12)

Text's Other has found its listener, and we see what radical disruption this Other might produce in Par-is through the convulsions and shock-waves it sends through the academy. The father's sturdy house explodes, and professors erupt into a frenzy of car chases, fisticuffs and grave-robbing.

It seems that the Victorians intentionally bequeathed their story to a time that might be more propitious for its hearing. Ellen 'took care to write down that her box was there' (p. 527), and Blanche, in her suicide note, appeals to another world and time where she might 'be known' (p. 335). Christabel wants her letters to be found by 'the one' who will hear her playful clues, not by a rational being who would ignore toy dolls. Maia worlds their story in her blood. Christabel, incinerated in her own time, hopes that some 'Phoenix' will be born from her 'ashy womb' (p. 546). She gives her daughter the name of the mother of Hermes, the phallic god who represents the potent, creative aspects of agonic energy. In a complex symbolic flourish, Byatt suggests that Maia begets both Maud (who is learning Aphrodite's power) and Roland-as-Hermes, the 'thief, artist, psychopomp' (p. 553), and therefore the possibility of the herm-aphrodite, ancient icon of the syzygy.

The question remains, is our time the right time for the rebirth of the hermaphrodite? Certainly the contemporary plot, with its gargantuan characters, hyperbolic symbolism and audacious coincidences, suggests a movement from heavy Victorian tragedy to comedy, with its promise of marriage at the end. Roland does not become the tormented Ash, but walks the path of the little tailor. Like the tailor, he feeds the animals, the cats whom he had once demonised. No longer a vampire of Ash's poetry, and having slain the Black Artist in himself, he begins to write his own poetry, finding that 'an hour ago there had been no poems, and now they came like rain and were real' (p. 516). Unlike Raimondin, he finds the water of life, the rain, in himself.

In their room at the inn Maud begins to waken and says, 'I feel – ' (p.

549), but she cannot finish her sentence. She goes on, 'When I feel – anything – I go cold all over. I freeze' (p. 549), but Roland insists that she is '*alive*' (p. 550). Their speaking gives way to the final language of bodies: 'all her white coolness . . . grew warm against him, so that there seemed to be no boundaries' (p. 551). Their boundary-less sexual union images the birth of the hermaphrodite in the Hieros Gamos, the *mysterium coniunctionis,* the sacred marriage. In the room is the 'smell of death and destruction and it smelled fresh and lively and hopeful' (p. 551). Perhaps their alchemical marriage gives the lie to Loki's prediction and affirms that from the corpse of the dead plot of fate, Ask and Embla might be reborn.

FOR FURTHER READING

For a list of A. S. Byatt's works, see the British Council website: <http://www.contemporarywriters.com/authors/>.

Chodorow, Nancy, *The Reproduction of Mothering: Psychoanalysis and the Sociology of Gender* (Berkeley: University of California Press, 1978).

Creed, Barbara, *The Monstrous Feminine: Film, Feminism, Psychoanalysis* (London: Routledge, 1993).

Dinnerstein, Dorothy, *The Mermaid and the Minotaur: Sexual Arrangements and Human Malaise* (New York: HarperColophon Books, 1977).

Hays-Gilpin, Kelley and David S. Whitley, *Reader in Gender Archaeology* (London: Routledge, 1998).

Marlan, Stanton, ed., *Fire in the Stone: the Alchemy of Desire* (Wilmette: Chiron Publications, 1997).

Young-Eisendrath, Polly, *Gender and Desire: Uncursing Pandora* (College Station, Texas: A&M University Press, 1997).

NOTES

1 Jane Flax, *Thinking Fragments: Psychoanalysis, Feminism, and Postmodernism in the Contemporary West* (Berkeley: University of California Press, 1990), p. 21.

2 A. S. Byatt, *Possession* (New York: Vintage Books, 1990). All quotations are from this edition; page numbers are given in the text.

3 Nathan Schwartz-Salant, 'Anima and Animus in Jung's Alchemical Mirror', in *Gender and Soul in Psychotherapy*, ed. Nathan Schwartz-Slant and Murray Stein (Wilmette: Chiron, 1992), p. 6.

4 James Hillman, *Anima* (Dallas: Spring Publications, 1992), p. 177.

5 James Hillman, *Healing Fiction* (Barrytown: Station Hill Press, 1983), p. 103.

6 Anthony Stevens and John Price, *Evolutionary Psychiatry* (London: Routledge, 1996), pp. 47–50.

7 Jonathan Lear, *Love and its Place in Nature: a Philosophical Interpretation of Freudian Psychoanalysis* (New York: Farrar, Straus and Giroux, 1990), p. 194.

8 Philippe Sollers, *Writing and the Experience of Limits* (New York: Columbia University Press, 1983), p. 197.

9 Peter Brooks, *Reading for the Plot: Design and Intention in Narrative* (New York: Knopf, 1984), p. 61.

10 Ibid., p. 261.

16

Jeanette Winterson and the Lesbian Postmodern: Story-telling, Performativity and the Gay Aesthetic

Paulina Palmer

To Cambridge Lesbian Line

INTRODUCTION: LESBIAN/ POSTMODERN PERSPECTIVES

In exploring the lesbian postmodern as exemplified in the fiction of Jeanette Winterson, I shall centre my discussion on *The Passion* (1987) and *The Power Book* (2001). My decision to focus on these two texts reflects the fact that, since they were written at different stages of Winterson's career, they give an insight into the development of her intellectual interests and her viewpoint on postmodernism. They also illustrate the different approaches she adopts toward time. Whereas *The Passion* is a work of historiographic metafiction located in the period of the Napoleonic Wars, *The Power Book*, though set in the present, is futuristic in emphasis in that it treats a relationship between two women that takes place in virtual reality.

The interrelation between the lesbian and the postmodern that characterises the two novels, though taking a highly individualistic form, is far from merely personal and idiosyncratic. It reflects the wider cultural and ideological connections existing between the two perspectives. A significant point of connection between the lesbian and the postmodern is that both are characterised by the concept of 'excess'. While lesbian desire and the figure of the lesbian herself, as Bonnie Zimmerman argues,[1] are excessive to a phallocentric economy that has traditionally relegated woman to the positions of object of exchange and specular mirror of man, postmodern fiction is typified by an excess of narrative. Postmodern texts tend not only to inscribe a proliferation and interplay of 'small' minority storylines, but also, influenced by psychoanalysis, frequently depict other concepts such as memory and identity in terms of narrative.[2] Excess is also reflected in such fiction in its 'inability to stay within historical and aesthetic boundaries'.[3] This is exemplified both by the juxtaposing of different historical eras within a single novel and by the recasting and interweaving of different generic forms.

Other connections also exist between postmodern and lesbian perspectives. Just as the postmodern, according to Jean-François Lyotard, rejects a single totalising vision and the idea of a centre,[4] so lesbian and queer politics rejects a norm of sexual behaviour by foregrounding the different sexualities and ways of life available to the individual. And whereas the postmodern aims to deconstruct the master narratives that dominate Western culture, lesbian theoretical and representational practices seek to interrogate and denaturalise ideological and cultural concepts and institutions such as gender and sexuality that have been regarded as unchanging and, as a result, remained unquestioned. As Judith Roof, summing up the affinity between the two, observes, both aim to 'challenge centred logic and identity, the lesbian confronting heterosexuality and gender, the postmodern questioning subjectivity, knowledge and truth' (p. 49). In many cases, in fact, lesbian theory and fiction, rather than merely reflecting the influence of postmodern theoretical and representational trends, have been in the vanguard and contributed to their formation. The work of Eve Sedgwick, Judith Butler and, in the field of fiction, Winterson herself, represent key examples.

However, the connections between the lesbian and the postmodern, summarised above, are complicated and to a degree undermined by certain tensions and differences. These centre on the concepts of 'politics' and 'agency'. Whereas the postmodern, according to Linda Hutcheon, is 'politically ambivalent, doubly encoded as both complicity and critique',[5] the lesbian, like the feminist, is committed to a political agenda. It aims to combat homophobia and achieve social and political change by challenging the oppressive role of 'threatening spectre'[6] which, despite the work of lesbian and gay campaigning organisations, many sections of society still assign to lesbians and gay men. Butler recommends that we challenge these attitudes by the 'reworking of abjection into political agency' with the aim of 'resignifying the abjection of homosexuality into defiance and legitimacy'(p. 21). As is indicated by Butler's emphasis on 'political agency', another point of difference between the postmodern and the lesbian is that, whereas the former tends to foreground the fluid nature of subjectivity, the latter, while accepting the formation of the subject through history and culture and the existence of her/his multiple identities and desires, affirms the importance of personal agency and decision-making both on an individual plane and in terms of the les-bi-gay-trans community.

Butler's theory of the performative nature of gender furnishes a strategy to challenge the typecasting of lesbians and gay men as abject. Instead of regarding gender as natural, she defines it as 'the repeated stylisation of the body, a set of repeated acts within a highly rigid regulatory frame that congeal over time to produce the appearance of substance, of a natural sort of being'. If gender, as Butler argues, is performative, then it is by no means fixed. Its conventions may be appropriated and re-enacted in a manner subverting heterosexual dominance. Different forms of lesbian cross dressing and male gay drag can, in fact, challenge and subvert heterosexual norms by demonstrating their instability. Even though, as Butler herself admits, it is difficult to ascertain which of these forms are transgressive in effect and which serve merely as heterosexual entertainment, the potential for subversion nonetheless exists.[8]

Winterson's *The Passion* and *The Power Book,* the two novels I have selected for analysis, as well as being of interest in their own right, furnish excellent material to explore the interaction and tensions between the lesbian and the postmodern. Though differing in period and focus, they none the less display common features. Both, for example, recast a romance narrative. Commenting on the provisionality of this kind of fiction, Diane Elam observes, 'Exactly what the genre of romance is remains an uncertainty: each text must in some way redefine what it means by "romance", must in the process of this redefinition create a meaning for the genre of romance to which it addresses itself' (p. 7). Winterson's two novels certainly achieve this. Challenging the heterosoexist associations that the term 'romance' evokes, they utilise perceptions and strategies associated with the postmodern to redefine and transform the genre from a lesbian viewpoint. These include, an emphasis on storytelling and intertextual references, the recasting of the love stories of the past in the light of present day lesbian concerns, and the introduction of episodes of fantasy and magic realism to create a gay aesthetic of role-play and artifice. In addition, while referring to the subject's multiple identities and desires and the performative dimension of gender, Winterson utilises these postmodern concepts with the sexual-political aim of exploring love between women. She also interweaves a postmodern focus on woman as subject to desire and the forces of history and culture, with a lesbian/feminist emphasis on female agency and self-assertion.

THE PASSION AND THE GAY AESTHETIC

Like many postmodern novels, *The Passion* is strongly preoccupied with the rhetoric of story-telling, its pleasures and contradictions. The novel teems with numerous interrelating narratives. In typical postmodern fashion, the public metanarrative of the Napoleonic Wars narrated by the French peasant Henri, which in the opening pages Winterson teasingly leads the reader to believe will assume centre-stage, becomes increasingly marginalised, serving chiefly as a frame for the characters' accounts of the different passions (love, religion, hero-worship) that motivate them, and the acts of folly and rashness they prompt them to commit. A story which plays a key role in the novel, the one on which I intend to concentrate, is that of Villanelle, the Venetian girl with whom Henri falls in love. This, instead of being a linear narrative, the episodes of which are recounted consecutively, is interrupted by the stories recounted by other characters. Its content is further complicated and, on occasion, put in question by the fact that, instead of being related entirely by Villanelle, it is told in part by Henri.

Villanelle features in the novel as the signifier of lesbian desire, and, in keeping with this, her story centres on the brief but passionate love affair in which she engages with the mysterious woman she terms 'the Queen of Spades',[9] whom she encounters while working at the Casino in Venice. Villanelle's recognition of the transgressive nature of lesbian love in the hetero-patriarchal context of eighteenth-century Europe is signalled by her comment to Henri, 'It was a woman I loved and you will admit that is not the usual thing' (p. 94). The fact that the Queen of Spades is married increases the illicit nature of the two women's relationship, causing it to take place under conditions of secrecy, masquerade and lack of social recognition – all the features, in fact, which today we encompass in the term 'the closet'. The centrality that the concept of the closet assumes in Villanelle's narrative is advertised, as we shall see, by Winterson herself in the punning reference she makes to the term in the later stages of Villanelle's story. Linda Hutcheon argues that the reconstruction of material from the past in the light of present-day issues typifies the genre of historiographic metafiction.[10] Adopting this device, Winterson treats a topic which, as illustrated by the number of women identifying as lesbian or bisexual who still feel socially compelled to pass as heterosexual, is of key interest to the lesbian/queer community today. Postmodern strategies of metaphor, magic realism and inter-textuality are the tools she utilises to achieve this.

Two different approaches to the closet are discernible in lesbian/gay culture and politics. The one, associated with the Gay Liberation and Lesbian Feminist movements of the 1970s and 1980s, concentrates on exposing its oppressive effects and foregrounding the psychological damage which the social and ideological pressures to conceal their sexual orientation inflict on lesbians and gay men. The other reflects poststructuralist perspectives and develops the aesthetic of artifice, style and wit associated with the writing of Marcel Proust and Oscar Wilde. Though acknowledging the closet's oppressive effects, this second approach seeks to investigate the richly inventive language of counter-codes, masquerade and parody which lesbians and gay men have traditionally used to perform the complex feat of concealing their sexual orientation from heterosexual society while disclosing it to their homosexual peers. As Lisabeth During and Terri Fealy, contributing to the latter approach, comment, 'Mimicry, innuendo and inversion, originally strategies of self-protection, have become part of the production of gayness, a distinctive aesthetic'.[11] Sue Ellen Case, investigating the aesthetic the closet has produced, remarks on the way in which 'The survival tactic of hiding and lying [has] produced a camp discourse . . . in which gender referents are suppressed, or slip into one another, fictional lovers are constructed [and] metaphors substitute for literal descriptions'.[12] She argues that this strategy of indirection 'works to defeat the reign of realism' and alerts attention to the aesthetic of 'artifice, wit, irony, and the distancing of straight reality and its conventions'[13] that it promotes. The idea of a gay aesthetic, itself a postmodern concept, furnishes an appropriate context for discussing Winterson's narrative of Villanelle and her love-affair with the Queen of Spades, illuminating its focus on performativity, metaphor and wit. In recounting it, Winterson introduces instances of masquerade and, as suits the topic of her heroine's closeted relationship and the acts of role-play and subterfuge it involves, moves, in the course of the text, from a naturalistic plane to a fantasy realm of magic realism and parodic intertexts.

Two motifs with fantasy connotations play a prominent part in Villanelle's story: her webbed feet, interpreted by critics as a signifier of her sexual difference, and her heart which, as a result of the intensity of her infatuation, she loses to the Queen of Spades. Both carry intertextual resonance, representing a lesbian recasting of motifs traditionally utilised in a heterosexual context in literature and art.

Villanelle's webbed feet, to which the reader is introduced at the start of her narrative, position her as sexually transgressive, since they carry demonic, perverse connotations. Marina Warner illustrates how the devil and his minions are sometimes depicted in medieval art with webbed feet and, commenting on representations of witches and succubi, describes webbed feet as 'a recurrent sign of contrariness, and, in women of deviancy'.[14] The grotesque appearance of Villanelle's feet and the deviancy they signify understandably result in her seeking to conceal them.

As well as carrying connotations of deviancy, Villanelle is also associated with performativity and masquerade. This is illustrated both by the male drag that she wears while working at the Casino and by the admiration she expresses for the acts of daring, sexual as well as gymnastic, performed by the acrobats during Carnival. She describes how: 'Now and again, one will dangle by the knees and snatch a kiss from whoever is standing below. I like such kisses. They fill the mouth and leave the body free. To kiss well one must kiss solely. No groping hands or stammering hearts. The lips and the lips alone are the pleasure' (p. 59). This description of the acrobats' movements and the kisses they steal anticipates, and acts as a metaphor for, Villanelle's love affair with the Queen of Spades which resembles them in being precarious, illicit and sexually exciting. Villanelle's account of the stylised positions that she and her lover adopt and their exclusive focus on mouth recalls the acrobats' positions:

> She [the Queen of Spades] lay on the rug and I lay at right angles to her so that only our lips might meet. Kissing in this way is the strangest of distractions. The greedy body that clamours for satisfaction is forced to content itself with a single sensation and, just as the blind hear more acutely and the deaf can feel the grass grow, so the mouth becomes the focus of love and all things pass through it and are re-defined. It is a sweet and precise torture. (p. 67)

This passage, in describing the artificial positions that Villanelle feels forced to adopt to conceal her gender and sexual orientation, can be read as wittily parodying the strategies of subterfuge and masquerade that, throughout the ages, lesbians and gay men have adopted to conceal their sexual identities, while none the less forming relationships and achieving sexual pleasure. Referring to the aesthetic of masquerade and artifice which the role-play and subterfuge associated with the closet have produced, Danae Clark comments, 'Lesbians are accustomed to playing out multiple styles and sexual roles as a tactic of survival and have thus learned the artifice of invention in defeating heterosexual codes of naturalism' (p. 194).

Winterson continues Villanelle's narrative of the closet, developing the themes of secrecy and deceit it involves, in the little episode of magic realism she introduces subsequently, focusing on Villanelle's loss of her heart to the Queen of Spades. This again foregrounds a gay aesthetic of fantasy, metaphor and wit. The literal manner in which Villanelle treats the conceit of the lost heart and her insistence that her own heart is no longer in her possession astonishes Henri. It prompts him to question her sanity. 'Was she mad?' he wonders. 'We had been talking figuratively. Her heart was in her body like mine' (p. 115). Only when she invites him to ascertain for himself the absence of a heart, does he credit her words: 'I put my ear to her body and crouched quite still in the bottom of the boat and a passing gondolier gave us a knowing smile. I could hear nothing' (p. 116).

Winterson's introduction of the conceit of the lover's loss of his heart, while recalling the lyrics of John Donne and Sir Philip Sidney, radically recasts it, employing it to demonstrate both the intensity of lesbian love and the closeted existence to which hetero-patriarchal society conventionally relegates it. Refusing to remain the passive victim of love and asserting a degree of agency, Villanelle, as is typical of Winterson's dynamic heroine, assumes the initiative and persuades the astonished Henri to retrieve her heart from the Queen of Spades' thrall. Determined to prove his devotion, he surreptitiously enters the latter's house at night and, alerted by the tell-tale beating of the heart, discovers it, just as Villanelle said he would. It lies concealed in a jar in a location which Winterson, punning on the secretive nature of the two women's love affair while also signalling to the reader the word's modern meaning, wittily describes as 'a vast walk-in closet' (p. 120). Henri takes the jar and, leaving the house unobserved, gives it to Villanelle. She uncorks it and pops 'this valuable, fabulous thing' (p. 120) back in her breast, apparently none the worse. The action signifies her regaining of control of her life, appropriately concluding on a note of postmodern fantasy this particular episode in her romance narrative.

VIRTUAL ROMANCE IN *THE POWER BOOK*

Like *The Passion*, *The Power Book* foregrounds the art of story-telling, its pleasures and contradictions. Winterson's decision to centre the latter novel on an encounter between two women on the internet enables her, in fact, to develop the postmodern focus on narrativity by giving it a new and fashionable slant, increasing the emphasis on story-telling, and accentuating the ambiguity of the division between fact and fiction, life and art. The concept of a gay aesthetic, associated with the prioritising of fantasy, magic realism and wit and representing character in terms of masquerade, is also developed.

The premise of *The Power Book* is relatively simple, belying both the novel's narrative intricacy and its complex treatment of subjectivity. Sitting at her screen one night, Ali – or rather the woman who uses the name as an alias, for in this world of virtual reality it is difficult, if not impossible, to distinguish identity from masquerade – receives an email reading, '*Freedom, just for one night*'.[15] It comes from an unknown correspondent who signs herself 'Tulip'. Interpreting the words as signifying 'Just for one night the freedom to be somebody else' (p. 4), Ali, a writer by profession and, as is indicated by her reference to *The Passion*, a stand-in in certain respects for Winterson herself, accepts the challenge of inventing a set of narratives depicting Tulip and herself meeting in exotic locations, their identities transformed. Comparing herself to the owner of a shop selling theatrical costumes where 'people arrive as themselves and leave as someone else' (p. 3), she triumphantly announces, 'I can change the story. I am the story' (p. 5).

The representation of subjectivity as constructed through narrative, which Ali's words imply, is developed in the stories she narrates. The first, a tale in the style of *The Book of The Thousand and One Nights*, develops the motif of lesbian role-play introduced in *The Passion* in Villanelle's adoption of masculine attire. The tale opens on a fantastic note, with Ali portraying herself as a Turkish girl who masquerades as a boy substituting tulip bulbs for balls and a tulip stem for a penis, and concludes with her making love with Tulip herself, who appears in the guise of a beautiful princess. Like Villanelle, whose experience of wearing drag leads her to question, 'What was myself? Was this breeches and boots self any less real than my garters?' (p. 66), Ali's performance of masculinity problematises the existence of an authentic, original gender. It exemplifies Butler's postmodern dictum that '*in imitating gender, drag implicitly reveals the imitative structure of gender itself – as well as its contingency*'.[16] However, in contrast to Villanelle who, as we have seen, in her initial sexual encounter with the Queen of Spades feels compelled to disguise her lack of male sex organs by limiting her lovemaking to kissing, Ali, as a result of Winterson's movement into the realm of magic realism, is able to enjoy full sexual congress. As she comments in amazement:

> Then a strange thing began to happen. As the Princess kneeled and petted my tulip, my own sensations grew exquisite, but as yet no stronger than my astonishment, as I felt my disguise come to life. The tulip began to stand. I looked down. There it was, making a bridge from my body to hers. . . . Very

gently the Princess lowered herself across my knees and I felt the firm red head
and pale shaft of the plant itself in her body. A delicate green – tinted sap drib-
bled down her brown thighs. All afternoon I fucked her. (p. 22)

The gay aesthetic has been described as comprising the 'masquerade of men
and women who self-consciously act; who flaunt incongruous allusions, par-
odies, transvestite travesties . . . who continue to proliferate a protean, and
never normative, range of fantasies in social dramas of their own choosing'.[17] Winterson's playful recasting, in the passage from the novel cited
above, of the early modern concept of 'a vegetable love' (a love characterised only by growth) introduced by Andrew Marvell in his famous seduction
lyric 'To his Coy Mistress', vividly fulfils these criteria. Ironically, however,
Tulip is by no means amused by Ali's description of her being penetrated by
a tumescent tulip stem. Objecting to being transformed into 'a flower-
fucking princess', she playfully protests by email, 'That was a terrible thing
to do to a flower!' (p. 25).

Winterson's representation of Ali and Tulip engaging in a love affair on
the web gives her the opportunity to explore the postmodern concept of the
feminine masquerade. She prompts us to perceive that the difficulty of dis-
tinguishing between the persona that the female subject adopts on the web
and her real-life identity is not unique to the world of virtual reality, but
reflects woman's everyday situation. Joan Riviere, answering the question,
'Where [do] I draw the line between genuine womanliness and the "masquerade"?' concludes that no such line exists since 'they are the same thing'.[18]
The postmodern refusal to postulate an authentic femininity that exists prior
to the masquerade, posited by Riviere and discussed by Stephen Heath and
Judith Butler, is, in fact, a key premise of Winterson's novel.[19]

Ali's tour-de-force of story-telling, as well as enabling her to display her
narrative skills, also signifies an act of courtship and seduction. Sexually
infatuated with Tulip and, like her predecessor Villanelle, risking her heart
in the game of chance that love represents, she utilises the stories she tells
and the flirtatious exchanges, punctuating them as a strategy to develop
the burgeoning relationship. Like that archetypal female story-teller
Sheherazade who succeeds in eternally postponing the date of her execution
and, to cite Adriana Cavarero, 'keeping death outside the circle of life'[20] by
delighting the Sultan Shahriyar with her narrative expertise, Ali, by means
of her imaginative fecundity and rhetorical skill, manages to keep the attraction between Tulip and herself alive, thus postponing the death of love.

The Power Book, like Winterson's other novels and postmodern fiction
in general, brings together conventions from different genres, including
quest narrative (reflected in the erotic games of pursuit which Ali and Tulip
play on the web and the recurring metaphor of buried treasure), travelogue
(illustrated by the exotic locations of Paris and Capri depicted in images
resembling 'a grainy movie' [p. 47], which Ali selects for their virtual reality

assignations), and fantasy (exemplified by her recasting of myth and legend). However, the genre which the novel prioritises is the romance and, as in *The Passion*, Winterson utilises the postmodern strategy of intertextuality to construct a lesbian version of the form. In the persona of Ali, she also discusses the meaning of the term 'romance' and investigates its ambiguities. In contrast to Tulip, who is portrayed as a sophisticated rich girl with her heart set on real-life amours, the writer Ali associates the term with romantic literature. This is illustrated by her flippant suggestion that, if it is romance that Tulip is looking for, she should download *Romeo and Juliet*!

In addition to commenting on the form of the romance and illustrating its development from medieval tales of chivalry to present-day love stories, Ali examines the contradictions between life and art that the term embodies by juxtaposing episodes describing her involvement with Tulip with tales from romantic myth and legend portraying 'great and ruinous lovers' (p. 77). She also contrasts the imperfections of real-life relationships with the idealised image of love that romantic fiction creates. Aware that Tulip is married and is reluctant to leave her husband, she laments, 'The trouble is that in imagination anything can be perfect. Downloaded into real life, it was messy. She was messy. I was messy. I blamed myself. I had wanted to be caught' (p. 46). She painfully acknowledges the fact that, due to 'the immensity' of love and the disruptive power it wields, the emotional tumult to which it gives rise 'is not clean, it's not containable' (p. 51).

However, the contrast between real-life romance and its literary counterpart, which, as her relationship with Tulip becomes emotionally fraught, increasingly preoccupies Ali, is problematised by the fact that the affair between the two women, though appearing to belong to the category of 'real life', exists, in actual fact, chiefly on a fantasy plane. The majority of the encounters between them take place in virtual reality and, although certain episodes appear to imply that they do, in fact, eventually meet in person and make love in the flesh (in 'meatspace' [p. 174], as Ali irreverently puts it), it is difficult to determine at which point, if any, the shift from virtual to actual reality occurs. This ambiguity, though disappointing the reader who is hoping for a focus on tangible bodies and a conventional narrative development from fantasy to real-life, suits, of course, the concept of a gay aesthetic which, endorsing postmodern perspectives, prioritises masquerade, façade and surface over authentic identity, body and depth.

Another striking ambiguity that informs the novel hinges on the interplay between subjectivity and agency. To what degree is Ali, like Villanelle, the subject of desire and to what degree is she, in manipulating the rhetoric of story-telling as a strategy of seduction, the active agent? When she at last succeeds in forming a relationship with Tulip, the issue of agency continues to worry her since she recognises that, paradoxically, 'The only power I have is the negative power of withdrawal' (p. 187). Even her narrative skills furnish no proof that she is in control since, as she uneasily recognises, she 'is not telling stories . . . the stories are telling her' (p. 215). A similar contradiction informs, of course, Winterson's own efforts as a writer to challenge convention by constructing a lesbian romance. As her retelling of *Paolo and Francesca* and *Lancelot and Guinevere* illustrate, the stories of lesbian love she creates come out of, and are inevitably influenced and tainted by, the heterosexist ideology of the classic romances of the past, even though, at the same time, they actively recast and transform them.

As indicated above, in both *The Passion* and *The Power Book* Winterson utilises perceptions and strategies associated with postmodernism, such as an emphasis on performativity, story-telling and intertextuality and the recasting of conventional motifs, to construct two imaginative lesbian love-stories that transform and subvert the heterosexist connotations of the romance genre. Whereas in the former she explores the gay aesthetic related to the closet, in the latter she situates the relationship between her two female lovers in virtual reality, a move which enables her to develop her investigation into the performative aspects of gender and subjectivity. And by reworking motifs appropriated not only from other writers' texts but also from her own earlier novel *The Passion*, she develops the device of intertextuality, giving it a playfully self-reflexive slant. By interrelating lesbian and postmodern perspectives, she thus creates an innovative and, in terms of sexual politics, intellectually challenging form of fiction.

FOR FURTHER READING

For a hard copy list of Jeanette Winterson's work up to 2001, see *Contemporary Novelists*, ed. David Madden et al., 7th edn (New York: St James Press, 2001). For a more up-to-date list on the internet, see the British Council website: <http://www.contemporarywriters.com/authors/>.

Farwell, Marilyn R., *Heterosexual Plots and Lesbian Narratives* (New York: New York University Press, 1996).
Doan, Laura, ed., *The Lesbian Postmodern* (New York: Columbia University Press, 1994).
Munt, Sally, ed., *New Lesbian Criticism: Literary and Cultural Reading* (Hemel Hempstead: Harvester Wheatsheaf, 1992).
Palmer, Paulina, *Lesbian Gothic: Transgressive Fictions* (London: Cassell-Continuum, 1999).

NOTES

1 Bonnie Zimmerman, 'Lesbians Like This and That', in *New Lesbian Criticism: Literary and Cultural Readings*, ed. Sally Munt (Hemel Hempstead: Harvester Wheatsheaf, 1992), pp. 1–15, p. 4.

2 Mark Currie, *Postmodern Narrative Theory* (London: Macmillan, 1998), pp. 1–5.

3 Diane Elam, *Romancing the Postmodern* (London: Routledge, 1992), p. 12.

4 See Judith Roof's discussion in 'Lesbians and Lyotard: Legitimation and the Politics of the Name', in *The Lesbian Postmodern*, ed. Laura Doan (New York: Columbia University Press, 1994), pp. 47–66.

5 Linda Hutcheon, *The Politics of Postmodernism* (London: Routledge, 1989), p. 168.

6 Judith Butler, *Bodies that Matter: On the Discursive Limits of 'Sex'* (London: Routledge, 1993), p. 3.

7 Judith Butler, *Gender Trouble: Feminism and the Subversion of Identity* (New York: Routledge, 1990), p. 33.

8 See my essay, 'Gender as Performance in the fiction of Angela Carter and Margaret Atwood', in *The Infernal Desires of Angela Carter: Fiction, Femininity, Feminism*, ed. Joseph Bristow and Trev Lynn Broughton (New York: Longman, 1997), pp. 24–42, pp. 26–7.

9 Jeanette Winterson, *The Passion* (Harmondsworth: Penguin, 1988), p. 94. All quotations are from this edition.

10 Linda Hutcheon, *A Poetics of Postmodernism: History, Theory, Fiction* (London: Routledge, 1988), p. 137.

11 Lisabeth During and Terri Fealy, 'Philosophy', in *Lesbian and Gay Studies: a Critical Introduction*, ed. Andy Medhurst and Sally Munt (London: Cassell, 1997), pp. 113–32, p. 127.

12 Sue Ellen Case, 'Toward a Butch-Femme Aesthetic', cited by Danae Clark in 'Commodity Lesbianism', in *The Lesbian and Gay Studies Reader*, ed. Henry Abelove, Michele Aina Barale and David M. Halperin (London: Routledge, 1993), pp. 186–201, p. 194.

13 Sue Ellen Case, 'Toward a Butch-Femme Aesthetic', in *The Lesbian and Gay Studies Reader*, pp. 294–306, p. 298.

14 Marina Warner, *From the Beast to the Blonde: on Fairy Tales and their Tellers* (London: Chatto and Windus, 1994), p. 121.

15 Jeanette Winterson, *The Power Book* (London: Vintage, 2001), p. 3. All quotations are from this edition.

16 Butler, *Gender Trouble*, p. 37.

17 Harold Beaver, 'Homosexual Signs', *Critical Inquiry*, 8, 1 (1981), 99–119, 106.

18 Joan Riviere, 'Womanliness as a Masquerade', in *Formations of Fantasy*, ed. Victor Burgin, James Donald and Cora Kaplan (London: Methuen, 1986), pp. 35–44, p. 38.

19 See Stephen Heath, 'Joan Riviere and the Masquerade', in *Formations of Fantasy*, pp. 45–61; and Butler, *Gender Trouble*, pp. 50–7.

20 Adriana Cavarero, *Relating Narratives: Storytelling and Selfhood*, trans. Paul A. Kottman (London: Routledge, 2000), p. 123.

PART IV

Postmodernism and other -isms

17

(Re)Constituted Pasts: Postmodern Historicism in the Novels of Graham Swift and Julian Barnes

Daniel Bedggood

To articulate the past historically does not mean to recognise it 'the way it really was' (Ranke). It means to seize hold of a memory as it flashes up at a moment of danger.

Walter Benjamin[1]

British novelists Graham Swift and Julian Barnes share a fascination with troubled histories. At one point in Swift's novel *Waterland*, a character asserts that 'the only important thing about history . . . is that it's got to the point where it's probably about to end'.[2] Although within the book this particular character's fear of nuclear annihilation is not realised, the concern displayed towards history at this moment of postmodernity may be considered emblematic of a more widespread anxiety with history as a subject within literary representations in the late twentieth century. In the conditions of today's world, the place of history and its role in searching for meaning and facts seems uncertain to many. Compounding this, among those theorists who perceive an approaching 'end of history', opinions are even split as to whether this would be a negative thing: at least one theorist, Francis Fukuyama, doubts history's relevance in the face of the 'triumph' of capitalism, (prematurely) welcoming an 'end of history' as a sign of class victory.[3]

Despite the confidence of some of these critics, though, 'history' is hard to target, let alone dispatch. It seems that uncertainty about the significance of *some* forms of history has not led to a complete 'end of history'; in particular, the direction in anxiety about the representation of historical subjects within fictional narratives seems misrepresented by some critics. Instead of 'dying', history's significance has changed, and, if historical representation in literature is anything to go by, proliferated into 'histories'. The compounding of postmodern historiographic theory with postmodern literary techniques gives rise, in authors such as Swift and Barnes, to greater focus on the contingency of historical records and interpretation of events; to emphasis on the constructedness of history as a discourse or text; to an opening-up of history to include multiple perspectives on events; to an acknowledgement of different sorts of 'records' as having historical relevance; and to the awareness that looking back at the past is never the disinterested, objective activity it can be portrayed as.

Swift's and Barnes' writings reveal the constant remaking of the past to fit into concerns of the present as problematic. It is clear that Swift and Barnes have been particularly attentive to concerns with postmodern discourse, and that they have reformulated and extended the parameters of that which constitutes 'history' in their novels. Swift's career as a lecturer and researcher of literature and Barnes' own academic focus on French writing and culture place them inside the contemporary debates about literary and historical theory that are bound to influence their own writing. Characteristically postmodern, their texts represent not only the influence of literary theory on historical representation but also of historical theory on literature.[4]

A literature influenced by postmodern poetics engages with history by making the writerly or constructed qualities of history more obvious: in this practice, questions of ideological construction or perspective become apparent. As Keith Jenkins suggests, some of our previous assumptions about history, and the forms it has been expressed as, are no longer so readily acceptable.[5] Robert Young theorises that, as a trait within recent historiography, 'postmodernism can best be defined as European culture's awareness that it is no longer the unquestioned and dominant centre of the world'.[6] As a reflection of this, a postmodern historiography would represent the discourse of history as 'opened up': that is, no longer singular or subservient to a particular cultural perspective. The cause of this distrust of the relatively stable previous view is what Fredric Jameson defines as postmodernity: a condition brought about by the 'radical break' in cultural forms and systems in the 1950s and 1960s, with the wane of political, social and philosophical models of modernity.[7] Jameson suggests that the old certainties, aims and ideals of modernity are now insecure and debatable, and this is expressed in postmodern cultural forms as diverse as architecture, film, advertising and literature.

Jean-François Lyotard further articulates this view, expressing his distrust of 'metanarrative' or 'grand narratives'. Lyotard feels that traditional sciences and academic disciplines are often 'legitimated' through their recourse to such irrational metanarrative traits as 'the dialectics of Spirit, the hermeneutics of meaning, the emancipation of the rational or working subject, or the creation of wealth'; his response to these traits, then, is to 'define *postmodern* as incredulity towards metanarrative'.[8] Modernity's conception of history prescribes the significance of events into an understandable order (for example, within an overarching modern concept like 'progress', the causal logic of events is presented as given). In contrast, instead of this metanarrative prescriptiveness, postmodern narrative is more disjunctive, inhabited by the stories of those excluded by previous historical accounts told and a more 'heteroglossic' awareness of the way that history can be found in a wider range of 'types' of sources (after Bakhtin's 'heteroglossia': the 'polyphony of social and discursive forces' that constitute a text's production and which are necessary to recognise in the text's reading).[9] Such an awareness acknowledges the contingency of historical 'fact' and 'meaning'.

The 'metafictional' qualities of historiography, the self-awareness and acknowledgement of its writing, re-emphasising its constructedness, are further instrumental in blurring the distinctions between the disciplines of literature and history.[10] Linda Hutcheon formulates this movement towards recognition of 'history' as just one of the modes of discourse available:

> What the postmodern writing of both history and literature has taught us is that both history and fiction are discourses, that both constitute systems of signification by which we make sense of the past ('exertions of the shaping, ordering imagination'). In other words, the meaning and shape are not *in the events,* but *in the systems* which make those past 'events' into present historical 'facts'.[11]

'History' is, then, just another genre of discourse or narrative which imposes order on events through writing, and its peculiar claim to produce 'facts' that illuminate the past is questionable. References to history in literature, or to historiography 'proper', are equally unable to claim a privileged association with the reality of events: the very reporting and ordering of events reconstitutes them, with the act of writing or representation replacing the event as the subject of history. Literature and history are parallel forms of writing, and their differences are matters of style rather than content. Postmodern literature plays with a wide range of documents and literary styles, treating the wealth of different stories and ways of telling them as an important consolation to the loss of the illusion of historical certitude. As artists aware of these conditions and able to acutely comment upon them, Swift's and Barnes' postmodernist concerns shape both the subjects they write about and also their writing itself, leading to an opening up for historical examination of concerns like feats of memory, family stories, oral traditions, simulacra and mythologising.

Up to this time, Swift has produced seven novels alongside collections of shorter fiction. Throughout his *oeuvre,* there is a continuity of treatment concerning historical material, a treatment that often appears to resort to a critical reassessment of history, or *histories,* more properly, in reaction to crises of the present. Swift's view is not *reactionary,* in the sense of being politically nostalgic or elegiac in tone, mourning the loss of an epoch that made more sense than the current one, nor does he conceive of a unifying model of 'history' clearly formulated to reflect the present. Instead, he is engaged in an eclectic style of 'detective work' that establishes many different orders of historical referentiality, often in discursive modes not found in more conventional historical representation. In particular, Swift delves into demotic, 'personal', narrative modes and material that are then placed against the other historical subjects and features of his writing in a revealing manner.

Illustrating this in *The Sweet Shop Owner* (1980), his first novel, Swift deals with the personal history of Willy Chapman, the shopkeeper of the title, looking back at his dysfunctional family's past, episodically, on the day of his 'suicide'. Material proof of this history is found in a heteroglossic range of evidence: for instance, the memories of his daughter, Dorry, substantiated through the bedroom archive of old schoolbooks and plays inaccessible to an undereducated father, and the many dresses gifted but unused.[12] Further material evidence matches the familial patterns of behaviour, with Willy 'plotted' into the roles of his marriage, his business and fatherhood, going through the motions 'expected' by others long after these relationships have ceased to function as anything but caricature. While Willy is complicit in his 'role-playing', his observations as an outsider in his own life express his dissatisfaction. These objects and behaviours indicate the distance between characters, where the heteroglossic method gives voice to the varying perspectives within the family: for Willy, objects and money substitute for personal expression in the desire for closeness with his emotionally detached wife, Irene and the estranged Dorry. Dorry's reclamation of some of her mother's possessions effectively steals elements of Willy's story to construct her own, differing, materialist history, but Willy incorporates even these losses into the 'secret history' articulated for Dorry's benefit. In the face of Dorry's concurrent acceptance of a cheque for £15,000 but rejection of this as an overture to reconciliation, Willy's dual acts of storytelling and suicide are designed to reclaim family history: 'he would be history' (p. 10).

Shuttlecock (1981), Swift's next book, also engages in this kind of reflective method applied to family history, in this case to the investigation, by his son, of a Second World War spy's activities, filling in the blanks of the father's past into a kind of filial dossier of remnants and detritus. Again, Swift plays with a heteroglossic mode of writing, balancing the past and the present through a multiple awareness of and anxiety over different stories and concerns. Prentis, attempting an understanding of his family through his own act of writing, none the less cannot face constructing a unifying history of events that fulfils the 'conflicting demands of the text'.[13] Although increasingly anxious and even 'intimidated' by unsavoury possibilities in the stories and character of his family and colleagues, Prentis still chooses ignorance over the chance of knowing for certain his history's end. When presented with papers which could potentially illuminate his father's story, he decides that burning this evidence would match a newly discovered desire to 'be in the dark':[14] uncertainty becomes a stance portrayed as preferable to the death of possibilities presented by the prospect of historical closure.

Waterland (1983), Swift's third novel, may be seen as his most clearly 'historical' book yet, and this book similarly 'reconstitutes' the subject of history through an opening up of what can be considered 'historical'. The cycling, anti-linear, disjointed process of narrative in this book challenges an unquestioning privileging of more conventional 'history'. The intense, metafictional focus on the historical leads to a rich diffusion of 'histories' in the novel without *one* becoming dominant. Swift may seem to be 'betraying' history, at key points, and his protagonist certainly expresses fears of this activity, yet what emerges through Swift's technique is the dispersal of historical signification into other, less traditionally recognised historical registers.

The narrator, Tom Crick, has many of the traits characteristic of Swift's writing. Crick is absorbed in the past: retrospection, 'the art of looking backwards and reviewing past events', has become a fixation for the history teacher.[15] At a point of crisis in the present, when history itself is 'ending', Crick appears to be retreating into history from the anarchic 'here and now'. The 'end of history' is signalled by the challenges of his pupils, the closure of the history department, Crick's forced retirement and his wife's committal to an asylum: his comfortable, middle-class world, a material existence based on history, has been 'easily punctured by a knifeblade called Now' (p. 27). In the 'Now', the media circus pitched around his wife's kidnapping of a baby from a supermarket has enabled the headmaster of Tom's school to make some changes. Lewis uses the leverage of the publicity not only to force Tom's resignation, but also to abolish the 'rag-bag of pointless information' that is 'history' (p. 12). The rationale of such a Thatcherite 'Now' is economically based (akin to Fukuyama's disavowal of history) and, as such, is a policy that leaves little room for an epistemological tool in education to challenge that of the neo-conservative ideology of the day. Under attack by an 'official' warping of imagination, 'history' is also assaulted by pupils' anxiety-ridden view of the future. The pupils of Crick's class question the relevance of 'history', based on their fear of nuclear holocaust. What becomes apparent is that both the teacher and his pupils are at a point where 'the symptoms of fear' (p. 7) are overwhelming their existence. Price and his fellow pupils live in a world of 'posthistory', where the threat of nuclear annihilation inhabits their waking dreams.

In reaction to this, Crick tries to validate the worth of history for his pupils and himself. Yet in veering off the syllabus, he focuses on 'history' as it relates to his personal past, warping his pedagogic expertise into a self-centred piece of 'detective work' – one that reflects the heterogeneous or mixed-sourced content of a postmodern historiography. Crick's historical reclamation of the past is an 'interminable and ambiguous process' (p. ix), open to interpretation where professional detachment is doomed by his very involvement within both the events and their *telling*.

First, Crick sets up a history of the fen country, both a geographical and geological depiction, but one which may suggest, fleetingly, the possibility of progress in the imaginary landscape of the narrator. As such, the Fens establish the evidentiary groundwork for the historical metanarrative of 'progress' within the book. The Fens are charted and subjected to the structured enterprise of reclamation; with the arrival of Dutch engineers, those 'practical and forward-looking people', human control becomes an influence on the landscape, and the pace of history alters, and 'progress' (p. 11) seems to be achievable. Changes are made, cutting new courses of rivers to the sea, and draining land. Crick's ancestors 'became land people' (p. 13), engaged in what is still a 'slow and arduous process, the interminable and ambiguous process . . . of land reclamation' (p. 10). Later in the novel he suggests that his 'humble model for progress is the reclamation of land. Which is repeatedly, never-endingly retrieving what is lost' (p. 254).

Yet the resisting topography of *Waterland* is also the return of a 'natural' narrative in contrast to that historic artificiality of 'progress' constructed by humanity. Over the years, the waterways of the Fens are obstructed by the very silt that forms the land, and intense flooding periodically wipes out humanity's attempts at control. Draining the land only emphasises the instability of the area, with the 'reclaimed land . . . shrinking and sinking' (p. 12) below sea level, inviting disaster. Similarly, the flatness of the landscape also negates the presence of humanity and its rational history. Just as water is a 'liquid form of Nothing', the Fens, are 'a landscape, of all landscapes, most approximate to Nothing' (p. 13). Water takes on a mythic significance, an 'agent of dissolution, devolution, and loss', that challenges history's search for 'something'.[16]

The regression of empirical reclamation, the 'scientific' accumulation of facts and evidence, reaches an even more personal level when Tom Crick envisages the failure of Victorian certainties, the fall of his mother's family, the Atkinsons, and their levelling union with the Cricks in the production of various emblems within his own personal experience and memory. The evidence of a bottle of Ernest Atkinson's ale and the 'potato-head' brother Dick are essential clues in the 'detective work' of his personal past of the early 1940s. The death of Freddie Parr, Mary Metcalf's abortion, and Dick's self-drowning are all linked by a methodical observation of detail. Crick dispassionately records the sequence of events: the budding relationship of Mary and himself; the rivalry with Dick for Mary's sexual curiosity; the drowning of Freddie and subsequent inquiry; the discovery of the bottle linking Dick to murder; Mary's pregnancy and subsequent abortion; Tom's revelation of Dick's incestuous origin; and the witnessed fall of Dick. Yet despite his role as an historical scribe, Crick is still a participant in these events. There are clear implications in this inquiry of his culpability in this past crisis, implications that link his guilt to the repercussions of the present one. The past events have signalled a personal 'end of history' that can only be observed, not retrieved. The crisis of the abortion and subsequent death of Dick, in particular, are emblems for the dead-ends that Tom's inquiry has difficulty negotiating despite his efforts at empirical 'reclamation'.

Though the narrator works very hard to dredge up plausible explanations, the pages of *Waterland* are saturated with elements that drift from the official, empirical history into other historically imaginative landscapes. The history of the Fens is in actuality a composite structure of narratives that challenge any claim to historical stability, with the evidence often coming from mythological sources. A phrase from the beginning of Dickens's *Great Expectations*, 'Ours was the marsh country . . .', is used as an epigraph that not only confirms a similarly amphibious and ambiguous setting, but describes a place bereft of historical sequence, a land that has reclaimed the reclaimers before their time. Similarly, even in his discussion of historical models, Crick consistently observes a cyclic symbolism, 'which perpetually travels back to where it came from,' erasing the possibility of the rational continuity, or 'Progress' (p. 205). This imaginary model is applied to the French Revolution, the ultra-conservative 'return', and a 'nostalgia' for a lost 'Golden Age': 'we believe we are going forward, towards the oasis of Utopia. But how do we know – only some imaginary figure looking down from the sky (let's call him God) can know – that we are not moving in a great circle?' (p. 135).

Such questionings of the very exemplary models on which conventional historiography is based are not unique to this book. Reflecting some of the material referentiality of both *Shuttlecock* and *Waterland*, Swift's next novel, *Out of This World* (1988) effectively develops an episodic examination of the effects of war (including, in this case, terrorism) on personal history further, depicting yet another dysfunctional family, whose involvements emphasise war as a commodity (arms sales and war journalism) and leave a legacy of fatality and emotional scars in their wake. The persistent return to familial history is further maintained and extended in *Ever After* (1992), which narrates the reflections and research of two centuries of family past by a troubled academic: emotionally bereft and concerned with questions of mortality.

Such considerations of mortality and the possibility of a kind of survival within the memory of those who know you are more fully explicated in the novel that follows *Ever After*. *Last Orders* (1996) reveals Swift's postmodern duality of perspective towards history and mortality particularly strongly. The now-familiar subject matter, personal histories and how they relate to each other in the aftermath of a death, is given an added multiplicity of perspective by sharing out the narrative in first-person accounts between the central characters. Although there is a narrative sequence within the novel, with an increasingly protracted journey taken to dispose of Jack Dodds' ashes, this trip is constantly broken in the narrative by the insertion of flashbacks that complicate the historical connection of these characters. While, as in all Swift's novels, there is an element of connectedness to a larger context (such as reflections on the Second World War), this level of referentiality is mediated by the demotic narration of the characters' personal accounts. Correlative to *Waterland*'s historical figuration as 'human siltation', *Last*

Orders is constructed incrementally by these overlapping confessions. In their interconnected personal histories, familiarity with the life of the dead butcher and with each other 'defines' each of the characters on the journey, through friendship, bitterness, secret betrayal and open hostility, yet the constant 'confessional' quality and content of the text functions to unsettle the reader's expectations that have been based on each of the previous accounts. Towards the end of this novel, the reader may come to the realisation that the apparently 'ordinary' tale and 'ordinary' characters that populate it are anything but; the postmodern tactic of presenting the narrative through overlapping accounts, erasure and multiplication of 'histories' undercuts the assumptions made about the situation from the start, requiring a vigilant readerly detective work.

The most recent of Swift's novels, *Light of Day* (2003), also returns to *Shuttlecock*'s most literal incarnation of 'detective' work involved with the postmodern reclamation or reconstitution of history. The title signifies a kind of illumination of the past, achieved through (disgraced) ex-police detective turned private investigator, George, and his fixation on explaining key events that have caused his current situation. Yet the first-person narration also functions as a monologue addressed to the object of an obsession, and the central figure in his most (in)famous case, client and murderess Sarah Nash, in anticipation of her future release from prison into the 'light of day' and into his 'care'. The slippage between the different orders of reference within the title is exemplary of the type of reordering of historical signification within the narrative. The self-awareness in the address to Sarah reveals a document perhaps anticipating a reading at a later date, as an historical account; yet the slippage between the present of the speaking voice and several, alternative orders of time, which seem to be maintained in parallel to the present time, reveals a different control of historical perspective. The particular pattern of reference commemorating the present day's primary significance is tightly maintained: the day illuminated particularly throughout the plot is the second anniversary of the slaying of Sarah's husband after he farewells his lover. Yet the authority of the narrator, speaking as a former policeman, is also complicated by other historical mirroring which reveals his own implicit relationship with criminality. As representative in his roles as a 'bent copper' and a keeper of the secret of his father's infidelity, George remains as much a part of other people's histories (his daughter's, his ex-wife's, that of the thug he attempted to 'frame'): yet as much as he is an observer of others, he observes himself in the act of watching others, and makes a history of this. The postmodern indeterminacy with which he revisits the past, and re-interrogates it, reflects the duality of his position as both observer and one who is inextricably involved by the telling of his histories.

Julian Barnes' production of novels to date also demonstrates a fascination with what I have addressed as the postmodern historical concerns present in Swift's writing. Barnes has attracted his fair share of critical acclaim for his fiction; this is partly in recognition of his skills at steadily extending the genre's innovative reconstitution of the past. His eight novels to date provide evidence of his interest in the postmodern view of history, with the narrative emphasis of contingency in historical representation through an undermining of causal evidence in personal and biographical history; a reconfiguration of a 'series' of historical events, linked haphazardly; and a play on simulation and the representation of national history.

Metroland (1980), Barnes' first book, has been described as a 'fairly conventional coming-of-age novel';[17] yet it also provides an effective introduction to the trope of national identity and its history that Barnes effectively revisits in later books. The protagonist, Chris Lloyd, grows up in suburban London with French 'bohemian' ideals, yet has very 'safe' experiences in 1968 Paris, culminating in marriage and settling down to the suburban British lifestyle of his parents. Barnes' ironic treatment of the cultural history and refashioning of 1960s and 1970s Britain and France is represented in full bathetic force when the reader is introduced to a maturing Chris, trapped in this return to suburbia: 'on Saturday afternoon, as I track the lawn mower carefully across our sloping stretch of grass, rev, slow, brake, turn and rev again, making sure to overlap the previous stripe, don't think I can't still quote you Mallarmé'.[18]

In his next two novels, *Before She Met Me* (1982) and *Flaubert's Parrot* (1984), Barnes' commentary on historical 'appearance' and 'reality' is more firmly established in the retrospective vision towards versions of matrimony. In the former, Graham Hendrick is manipulated by his ex-wife into fantasies of his current wife's lurid past and present. This 'imaginary' past leads to an increasing paranoia that culminates in the violent outcome, with Hendrick committing both homicide and suicide. Similarly, in *Flaubert's Parrot*, Geoffrey Braithwaite, a retired doctor, is 'haunted' by his dead wife's apparent adultery and suicide. However, in this novel, Barnes' postmodern bricolage of the past, seemingly in the 'control' of his protagonist, is represented in a transferral from the subject of his dead wife to an apparent obsession with Gustave Flaubert. While undeniably unbalanced in his obsession, Braithwaite seems to avoid Hendrick's fate through this very distraction and mania with detail; however, Braithwaite's compulsive review of that other great adulteress, Emma Bovary, may indicate that his wife's presence is never far from his mind.

Combining literary 'detective work' with concrete traces of the great French writer's life, Braithwaite creates an historical collage that is revealing of his own mental process, with the need for tangible history made particularly apparent; yet Barnes' clever bricolage, putting together a new functional whole from fragments of disparate pasts, is also a fundamentally entertaining and convincing example of postmodernist salvage work. Braithwaite's highly amusing play with different 'systems' of recording and reordering the impact of Flaubert's writings and life provides a typically postmodern vision of the contingent decisions that make problematic the selection of one 'correct' or 'authentic' historical version. In particular, a number of chapters, including 'Chronology', 'Train-spotter's Guide to Flaubert', 'The Flaubert Apocrypha', 'Braithwaite's Dictionary of Accepted Ideas' and 'Examination Paper', present many different possible orders of 'containing' Flaubert in the historical record, in a manner that effectively exposes this contingency of selecting the 'truth' and makes ridiculous claims to 'priority' for any one order. In just such a way, the narrator's search for the title's 'authentic' parrot of Flaubert is doomed to indeterminacy, represented at one point by the equally strident claims of two opponent parrots. This indeterminacy burgeons on the last page of the novel, when narrator and reader are presented with some fifty candidates: 'everywhere I looked there were birds. Shelf after shelf of birds . . . They did look – I had to admit it – a little cranky. I stared at them for a minute or so, and then dodged away. Perhaps it was one of them'.[19] Braithwaite's former certainty, which actually rests on which parrot he *prefers* rather than on the basis of incremental proof, is thus interrogated and found implausible.

The placing of the narrator within the schematic consideration of historical 'proof' also alerts the reader to the postmodern referential presence of metafiction, the self-conscious acknowledgement or emphasis of the text as a literary object. Barnes, in this, shows his alignment with the literary stylings of Swift, who, especially in his narrators of *Waterland* and *Light of Day*, creates intricate patterns of self-reference and awareness within the construction of historical 'textuality'. In the reordering of basic information into different forms, such as when several different emphases on Flaubert's life are presented (for example, in 'Chronology'), or in the proliferation of parrots, a key self-conscious focus on elements such as repetition and imitation is clearly presented, and a self-critical awareness perceived in Barnes' first-person reflexive control. In the end, however, Braithwaite's self-referencing and the deconstruction of his own narrative give rise to an uneasy semblance of 'erudition', in conjunction with a lack of knowledge about his own wife. For all the historical conjuring evident where Flaubert is the subject, the narrator's wife, Ellen, proves a blind spot that Braithwaite cannot, or will not, illuminate.

Barnes' next book, *Staring at the Sun* (1986), has been labelled by one critic as 'an honourable failure . . . a broken-backed whole',[20] yet in its postmodern styling, it sets up the experimental structure of *A History of the World in 10½ Chapters* (1989). The former novel is characterised by a thematic, cyclic reference to a 'visionary' element, positing an historical model of 'return' that maintains a sense of historical continuity in its repeated elements (especially in the repetition of the beginning's setting at the novel's end), set against a period of apparent frenetic change. Similarly, *A History of the World in 10½ Chapters*, with its more elaborate structural organisation, relies heavily on thematic connectivity and 'returns' in focus, to offer a loose order within the divergence of its offerings. In some respects this 'novel' resembles a Barnes collection of short stories, and some critics condemn the lack of 'purpose' implicit in what is claimed to be a 'sprawl of disconnected episodes and reflections'.[21] Yet there is an order here, postmodern in nature: the kind of order that links the book's material into a bricolage. The proliferation of historical reference in the work stems from a few pivotal features in content (including the Ark, boats in general and a reappearance of insects that exist as privileged observers of human history), and plays on different modes of discourse (including the short story, essay, art criticism, historical abstract) that effectively deconstruct the novel's articulation of the past.

Metafictional awareness is equally foregrounded in Barnes' next two novels: *Talking it Over* (1991) and *The Porcupine* (1992). In the former, Barnes uses the narrative ploy of three, alternating first-person 'talking heads', who directly address the reader. They provide us with a largely superficial commentary on a 'love triangle', yet there is also a light-hearted play with allusions and reported details in the disjointed narrative. *The Porcupine*, the novel with, perhaps, the most mixed reception yet from critics, combines postmodernist stylistics with politics and recent history, fabricating on the trial of an Eastern European former leader that has resonance with the 'real life' Bulgarian and East German leaders' experience. Both in methodology and content, Barnes plays with a referentiality that ensures readers concentrate on issues of appearance and 'reality'.

Barnes' latest novel, *England, England* (1998), takes such a focus on the boundary between the 'real' and its simulation to a further level, with the primary subject of a theme-park, the essentialised, miniature copy of the title reference. As a postmodern reassessment of national identity, particularly as it focuses on key, 'mythologised', emblems from history (encapsulated, for instance, in the 'Fifty Quintessences of Englishness'), this novel works as an effective satire of both the selection of what constitutes 'essential' national characteristics, and the processes of commodification that go hand-in-hand with marketing these for tourist consumption. In effect, the replica 'England', located compactly on the Isle of Wight, comes to supplant the 'original' version, both in terms of economic importance and cultural significance. While the details of its 'authenticity' slip, for instance, when 'Robin Hood's Merrie Men' transgress by eating other elements on display, the replica's influence on the authentic model result in 'real' England's regression to a backward state. In a typical postmodernist juxtaposition, then, the 'authenticity' of the original is seen to be transferable to the copy: a desire for easily formulated symbols of national identity reveals itself potentially destructive of the 'real' nation and the 'sign' replaces the 'real' object being represented.[22] However, the 'real' England's regression into the past also creates a doubling of historical simulation, both as a result of this theme-park construction. What may appear to be an uncomfortable convergence

of pasts, raising concerns about authenticity and precedence, is not totally
unsalvageable, though: in a scene where Ray Stout dressed as Queen Victoria
is observed by children, the children's ability to believe in both characters at
the same time, the 'willing yet complex trust in reality',[23] displays the potential for postmodern historicism to be acceptable within its several layers of
reference, concurrently. The children have no problem dealing with the competing histories on display in the one performance.

Examining the novels of Graham Swift and Julian Barnes reveals an articulation of postmodern concerns and methodologies in the representation of
'history' in their texts. Fiction, in its own way, is an historical record reflecting the changes in ideological concerns of the time of its production. This is
particularly apparent when history itself is a prominent subject within
fiction. These authors' use of referentiality and a greater diversity in considering what can be 'history,' present in both historical material and histori-
cised narratives, is combined to produce complementary effects of
inclusiveness without conclusiveness. Swift's and Barnes' work constitutes
an 'opening up' of possibilities for finding meanings from the fictive pasts,
yet one that resists the desire for stability in those meanings. As the continuing postmodern representation of history in literature demonstrates,
history is not dead; it is just not the same as it was. Now plural, self-aware
of its constructed status, and reliant on a larger range of mediums of recording, history resists the threat of closure.

FOR FURTHER READING

For a hard copy list of the works of Graham Swift and Julian Barnes up to 2001,
see *Contemporary Novelists*, ed. David Madden et al., 7th edn (New York: St
James Press, 2001). For a more up-to-date list on the internet, see the British
Council website:
<http://www.contemporarywriters.com/authors/>.

Anderson, Benedict, *Imagined Communities: Reflections on the Origin and
    Spread of Nationalism*. Rev. edn. (London: Verso, 1991).
Brown, Marshall, ed., *The Uses of Literary History* (Durham, NC: Duke
    University Press, 1995).
Eagleton, Terry, *Literary Theory: an Introduction*. 2nd edn. (Oxford: Blackwell,
    1996).
Holton, Robert, *Jarring Witnesses: Modern Fiction and the Representation of
    History* (New York: Harvester Wheatsheaf, 1994).
Hutcheon, Linda, and Joseph P. Natoli, *A Postmodern Reader* (Albany: State
    University of New York Press, 1993).
Thompson, Willie, *Postmodernism and History* (Basingstoke: Palgrave
    Macmillan, 2004).

NOTES

1 Walter Benjamin, 'Theses on the Philosophy of History', in *Illuminations*, ed. Hannah Arendt, trans. Harry Zorn (London: Pimlico, 1999), p. 247.

2 Graham Swift, *Waterland* (London: Picador, 1992), p. 7. All quotations are from this edition; page numbers are given in the text.

3 Francis Fukuyama, *The End of History and the Last Man* (New York: Free Press, 1992).

4 See Tony Bennett, *Outside Literature* (London: Routledge, 1990), pp. 46–7.

5 Keith Jenkins, 'Introduction', in *The Postmodern History Reader*, ed. Keith Jenkins (London: Routledge, 1997), p. 6.

6 Robert Young, 'White Mythology,' in ibid., pp. 75–6.

7 Fredric Jameson, 'Postmodernism, or the Cultural Logic of Late Capitalism', in K. M. Newton, ed., *Twentieth-Century Literary Theory: a Reader*, 2nd edn (New York: St. Martin's Press, 1997), p. 267.

8 Jean-François Lyotard, 'The Postmodern Condition', in Jenkins, *The Postmodern History Reader*, p. 36.

9 Michael Holquist, *Dialogism: Bakhtin and His World* (London: Routledge, 1990), pp. 69–70.

10 Robert Scholes, *Fabulation and Metafiction* (Urbana: University of Illinois Press, 1979), p. 114. Scholes avers that the metafictional text draws explicit attention to its own constructedness.

11 Linda Hutcheon, 'Historicising the Postmodern', in *A Poetics of Post-modernism: History, Theory, Fiction* (London: Routledge, 1988), p. 89.

12 See Graham Swift, *The Sweet Shop Owner* (London: Picador, 1997), pp. 146–8. All quotations are from this edition; page numbers are given in the text.

13 David Leon Higdon, 'Double Closures in Postmodern British Fiction: the Example of Graham Swift', *Critical Survey*, 3, 1 (1991), 94.

14 Graham Swift, *Shuttlecock* (Harmondsworth: Penguin, 1982), p. 199. All quotations are from this edition; page numbers are given in the text.

15 David Leon Higdon, *Shadows of the Past in Contemporary British Fiction* (Athens, GA: University of Georgia Press, 1984), p. 19.

16 Pamela Cooper, 'Imperial Topography: the Spaces of History in *Waterland*', *Modern Fiction Studies*, 42, 2 (Summer 1996), 373.

17 Sven Birkets, 'Julian Barnes (1946)', in *British Writers*, ed. George Stade and Carol Howard (London: Charles Scribner, 1997), p. 65.

18 Julian Barnes, *Metroland* (London: Jonathan Cape, 1980), p. 174. All quotations are from this edition; page numbers are given in the text.

19 Julian Barnes, *Flaubert's Parrot* (London: Picador, 1985), p. 190. All quotations are from this edition; page numbers are given in the text.

20 David Lodge, '[Review of] *Staring at the Sun*', *New York Review of Books*, 34 (7 May 1987), 3.

21 Birkerts, 'Julian Barnes (1946)', p. 70.

22 For an extensive discussion of this postmodern trait, see Jean Baudrillard, *Simulacra and Simulation*, trans. Sheila Faria Glasser (Ann Arbor: University of Michigan Press, 1994).
23 Dominic Head, *The Cambridge Introduction to Modern British Fiction, 1950–2000* (Cambridge: Cambridge University Press, 2002), p. 121.

18

Colonising the Past: The Novels of Peter Ackroyd

David Leon Higdon

In a mere thirty years, Peter Ackroyd has published ten densely intertextual novels, five well-received biographies, studies of the English imagination, drag and postmodern theory, four studies of London, an estimated million words in reviews, essays, introductions and short stories. Although these works involve historical figures, constantly question the continuities between past and present, and foray deep into metafictional experiments, Ackroyd rejects being called either an historical novelist or a postmodernist, preferring to identify with what he calls 'English music' and the Cockney visionary traditions, a stance which marks him as both.

However much Ackroyd has rejected the label 'postmodern' in interviews, his position in his critical writing has been paradoxical, even contradictory. In book reviews written during the 1970s, he criticised such novelists as Thomas Pynchon, Gabriel García Márquez and Italo Calvino, among others, for creating 'a very deliberate rhetoric which is supposed to replace the conventional pieties of realistic narrative but [which] succeeds only in murdering them',[1] but simultaneously, his *Notes for a New Culture* recommended the major forces in postmodernism, Jacques Lacan and Jacques Derrida, as essential reading and polemically attacked the English tradition for being excessively grounded in the 'related values of humanism and subjectivity'.[2] When he began to write novels himself, he started within the bounds of realistic narrative; however, his novels increasingly exploited the full range of postmodern techniques, turning to anti-realism, grounding themselves in a range of structural play, steeping themselves in layers of intertextuality, foregrounding their fictionality, and fully exploiting historical discontinuities, pastiche and parody, and especially featuring types of impersonation he had theorised earlier in his history of drag and transvestism. In a 1986 review of Timothy Mo's *An Insular Possession*, he indirectly situated his own fictive world: 'If "post-modernism" means anything, it is in its disavowal both of conventional realism and self-conscious experimentalism; and this is precisely the area where historical fiction has come into its own' (*Collection*, p. 191).

In theorising novels combining literature, history and theory, Linda Hutcheon coined the term 'historiographic metafiction' to describe contemporary works which are 'both intensely self-reflexive and yet paradoxically also lay claim to historical events and personages',[3] an accurate description of most Ackroyd novels. Moreover, his alternative worlds, congruent with but strikingly different from the 'real' world, fall in line with Brian McHale's theory that postmodern writers dramatise 'the shift of dominant from problems of *knowing* to problems of *modes of being* – from an epistemological dominant to an *ontological one*.[4] Ackroyd may not deconstruct the page as do B. S. Johnson and Christine Brooke-Rose, but his interrogation of the reality claims of narration, use of polyphonic texts and exploitation of pastiche certainly place him in the company of John Fowles and David Lodge.

Ackroyd often praises Dickens' 'streaky bacon theory' in his critical writings and practises it fully in his novels.[5] English fascination with heterogeneity, he argues in 'The Englishness of English Literature', 'lies in a characteristic mixture of forms and styles, in the alternation between tragedy and comedy, in the unwillingness to maintain one mood for very long, in the manipulation of form for theatrical effect' (*Collection*, p. 338). This idea becomes the major theme in *Albion*, his perceptive, eccentric survey of English imagination as expressed in music, art, architecture and literature. Similarly, in *First Light* Ackroyd plays four distinctly male-dominated narratives against one another, skilfully crossing and re-crossing them until they become one; and in two of his most accomplished novels, *Dan Leno and the Limehouse Golem* and *Milton in America*, he finds ways of letting the narratives inhabit one another's space without necessarily resolving them into one current.

No account of Ackroyd's fiction would be complete without noting the major role London plays in his novels, because London supplies the cultural vitality, historical depths, and thematic energy of his urban art, largely confined to the geography and timescape of central London, stretching from Trafalgar Square to the Tower. As Ackroyd has said, 'London has always provided the landscape for my imagination. It becomes a character – a living being – within each of my books'. Of course, Ackroyd's engagement with and immersion in London are nowhere more apparent than in his 'biography' of the city which personifies it 'as a human shape with its own laws of life and growth'.[6] This biography provides a general tour through time and space, by topics, recording the oddities of speech, habits and customs, which make up the diverse continuities of a 2000-year-old city. Fascinated by the eccentricities, vitalities and permanence of London's lower classes, Ackroyd's is the city of 'those nightmares and fantasies which turned London into some mighty vision akin to that of Piranesi, a labyrinth of stone, a wilderness of blank walls and doors'.[7]

It may be disconcerting for the reader to learn that Ackroyd wrote *The Great Fire of London* 'out of sheer boredom'. He told his interviewer, 'I wanted to write something and so I started writing it. I knew nothing very much about Dickens then'.[8] During a stay in Iceland, however, he began reading *Little Dorrit*, 'one of the great English sagas' (*Collection*, p. 99), and his own novel blossomed into a traditional realistic narrative populated with

Dickensian characters. *Little Dorrit*'s bankruptcies and revenge have never enjoyed the film popularity of Dickens' other 'dark works'. That is, until Spenser Spender, the unifying centre of *The Great Fire of London*, searching for a project to capitalise on his recent successful documentary, decides to film it after recalling a single line from *Little Dorrit*. Appropriately, he conceives of the project as a series of juxtaposed images of sepulchral houses, ghostly prison yards and decaying buildings. The novel, properly, is not about Dickens, but ways in which Dickens shadows every modern figure in it.

Little Dorrit, however, does not wish to be filmed in a contemporary idiom. Its relevance to the contemporary world and the problems of creating a script are summarised by Jeb Penstone, who declares it 'a subversive text ... significantly anti-capitalist, anti-industrial, anti-authoritarian'.[9] Spender wishes to register the ways Dickens 'understood London' (p. 16), but Ackroyd's grotesque and unashamedly Dickensian characters jinx his plans. Identifiable by their physical oddities, peculiar speech habits, quasi-allegorical names and general misfit in the modern world, they range from Michael Dickey's recognisably Dickensian speech impediment: '"He calls it a wecession. More like a wetweat, it seems to me"' (p. 128), to Little Arthur, one of several dwarfs in Ackroyd's world, to Audrey Skelton who, possessed by Amy Dorrit herself during a séance, becomes insane. Labour and financial difficulties shut down production. Leading a group of homeless men, Audrey sets fire to the film set, which collapses on Spender, killing him.

If *The Last Testament of Oscar Wilde* had a scholarly preface, readers might easily mistake Ackroyd's second novel for an authentic memoir, so well does it impersonate Wilde, even though at one point Frank Harris tells Wilde: '"You have quite obviously changed the facts to suit your own purpose"'.[10] *The Last Testament* purports to be the autobiography Wilde wrote in Paris during the three months before his death, a topic suggested to Ackroyd by Giles Gordon (*Collection*, p. xxi). Wilde struggles to find new vitality by searching the ruins of his past life, feeling that he 'must master the past by giving it the meaning which only now it possesses for me' (p. 75). Finding the words, style and voice of an author known for brilliant wit and memorable aphorisms was a genuine challenge for Ackroyd; however, he successfully mimics Wilde's habits of mind. Ackroyd's Wilde refers to most of his published works, creates several stories consistent in style and theme to his sophisticated fairy tales, and surrounds himself with the words and works of others.

Repeatedly, Ackroyd has asserted that 'there is very little difference between [biography and fiction] ... the biographer can make things up, but ... a novelist is compelled to tell the truth' (*Collection*, p. 367). Both must be concerned with narrative and be immersed in 'a similar act of recovery or revival' (*Collection*, p. 263) – very much a postmodern fusion of genres. The novel successfully straddles the boundaries between biography and fiction, between realism and postmodernism. Ackroyd shows every sign of agreeing with Richard Ellmann, Wilde's biographer, that 'Wilde had to live his life twice over, first in slow motion, then at top speed',[11] because Wilde's retrospection details a hurried search as death approaches. To 'master' the facts, Wilde is drawn into the language of the exile, the anchorite, the martyr, and aligns his victimisation with those of St Julian, Lazarus and St Sebastian. He combs his memory of the classics and finds kinship with Bellerophon, Tantalos, Medusa and Niobe. However, he has no regrets for his life as he turns his agenda from word-maker, to personality, to detached spectator of his own life.

Ackroyd found his unique postmodern voice in *Hawksmoor*, his third novel. From this point on, his works are studies in alternation, as twentieth-century settings and narratives run counterpoint with the eighteenth century in *Hawksmoor*, the sixteenth century in *The House of Doctor Dee*, and a full range of English arts in *English Music,* constantly forcing contrasts on the reader's attention and luring the reader into pulling the divergent narratives together – and Ackroyd fully expects his readers to be active. Architecturally, England would be quite different without the talents and works of Nicholas Hawksmoor, Ackroyd's inspiration, for there would be no Blenheim Palace or Easton Norton defining the power and prestige of eighteenth-century accomplishments; and London would lack the upper towers of Westminster Abbey. He will be remembered most, though, for the six 'English Gothick' churches he built to commemorate High Church and Tory power. In *Hawksmoor*, Ackroyd uses these London churches as the focal points of ritual murders intended to contaminate the churches from the moment of their foundation. Their 'significant topography', Ackroyd comments, 'marks a revival of the earth magic once practised by the Celtic tribes of this region, yet it also gives due recognition to the power of place' (*London*, p. 207).

Hawksmoor mechanically folds one narrative into another. Six odd-numbered chapters feature the activities, fears and crimes of Nicholas Dyer (the fictionalised Hawksmoor), using eighteenth-century diction, spelling and syntax, an effect Ackroyd achieved by reading period novels and journalism for some weeks in the British Library. Chief Superintendent Hawksmoor, the twentieth-century Scotland Yard authority attempting to locate the murderer replicating Dyer's crimes, is featured in the even-numbered chapters. This mysterious duel between criminal and detective exploits the contrast between the rational, scientific, hyper-pragmatic being and the obversely non-rational, passionate, spiritual self. The scientific laboratory confronts the magician's spells across three centuries in chapters which effectively echo and mirror one another by repeating names, phrases, objects and action. The conflict acutely depicts the opposition of the man who sees a world dominated by supernatural powers, which must be propitiated, and the rationalist detective who constantly strains to weave a causal narrative around each crime. These worlds threaten to cancel one another at times, but Ackroyd early described his novel as 'the art of Shaddowes . . . for there is no Light without Darknesse and no Substance without Shaddowe'.[12] Unfortunately, third-person perspective mutes Hawksmoor's personality, thoughts and actions, but the moment of epiphany is Hawksmoor's, though it brings no victory.

Invention of the written word brought the possibility of forging words, and perhaps the most famous 'forger' in English literature is Thomas Chatterton, who invented a fifteenth-century poet, Thomas Rowley, and created an entire Rowley canon which attracted admiration from a number of Romantic poets, including Wordsworth and Keats. Just as Chatterton invented Rowley, Ackroyd's brilliantly postmodern novel invents a new Chatterton, one who fakes his suicide and lives for thirty-five more years, 'facts' not known until a young modern poet discovers an 1802 portrait and a bundle of 'authentic' Chatterton papers. Ackroyd's novel builds complex layers around the question of what is authentic and original and what is forged and derivative by juxtaposing Chatterton with a novelist who has built a career by plagiarising, and a painter's assistant who has faked a number of the artist's works. The artist's assistant, Merk, puts the matter thus: "'But who is to say what is fake and what is real? You're sure you know the difference, yes?'"[13] In an allegorical moment, Merk attempts to strip the forged Chatterton portrait of its additions, only to discover an ever-receding original, but the layers begin to interact and slough away, collapsing the search for the original, truly an image of Derridean *différance*.

Because Chatterton rebels against the concept of originality and stands in many ways as a proto-postmodernist, he embodies the key issue the novel addresses: Is, as Plato asserted, all art but imitations of imitations? Ackroyd calls Chatterton, 'the most celebrated faker of the eighteenth century' and views his poetry as 'reverence for the past' which led him 'to re-create, rather than rescue, past time'.[14] Chatterton's confidence, boldness, creativity and joy in life form a telling contrast to Ackroyd's protagonist, Charles, a very sympathetic character, but a failure with his own poetry. Loved by his family, respected by his friends, Charles dies of a brain tumour, and his death sharply contrasts with Chatterton's more melodramatic end. Chatterton is obviously Charles' *alter-ego*, whom he hoped to authenticate and rescue with the unexpectedly discovered portrait and manuscript – both, unfortunately, forgeries.

First Light veered sharply back into realism and serious problems. Its very large cast of characters has no central focal point; its short chapters seem fragments at times; most significantly, it is not firmly enclosed by a historical figure or set in London. Set on the border of Dorset and Devon, *First Light* lacks the rich depths and historical echoes London brings to Ackroyd's earlier novels, even though Ackroyd vacationed and lived in Devon for a time. None the less, *First Light* retains Ackroyd's thematic preoccupations: the connections between past and present and the intense probing of the meaning of time itself. The novel's distinctly segregated plot-lines juxtapose very different temporal worlds: the academic worlds of astronomy and archaeology, the entertainment world of vaudeville, radio and television, and the rural world of a Dorset village. The perspectives on time range from cosmological vastness to shelves of antique clocks, from recent genealogical mysteries to lingering practices of ritual blood sacrifice and fertility dances.

Damian Fall, a fortyish astronomer, dominates eleven of the eighty chapters and repeats the novel's opening as its closing chapter. His world, the most confined and least populated, depicts a midlife crisis brought about by his panic in the face of the immensity of time and space and the ever-visible reminders from his posters of scientific greats of his professional failure. Last seen curled up in a corner of the Observatory, barking and screaming that Aldebaran is rushing towards Earth, Damian once explained to Mark Clare how everything in the universe is related because 'all the materials of life come from the cosmic trace elements'.[15]

Joey Hanover, in search of his biological parents now that he and his malapropish wife have retired from show business, inhabits a wider world, differing in tone and style. Knowing only that he was born in a Dorset cottage with faces carved in its plaster ceiling, Joey blunders onto this very cottage, and thus into his family's history. Quickly rejuvenated, Joey is allowed to share more family secrets when he dons antlers at the winter reunion of the Mint family and then hides the coffin of the ancestral Mint. Surprisingly, Joey, the vaudeville clown, experiences the crucial epiphany of the novel. Driven to open the prehistoric coffin, he has a vision of what this ancestor would have been to his tribe, 'hearing' his voice tell the people that stars were once souls, the eyes of the dead, even one's dreams. The relationship between humans and stars gives Joey a feeling of belonging, quite the opposite effect it had on Damian.

Mark Clare, the major protagonist, has made the archaeological find of a lifetime: a tumulus, a stone circle and a valley which obviously had great ritual significance at one time. Star maps of Aldebaran, the Pleiades and the Hyades are cut into the stone closing the entrance to the grave. Excavating this find should be the high point of Mark's career. However, Mark is oddly depthless, awkwardly distanced, primarily incapable of focusing his life. We learn little about his failed marriage, virtually nothing about his career and only bits about his opaque being. In other words, Mark is a colourless character unable to support the sophisticated framework and thematic depths of the novel. Excavation brings several surprises: the skeleton of a sacrificed man, a mysterious tunnel and finally an ancient wooden coffin, but the excavation of the tomb finds no counterpart in the excavation of Mark's soul. The novel ends with an unearned vision of metaphysical union telling the characters, 'No one is ever dead, and at this moment of communion a deep sigh arose from the earth and traveled upward to the stars' (p. 325).

English Music, which most reviewers rightly condemned as a failed postmodern experiment, follows Timothy Harcombe from childhood in the 1910s to young adulthood in the 1930s and his discovery that he possesses the gifts of healing and clairvoyance; his other gift, which either charms or alienates the reader, enables him to enter novels, music and paintings in what seem to be trances. The even-numbered chapters mechanically swirl him through *Pilgrim's Progress*, *Alice in Wonderland*, *Great Expectations*, *Robinson Crusoe* and *Morte d'Arthur*, poems by William Blake, and stories by Arthur Conan Doyle. Music takes him into the world of William Byrd; painting into canvases by Hogarth, Constable, Gainsborough and others. These excursions mostly reveal Timothy's passivity. We last see Timothy replacing his father in the circus troupe, circling England on tour – a moment of thematic clarity but also narrative weakness. Cristopher Nash has found such circular structures to be quite common in postmodern fiction: 'There may for the writer be the compensating gratification that, if the work forms a circle (or a sphere), it is a closed world, tautologically pure, autonomously perfect.'[16] *English Music*'s complicated genesis may account for some of its problems. Ackroyd was attracted to writing a novel about William Byrd, Thomas Tallis and John Dowland, but 'could find no vital clues in their lives to assist [him]' (*Collection*, p. 384). He also weighed the possibilities of creating a Borgesian character that would thus be trapped in a library. Waiting for sleep one night, his ideas coalesced into a narrative line with a father and son relationship taking priority and troping the relationship between an author and his or her characters.

Ackroyd's next three novels found successful ways to become true examples of historiographic metafiction. In little over a month, timid, withdrawn and methodical Matthew Palmer, the young professional researcher and protagonist of *The House of Doctor Dee*, is assaulted by news that his best friend is a transvestite as well as his father's lover, his inherited house once belonged to an Elizabethan 'black magician' and his supposed biological parents had adopted him. These epistemological shocks are framed by the story of Doctor John Dee, because Ackroyd has again energised his novel by resorting to disjunctive plots which valorise one another.

A Tudor scientist, Dee survived charges of treason, heresy and sorcery in an age little inclined to leniency. A true Renaissance polymath, he wrote seventy-nine books on astronomy, mathematics, alchemy, cartography and other topics. Ackroyd was more interested in Dee's mysterious crystals which supposedly enabled him to hold discourses with angels and his reputation as a conjuror or magus. Ackroyd recalls reading about Dee in the early 1980s: 'I thought he was a rather remote, rather esoteric figure', he told Anke Schulz – exactly the kind of eccentric being whose biography he might have written had he not found a fictional use.[17] Matthew becomes so interested in Dee that he reads six scholarly biographies and several of Dee's own works. Dee's dreams and visions offer spectacular forays into psychological fantasy, with Queen Elizabeth I anatomising his body in one dream and his dead wife inducting him into the universal dance of love set in a fantastic garden of flowers in another. The Dee chapters colourfully recreate Elizabethan life, celebrating the noise and rowdiness of a London tavern, the smell of London streets and the mustiness of an Elizabethan scientist's study – telling contrasts to Matthew's dreary world.

Ackroyd's Dee is a troubled, egotistical man, surrounded by actual or imagined attempts to discredit or destroy him. Destructively, he lusts for gold and wishes for immortality. He craves the knowledge of Paracelsus and Hegelius, but his true kin are Daedalus, Faust and Frankenstein, and his will concludes with his desperate claim for immortality: 'I, who made [the homunculus], will live within him for ever'.[18] Is Matthew 'the little man' created by Dee? Are putative father and son looking at one another across some four hundred years? The glass tubes in which a homunculus is incubated appear in both narratives, and Matthew is frequently called 'the little man'. In its thirtieth year, Dee's notes tell us, the homunculus will 'fall asleep and return to its first unformed state' (p. 123), to be nurtured once again into being by one of the Inspirati. Matthew, now twenty-nine, is nearing that point of transition. Both men inhabit the final chapter, 'The Vision', with considerable slippage between the two historical realities and personalities. Eschewing the closed endings of his earlier novels, Ackroyd provocatively and deliberately blurs the issues.

Dan Leno and the Limehouse Golem offers many firsts: a female protagonist, a fully exploited retrospective opening, a number of narratives left as polyphonic threads. In keeping with the murder mystery material, Ackroyd makes the reader share in the generation of meaning. More than one reader, however, will fall into every trap set in the text, where virtually nothing is what it at first seems.

Elizabeth Cree and John, her husband, cross paths with Dan Leno (the most famous music hall performer of the 1880s), the elderly Karl Marx, and the young George Gissing. Marx's economic theories, Gissing's class interests and John Cree's amateurish fascination with the London poor provide rich theoretical but unresolved, loose interpretative boundaries to Elizabeth's life. Indeed, Elizabeth's rags-to-riches life story could have been the basis for one of Gissing's novels. Born illegitimate to a religious fanatic and early orphaned, Elizabeth fortuitously falls in with Dan Leno's company. Soon 'Lambeth Marsh Lizzie' discovers her talents for comic songs and suggestive patter. As 'Little Victor's Daughter' and in drag as 'The Older Brother', Elizabeth becomes a spectacular hit in the East End music halls. Success brings marriage and middle-class respectability, but also murder.

Elizabeth's story is framed by male narratives, the most sensational of which spurs rumours of a golem loosed on East London. Both Marx and Gissing are suspected and questioned. Their narratives become adjuncts to the trial transcripts, descriptions of the execution, and the murderer's declaration of fidelity to Thomas De Quincey's 'On Murder as One of the Fine

Arts'. Since the reader has access to John's diaries, however, he becomes convinced that Cree is the savage murderer. We do not learn until the very end that Elizabeth has faked the diary and that she, in drag, actually committed the murders. Which narrative is 'true'? Did Elizabeth become a monster because of the economic conditions? Did her mother's emotional and sexual abuse of her spur the vengeful actions? Was she so sexually imbalanced that she turned her rage against the prostitutes she dismembered? Eight years later, the still unknown Jack the Ripper will replicate several of Elizabeth's crimes, making Dan Leno's closing line, 'Here we are *again*!'[19] capture the repetitive nature of human actions which so interests Ackroyd.

Milton in America builds on a simple premise: What if Milton, fearing execution, had fled England for the American colonies in 1660? What if, rather than writing *Paradise Lost*, Milton had become a colonial political leader? Unlike Chatterton, Milton is no particular hero to Ackroyd, who only mentions him in *London*, *Albion* and *The Collection*, to praise his 'capacity for abuse of the most disgusting kind' (*Collection*, p. 354), but his portrait of Milton does justice to the complexity of the man. His Milton is learned, intellectual, musical and utterly committed to the rightness of his ideas, but is also intolerant, vituperative, intensely anti-Catholic and rigidly distrustful of the American forest. The theocratic community he galvanises is harshly prohibitionist and suspicious of all its citizens. Milton signals its future by reminding the colonists 'of the urgent necessity of a prison to contain the evil seed and of a meeting-house to protect the good'.[20]

As with Wilde, Ackroyd creates the ring of authenticity by using incidents taken from the author's life, citations from his writings and actual historical events in the American colonies, though rearranged in time, so that he may successfully impersonate him. He also lets several voices establish the conflicts. Played against Milton's eloquence are Goosequill's London idioms, Katherine's Devon pronunciations, and the occasional scriptural and Latin citations. Goosequill, Milton's guide, helper and opposite, is telling Katherine how he met Milton hiding under straw in a wagon leaving London and how the two of them alone survived the New England shipwreck. He describes Milton's actively encountering difficulties with witchcraft, murder, sodomy and the Native Americans, as the now-pregnant Katherine sits sewing, while Goosequill flirts and teases. Not until the end of Part One do we learn that the memories of these events have been reawakened by the unexplained disappearance of Milton from the settlement in December 1661.

The novel's first half, 'Eden', intertextually echoes *Paradise Lost*. In their earthy, sexual, innocent, almost sceptical ways, Goosequill and Kate figure as Adam and Eve, constantly undermining Milton's grand, unreachable plans for the community. While Goosequill is 'the very pattern of a storyteller' (p. 72), undercutting Milton at every point, Milton is the very pattern of the allegorist, seeing England as Egypt, New Milton as Canaan, and himself as Moses. He envisages Massachusetts as his possible free commonwealth. Too soon, his dreams collapse into struggles against the symbolic and psychological wildernesses, the 'goblin world' to be destroyed by 'right reason and godly persuasion' (p. 134). The 'goblin world' assaults Milton from two sides: his journey alone into the woods to confront the Indians and the arrival of a group of new colonists led by Ralph Kemper intent on settling Mary Mount, a quasi-royalist and emphatically Catholic town earlier treated by Nathaniel Hawthorne.

Both the Catholics and Indians introduce Milton to a richly non-rational world. When the Indians heal Milton's broken leg by 'magic', induct him into a numinous world beyond his tools of reason, and temporarily restore his sight, his participation in the ceremonies and certainly his sexual pleasure with an Indian woman guiltily drive him to destroy what he sees as temptations. Jarred back into blindness, Milton echoes the closing lines of (the unwritten) *Paradise Lost*: '[This] is the beginning of all our woe. The blind man wandered ahead and, weeping, through the dark wood took his solitary way' (p. 277). In this mood, he and the colonists destroy Mary Mount.

Compared to Anthony Burgess's *The Wanting Seed* or Russell Hoban's *Pilgerman*, Ackroyd's *The Plato Papers* is a disappointingly thin exercise in futuristic fiction. Indeed, the work lacks characters, plot and intellectual tension, though it possesses some slight humour in the future's attempts to reconstruct the past. Although reviewers called it a 'rollicking and merry paean to the redemptive properties of ignorance' (a complete misreading) 'likely to challenge readers for generations to come', Eric Korn accurately labelled it a 'brief and intermittently arresting fantasy . . . But it is a sinewless skeleton, and will not stand alone'.[21]

And where will his future take Ackroyd? Ackroyd is only fifty-five – young for a novelist. He should have a number of novels yet in his future. He has indicated that he will write a biography of J. M. W. Turner, and he remains under contract to his publisher for at least six more books. The only certain prediction is that Ackroyd will continue to annex and colonise more territories in the past and that these territories will be bounded by London and probably foreground a known writer. Readers can also hope that after his eight-year absence from fiction he will return to more impersonations of historical figures and continue to give his comic talents free range in brilliantly realised alternative worlds and that he will continue to 're-create the past'.

FOR FURTHER READING

For a hard copy list of Peter Ackroyd's work up to 2001, see *Contemporary Novelists*, ed. David Madden et al., 7th edn (New York: St James Press, 2001). For a more up-to-date list on the internet, see the British Council website: <http://www.contemporarywriters.com/authors/>.

Gibson, Jeremy and Julian Wolfreys, *Peter Ackroyd: the Ludic and Labyrinthine Text* (London: Macmillan, 2000; New York: St. Martin's Press, 2000).
Hutcheon, Linda, *A Poetics of Postmodernism: History, Theory, Fiction* (London: Routledge, 1988).
McHale, Brian, *Postmodernist Fiction* (London: Methuen, 1987).
Nash, Cristopher, *World Postmodern Fiction: a Guide* (London: Longman, 1987).
Onega, Susana, *Metafiction and Myth in the Novels of Peter Ackroyd* (Columbia, SC: Camden House, 1999).

NOTES

1 Peter Ackroyd, *The Collection: Journalism, Reviews, Essays, Short Stories, Lectures*, ed. Thomas Wright (New York: Random House, 2001), p. 12. Hereafter cited as *Collection*.
2 Peter Ackroyd, *Notes for a New Culture* (New York: Barnes and Noble, 1976), p. 120.
3 Linda Hutcheon, *A Poetics of Postmodernism: History, Theory, Fiction* (London: Routledge, 1988), p. 5.
4 Brian McHale, *Postmodernist Fiction* (London: Methuen, 1987), p. 10.
5 In Chapter 17 of *Oliver Twist*, Dickens outlines the principle of comparison and contrast which captured the essence of structure in Victorian fiction. 'It is the custom on the stage', he notes, 'in all good, murderous melodramas: to present the tragic and the comic scenes, in regular alternation, as the layers of red and white in a side of streaky,well-cured bacon'. He sketches how such alternations can occur in tone, style, social status, location and/or time, and concludes that 'sudden shiftings of the scene, and rapid changes of time and place, are not only sanctioned in books of long usage, but are by many considered as the great art of authorship'.
6 *London: the Biography* (New York: Doubleday, 2000), p. 2. Hereafter cited as *London*.
7 *Dan Leno and the Limehouse Golem* (London: Sinclair-Stevenson, 1994), p. 34. In America, the title is *The Trial of Elizabeth Cree: A Novel of the Limehouse Murders* (first published New York: Doubleday, 1995).
8 'Contemporary Authors Interview' (18 November 1987), in *Contemporary Authors* (Detroit: Gale Press, 1988), Vol. 127, p. 44.
9 *The Great Fire of London* (London: Sphere, 1984), p. 80. All quotations are from this edition; page numbers are given in the text.
10 *The Last Testament of Oscar Wilde* (London: Penguin, 1993), p. 160. All quotations are from this edition; page numbers are given in the text.
11 Richard Ellman, *Oscar Wilde* (New York: Alfred A. Knopf, 1988), p. 586.
12 *Hawksmoor* (New York: Harper & Row, 1985), p. 5. All quotations are from this edition; page numbers are given in the text.
13 *Chatterton* (New York: Grove, 1987), p. 113. All quotations are from this edition; page numbers are given in the text.

14 *Albion: the Origins of the English Imagination* (New York: Doubleday, 2002), pp. 443, 440. All quotations are from this edition; page numbers are given in the text.
15 *First Light* (London: Sphere, 1989), p. 263. All quotations are from this edition; page numbers are given in the text.
16 Cristopher Nash, *World Postmodern Fiction: a Guide* (London: Longman, 1987), p. 197.
17 <http://webdoc.sub.gwdg.de/edoc/ia/eese/articles/schuetze/8_95.html>, p. 171.
18 *The House of Doctor Dee* (London: Hamish Hamilton, 1993), p. 226. All quotations are from this edition; page numbers are given in the text.
19 *Dan Leno and the Limehouse Golem* (London: Sinclair-Stevenson, 1994), p. 261.
20 *Milton in America* (London: Sinclair-Stevenson, 1996), p. 110. All quotations are from this edition; page numbers are given in the text.
21 'In the Unreal City', *Times Literary Supplement*, 2 April 1999, 21. The compliments come from reviews in American newspapers, the *Buffalo News* and the *Christian Science Monitor*.

19

Player of Games: Iain (M.) Banks, Jean-François Lyotard and Sublime Terror

Cairns Craig

If the key text shaping conceptions of postmodernity is Lyotard's *The Postmodern Condition*, then the crucial component in Lyotard's account is the collapse of the 'grand narratives' that have characterised Western culture since the Renaissance, together with the global success of consumer capitalism:

> The decline of narrative can be seen as an effect of the blossoming of techniques and technologies since the Second World War, which has shifted emphasis from the ends of action to its means; it can also be seen as an effect of the redeployment of advanced liberal capitalism after its retreat under the protection of Keynesianism during the period 1930–1960, a renewal that has eliminated the communist alternative and valorised the individual enjoyment of goods and services.[1]

The postmodern, in other words, is an epochal condition, and typical of this epoch is the swamping of the aesthetic – of the values of art – by the demands of capitalism. As Fredric Jameson puts it: 'What has happened is that aesthetic production today has become integrated into commodity production generally: the frantic economic urgency of producing fresh waves of ever more novel-seeming goods (from clothing to airplanes) at ever greater rates of turnover, now assigns an increasingly essential structural function and position to aesthetic innovation and experimentation'.[2] Postmodernism is nothing other than what Jameson describes as the 'cultural logic of late capitalism'.

If postmodernism is so historically circumscribed, then Jerome McGann's hailing of Walter Scott's 'postmodernity'[3] might look like a perverse and ahistorical misuse of the term. However, in an Appendix to *The Postmodern Condition*, Lyotard himself holds out an alternative to this *historical* development of the postmodern by suggesting that, in art at least, postmodernity does not develop out of modernity but is, rather, the inherent *ground* of the modern: 'A work can become modern only if it is first postmodern. Postmodernism thus understood is not modernism at its end but in the nascent state, and this state is constant' (p. 79). Postmodernity in its 'nascent state' makes it possible that, under certain conditions, typical features of the postmodern might emerge before the advent of postmodernity itself. Since the nation-state has been one of the fundamental 'grand narratives' of the modern era – the necessary complement, as Benedict Anderson has suggested, of secular modernity[4] – then the lack in nineteenth-century Scotland of a nation-state, or of a nationalist movement determined to establish such a state, may have made it precisely a place without a grand narrative of the kind that other 'modern' nations were developing. As a stateless nation, Scotland may have been postmodernism's 'nascent state' because it never fully entered that world of modernity in which the nation state was the norm.

'Incredulity toward metanarrative', which Lyotard regards as the consequence of the collapse of grand narratives, can be seen as one of the defining features of Scottish narrative in the period when 'British' history was identical with the narrative of English history, leaving Scotland in a kind of historical vacuum.[5] Scotland's cultural situation thus foreshadows the more general collapse of metanarrative since the Second World War, and produces those 'historiographic metafictions' and narratives of conflicting ontological levels identified by influential critics like Linda Hutcheon and Brian McHale as characteristically postmodern.[6] McGann's reading of Scott, then, underlines the extent to which an archetypal Scottish novel such as James Hogg's *Confessions of a Justified Sinner* (1824), with its conflicting double narrative and its self-reflexive inclusion of the author in his own novel, is only the most remarkable example of a kind of prescient postmodernism in Scottish writing.

Given this postmodern turn in Scotland's past culture, stylistic postmodernism in the contemporary Scottish scene has different resonances than elsewhere, and in this context, Iain Banks' fiction is both 'postmodernist' – in its development of those stylistic traits of the Scottish tradition which prefigure postmodernist styles – and either 'pre-' or 'post-postmodernist' in its refusal of the values which characterise the 'postmodern' as the condition of 'late capitalist' society.[7] Linda Hutcheon has suggested that we need to distinguish between the *stylistic* practices of the postmodern in art and postmodernism as a phase of modern capitalism, and has argued that writers who are 'postmodernist' in their styles and techniques are not therefore committed to the postmodernism of late capitalism in their social and political commitments.[8] Such an interplay of postmodernist styles with an anti-postmodernist value system has been characteristic of Banks' leading predecessors in Scottish postmodernism, Muriel Spark and Alasdair Gray, and this combination of Scottish tradition, postmodern style and anti-postmodern values can be seen clearly in Banks' *Complicity* (1993), which is at one and the same time a modernised version of Hogg's *Confessions*, a political thriller and a challenge to the values of the consumer capitalism that define the era of the postmodern.

The stylistic elements of Banks' postmodernism involve the fusion – or confusion – of high and popular culture; delight in the detail of new (or invented) technologies; the play of multiple and competing levels of ontology (human versus superhuman; author versus characters; art versus life); together with a great deal of black comedy that mocks the 'traditional' values of Western culture. Banks renders contemporary mass culture with the kind of ironic verve that an early postmodernist such as Vladimir Nabokov brought to his presentation of the America of cars and motels in the 1950s, and, like Kurt Vonnegut or Philip K. Dick, adopts the styles of popular modes of genre fiction for serious ends. *The Wasp Factory*, for instance, is a gothic black comedy; *Complicity* is a detection thriller in which, in classic fashion, the protagonist is, himself, the prime suspect; *Espedair Street* is fashioned as a rock 'n' roll autobiography, and in *Canal Dreams* the heroine is caught up in a James Bond world of international licences to kill. Banks' science fiction writing (published under the name of Iain M. Banks) often infuses itself into his 'serious' novels, most obviously in *Walking on Glass* (1985), in which Stephen Grout hears in the 'static' of tape recordings the engines of bombers from another world, believing himself to have discovered 'a Leak, a tiny slip they had made which let part of reality slip through into this prison of his life' (p. 113).[9] Reality, for Grout, is a science fiction world alongside which his 'real' world is an illusion. It is an ontology that the novel then seems to underwrite in the story of Quiss and Aja, exiles in a ruined castle in some future world who discover that it contains a technology allowing its inhabitants to enter the heads of people in the past and control them for their own pleasure. Grout fantasises alternative worlds more real than his; the novel suggests that his 'reality' is in fact a fiction played out at the behest of alien creatures. As in many of Vonnegut's and Gray's novels,[10] science fiction provides a means of undermining the ontological security of our common reality. The play of different ontological levels within the novel, each level implying that another level, previously assumed to be 'real', is no more than a fiction, reduces reality to a series of games, none of which can be assumed to have priority over any other.

It is exactly this transformation of the real into games that Lyotard identifies as characteristic of the postmodern. The disappearance of 'grand narrative' leaves behind only a series of 'language games' in which 'truth' is not the uncovering of the 'real' but a function of our construction of the world – or, rather, of *a* world – according to the rules of a particular game:

> It is useful to make the following three observations about language games. The first is that their rules do not carry within themselves their own legitimation, but are the object of a contract, explicit or not, between players (which is not to say that the players invent the rules). The second is that if there are no rules, there is no game, that even an infinitesimal modification of one rule alters the nature of the game, that a 'move' or utterance that does not satisfy the rules does not belong to the game they define. The third remark is suggested by what has just been said: every utterance should be thought of as a 'move' in a game. (Lyotard, p. 10)

This 'constructivist' conception of our relation to reality is often held to
justify the playfulness of postmodernist art, which recognises that its business is no longer to give an account of the 'real' but to play interesting games
with the *possible*. The transformation of the real into a series of games
matches the 'free play' of meaning by which the postmodern – in the guise
of the poststructural – is often defined. Since the very nature of language
games means that there will always be an 'indeterminate number' in play,
truth, 'unified or totalised', is redundant, and supposed truths will constantly
be displaced by new or alternative games.[11] The consequence of such a world
is what Prentice McHoan, in *The Crow Road*, recognises in his father: 'I
thought I could sense something like desperation in him, trying so hard to
equip us as best he could for the vicissitudes of life, while the world changed
all around us so fast that some of his ideas and theories – which had seemed
so important to him in his life, and so crucial for us to know in turn – became
irrelevant, were proved wrong, or just shown to be not so important after
all' (p. 324).[12] Immediately following this realisation, Prentice emerges from
a 'post-post-modernist concrete block' to look out upon a 'dark landscape
full of soft undulations, littered with chambered cairns, cup and ring marked
rocks, standing stones, tumuli and ancient forts' – the games of previous
eras. 'All the gods are false, I thought. Faith itself is idolatry' (p. 324). The
truths of the past are resolved into games; the games of the present dissolve
the very notion of truth.

Symptomatically, Banks' second science fiction novel was entitled *The
Player of Games*, and in all of Banks' novels characters are regularly the
'object of a contract, explicit or not, between players' in games. Thus in
Complicity, the narrator Colley has gradually to uncover the implicit contract once made with his childhood friend Andy, and to acknowledge 'the
burden of buried horror that bound me to Andy twenty years ago' (p. 235);[13]
and in *Whit*, the narrator, Isis, is spiritual inheritor of the invented faith of
her grandfather, a faith which forms a contract between her and the community which believes in her Grandfather's visions; while Kathryn Telman in
The Business is adopted on a whim by a rich woman who, having encountered the child when her car breaks down in a Scottish housing scheme,
decides on the role she will play in the future of the business. The contracts
by which these characters are defined are often accidental, but once made
determine the game in which they are necessarily players. The only choice,
as Gurgeh in *Player of Games* discovers, is that 'one can be the player, or one
can be . . . played upon' (p. 222).[14] It is a crisis that Isis encounters when her
grandfather, as founder of their religion, begins to change the rules to allow
even his granddaughter to be his bedmate: 'This is meant. We are the elect;
the chosen ones. The rules are different for us'; being the elect they 'don't
have to take any notice of the Unsaved's stupid rules' (p. 277). In order to
be a 'player of games', rather than the 'played upon', Isis has to leave the
self-contained world of her commune and negotiate the very different games

of the modern world, inventing ways in which she can continue to abide by the rules of her own 'faith' while traversing territory shaped by entirely different expectations. Abel, in *A Song of Stone*, on the other hand, finds the artificial social world that he has constructed quite literally overrun by an outside world whose games he has never learned to play: 'There are tensions between states, peoples, races, castes and classes which any given player – individual or group – simply neglects, takes for granted or attempts to manipulate for their advantage only at the risk of their very existence' (p. 78).

The conflict between being a player and being played upon, and the difficulty of discovering the rules of the game in which one is playing, are the insistent themes of Banks' fiction. In his first published novel, *The Wasp Factory*, the protagonist, Frank, believes himself to be a castrated male who takes revenge on the world for his castration by inventing a territory – centred on the Wasp Factory and bounded by his Sacrifice Poles – governed by his rules, and defiant of his father's rules:

> I was having a War at the time – the Mussels against the Dead Flies I think it was – and while I was in the library, soaking up all this damn silly Imperial measurement, the wind would be blowing my fly armies over half the island and the sea would first sink the mussel shells in their high pools and then cover them with sand. Luckily, my father grew tired of this grand scheme . . . (p. 12)[15]

Frank escapes from the 'game' that is his father's 'grand scheme' to one in which he has a god-like power to reshape and rename the world, treating reality as though it were the linguistic material of a literary fiction. What he and we discover, however, is that even in his escape he is still an actor in a game invented by his mad-scientist father. Frank is not actually a castrated male but a female. Deliberately deceived about his/her identity, s/he has been living in the Frank-enstein world of her father's imagination. Frank is a monster taking revenge upon the world for his mutilation, rather than Frances, who ought to be at home in it. Had she been Frances, however, she would have been no less insistently trapped in a world of games, like the Freudian theories of 'penis envy' which her supposed castration ironically mirrors. The creation of games whose rules are your own invention do not necessarily release you from the rules of the game from which you are fleeing. The same is true of Colley in *Complicity*, who is addicted to a computer game called *Despot*, a 'world-builder game' which gives him the illusion of being able to dominate past history but which 'actually *watches* you; it learns your playing style, it *knows* you, it will actually try its little damnedest to *become* you' (p. 53). This is precisely what happens to Colley in reality when he is caught up in a 'game' of revenge killings in which he is taken for his best friend Andy, who has in effect *become* him.

For some of Banks' characters, the discovery that they are playing in a game imposed on them by another requires that they accept responsibility for the very role scripted for them – that they play consciously and better the game in which they did not realise they were participants. Thus Isis, having discovered the real nature of the religion in which she has been brought up, decides to use it and to make it work more effectively, just as Kathryn Telman, in *The Business*, decides to fulfil what the Business wanted of her – marriage to the Prince of a Himalayan state – but for her *own* reasons rather than for theirs. Equally, in *Canal Dreams*, its Japanese protagonist, Hisako Onada, is apparently a victim of violence – her family having died in Hiroshima – and a person dedicated to international harmony, since she travels the world as a concert cellist. However, she is also a murderer, responsible for the death of a policeman in a student riot, and will survive the hijacking of the ship on which she is travelling only by becoming an even more effective player of the 'game' of killing.

Hisako's transformation from musician to murderer, however, points to the fundamental fact by which Banks' characters are confronted: games, too, operate on competing ontological levels. There are games that are played for aesthetic satisfaction and there are games played for life and death. So, in *The Player of Games*, Gurgeh, who is the highest-ranking player of intellectual games in a civilisation known simply as the Culture (which features in most of Banks' science fiction novels), finds himself pitted against the Emperor of the civilisation of Azad. Their game, like an infinitely more complex chess, imitates the rules of warfare, but what Gurgeh discovers is that this game is being played for real. To defend himself and the Culture, he has to become his own opposite, has to acquire the warrior virtues from which his civilisation had protected him: 'So now the man played like one of those carnivores he'd been listening to, stalking across the board, setting up traps and diversions and killing grounds; pouncing, pursuing, bringing down, consuming, absorbing . . .' (p. 247). The player of games discovers that he is playing the game for real, not for victory or defeat but for life or death. For Lyotard, 'to speak is to fight, in the sense of playing'(p. 10), but for Gurgeh to play is to fight, in the sense of killing. The aesthetic turns back into the violence it had apparently supplanted; the pleasure of play turns into the threat of terror; players become terrorists.

If *Dead Air* most explicitly charts the invasion of private life by public terrorism, dramatising the impact of 9/11, it only underlines that Banks' novels take place in wars or their aftermath, in territories where it is unclear if the rules are those of peace or of war. So in *The Crow Road*, the sight of a 'high-winged light aircraft' induces the reaction, 'It's a Mig on a bombing run; everybody down!' (p. 408); and in *The Wasp Factory* Frank's house sits on a cellar where an unstable arsenal of cordite left over from the Second World War is stored, representing, according to Frank, some 'link with the past, or an evil demon we have lurking, a symbol for all our family misdeeds; waiting, perhaps, one day to surprise us' (p. 53). In Banks' novels, violence is always waiting, in one form or another, to return upon us. For Andy, in *Complicity*, 'compassion and a few fair laws . . . exist against a background of global barbarism, they float on an ocean of bloody horror that can tear apart any petty social construction of ours in an instant' (p. 302). Not for nothing is the ship on which Hisako Onada is trapped in *Canal Dreams* called *Le Cercle*: the violence we seek to put behind us, turning it into a symbolic game, we are in fact sailing towards.

The return of terror in Banks' 'post-post modernist' novels reveals retrospectively the crucial 'move' made in Lyotard's postmodernism of 'language games'. For Lyotard, language games are fundamentally self-contained and self-enclosed. A '"move" or utterance that does not satisfy the rules does not belong to the game they define', and 'every utterance should be thought of as a "move" in a game' (Lyotard, p. 10). The singularity of moves and games – they are either part of *a* game or not – makes language games autotelic: you are either playing in this game or you are not. To make a wrong move is simply to stop playing this game and to open the possibility of another game whose truth-status is no different from the game you have failed to play. In this, Lyotard reveals his Kantian heritage: his 'language games' are the equivalent of Kant's 'categories' and, with equal determination, shape the world that we experience. For Lyotard, Kant is both 'the epilogue to modernity' and 'also a prologue to postmodernity'[16] precisely because the unknowability of the real in Kant's philosophy is repeated in the irrelevance of the real in the postmodern condition. But where, for Kant, the categories are few, and produce the shared world of our common human environment, for Lyotard the games are infinite and produce a world in which there are simply many different versions of the real.

The 'unknowability' of the real in Kantian philosophy could be overcome because, for Kant, our moral freedom both redeemed us from determinism and allowed us to escape the 'phenomena' of our ordinary experience by connecting with the 'noumenal' world otherwise known only to God. For Lyotard there is no God to salvage us from the limitations of our individual consciousnesses, but another of Kant's concepts, the 'sublime' – the ability of art to transcend the categories by which the rest of life is ruled – plays an equivalent role. The Kantian sublime is, for Lyotard, foundational to both modernist and postmodernist writing:

> A postmodern artist or writer is in the position of a philosopher: the text he writes, the work he produces are not in principle governed by preestablished rules, and they cannot be judged according to a determining judgement, by applying familiar categories to the text or to the work. Those rules and categories are what the work of art itself is looking for. The artist and the writer, then, are working without rules in order to formulate the rules of what will have been done. (Lyotard, p. 81)

The artist's ability to create something for which there are as yet no rules is the index of humanity's freedom – even if it is a freedom that belongs only to the visionary few. That Kantian 'sublime', however, has its dark *alter-ego* in Lyotard's writing. The sublime, of course, was originally defined in terms of terror. As Edmund Burke phrased it, whatever 'operates in a manner analogous to terrour, is a source of the sublime'.[17] For Lyotard, however, the terrifying threat of the sublime has been domesticated into the minor 'terror' that people experience when confronted by works of art for which there are no rules, works of art that invoke no pre-existing standards by which they can be judged or understood. It is a terror we can enjoy knowing that all novelties will eventually be accommodated into the rules of a future conception of art, and the 'sublime' object will once again have become part of a familiar game that we know how to play. Made irrelevant to the artistic sublime, however, terror returns as that which negates all language games, as that which refuses to enter into the world of 'language games' at all:

> I am excluding the case in which force operates by means of terror. This lies outside the realm of language games, because the efficacy of such force is based entirely on the threat to eliminate the opposing player, not on making a better 'move' than he. Whenever efficiency (that is, obtaining the desired effect) is derived from a 'Say or do this, or else you'll never speak again', then we are in the realm of terror, and the social bond is destroyed. (Lyotard, p. 46)

On one side is art, which joyously breaks the rules; on the other is terror, which refuses all rules.

By placing terror outside of our 'language games', Lyotard makes those games fundamentally benign: 'language games' are arenas in which we can play safely. For Banks, however, a self-contained, autotelic world of games is no more than a comforting illusion, because terror is not on the outside of language games: it is what happens when games overlap, collide, disperse, or transfer from the symbolic to the actual. And because the games in which we operate are porous, a rule-bound action in one game can also be (indeed, will inevitably be) an event in another game, one whose consequences are unimaginable – and therefore terrifying – from within the game we think we are playing. Thus in *Complicity*, Colley's sub-editor on the newspaper, Frank, delights in discovering how the spell-checker on his wordprocessor garbles Scottish places names: 'Yetts o' Muckart becomes Yetis o' Muscat under the spell-check' (p. 18). The spell-check has stepped into a game that does not accept its rules. This benign game, however, is mirror-image to the game in which Colley is caught, a game that goes back to events in a place called 'Strathspeld', a place whose meaning he is incapable of spelling out to himself. For Colley, the overlaying of games produces results very different from the comedy of Frank's spell-checker. He is asked to wait for a phone call from Andy beside a pub in Edinburgh's Grassmarket called *The Last Drop*, which might be a model for the games in Banks' novels, since its contemporary significance to pub drinkers – the last drop in the glass – conceals its grim historical reality – it is where criminals were taken for public hanging, a very final 'last drop'. The two meanings come together when it becomes the place where Andy indicates he will 'drop off' the last of his victims.

For Banks, our language games drop us, like the trapdoor on the gallows, from one level of game to another; from games structured by a benign symbolism to games in which terror spells death. It is an experience Banks dramatises towards the end of *Complicity* when Colley recalls that Andy had arranged, as a joke, the extinguishing of all lights when they were visiting the underground remains of old Edinburgh: 'But in those moments of blackness you stood there, as though you yourself were made of stone . . . you felt a touch of true and absolute terror . . . a fear rooted somewhere before your species had truly become human . . .' (p. 310). A joke opens a trapdoor to an entirely different game, a game played to the timescales of evolutionary history and played by the rules of terror. In that context, the postmodern dissolution of the real is the philosophical equivalent of Colley's drug-taking in *Complicity* or the fake belief-system of *Whit* – an evasion of the nature of the real rather than its confrontation.

Banks' 'post-postmodernism' provides an alternative commentary on Fredric Jameson's distinction between modernism and postmodernism in his discussion of Van Gogh's 'A Pair of Boots' and Andy Warhol's 'Diamond Dust Shoes'. The difference between them, according to Jameson, lies in the fact that for Van Gogh it was still possible to imagine, through the most banal objects, 'the willed and violent transformation of a drab peasant object world into the most glorious materialisation of pure colour, in oil paint'.[18] The painting, Jameson believes, invites its viewers to understand the boots as a symbol of art's potential to transform reality. Like Frank's Wasp Factory, it is 'an act of compensation which ends up producing a whole new Utopian realm of the senses'.[19] The Warhol image, on the other hand, is 'a random collection of dead objects hanging together on the canvas like so many turnips, as shorn of their earlier life world as the pile of shoes left over from Auschwitz'.[20] The postmodern, for Jameson, involves an increasing dematerialisation of the real, an increasing absence of humanity from art as it becomes simply another commodity in a world of capitalist commodification.

But in Banks' *Complicity*, the boot has a very different connotation: on the Basra Road, reporting the advance of allied troops in the battle against Saddam Hussein, Colley finds himself lost in a game he can no longer understand:

> I tried to imagine what it must have been like to be caught here, beaten, retreating, running desperately away in those thin-skinned civilian vehicles while the missiles and shells rained in like supersonic sleet and the belching fire burst billowing everywhere around. I tried, too, to imagine how many

people had died here, how many shredded, cindered bodies and bits of bodies had been bagged and removed and buried by the clean-up squads before we were allowed to see this icon of that long day's slaughter. (p. 291)

The imagination fails: we are in the presence of the sublime, but it is a sublime whose terror is far from aesthetic: 'The black, charred boot was a couple of metres away, half-buried in the sand. When I picked it up it was surprisingly heavy because it still had the foot inside it' (p. 292). The modernist and postmodernist footwear of Van Gogh and Warhol imply a rule-bound human life they have left behind for the unruled realm of art: Banks' boot contains the remnants of a human life whose loss is not redeemed by the fact that war is just another game that human beings play. Art, like terror, is not outside of the games we play but, like the foot in the apparently pictorial boot, inside, weighing it down, giving it gravity, refuting the self-contained game of art. In Banks' novels, Lyotard's translation of reality into game is reversed, and the games we play are for real – especially the games of (post-)postmodernist fiction.

FOR FURTHER READING

For an up-to-date list of the works of Iain (M.) Banks, see the British Council website:
<http://www.contemporarywriters.com/authors/>.

Craig, Cairns, Complicity: a Reader's Guide (New York: Continuum, 2002).
Malpas, Simon, Jean-François Lyotard (London: Routledge, 2003).
McCracken, Scott, Pulp: Reading Popular Fiction (Manchester: Manchester University Press, 1998).
Schoene, Berthold, Writing Men: Literary Masculinities from Frankenstein to the New Man (Edinburgh: Edinburgh University Press, 2000).
Smith, Anthony D., Nationalism and Modernism (London: Routledge, 1998).

NOTES

1 Jean-François Lyotard, The Postmodern Condition, trans. Geoff Bennington and Brian Massumi, in Theory and History of Literature, Vol. 10 (1979; rpt. Manchester: Manchester University Press, 1984), pp. 37–8.
2 Fredric Jameson, Postmodernism, or, the Cultural Logic of Late Capitalism (London: Verso, 1991), pp. 4–5.
3 Jerome McGann, lecture to the biannual Walter Scott conference, Eugene Oregon 2001; published as 'Walter Scott's Romantic Postmodernity', in The Borders of Romanticism, ed. Leith Davis, Ian Duncan and Janet Sorensen (Cambridge: Cambridge University Press, 2004), pp. 113–30.
4 Benedict Anderson, Imagined Communities: Reflections on the Origin and Spread of Nationalism (London: Verso, 1991), pp. 22ff.

5 See my *Out of History: Narrative Paradigms in Scottish and English Culture* (Edinburgh: Edinburgh University Press, 1996), for a detailed discussion of Scotland's dehistoricisation.

6 See Linda Hutcheon, *A Poetics of Postmodernism: History, Theory, Fiction* (London: Routledge, 1988); and Brian McHale, *Postmodernist Fiction* (London: Methuen, 1987).

7 See my 'Beyond Reason – Hume, Seth, Macmurray and Scotland's Postmodernity', in *Scotland in Theory*, ed. Eleanor Bell and Gavin Miller (Amsterdam: Rodopi, 2004), pp. 249–85.

8 Linda Hutcheon, *The Politics of Postmodernism* (London: Routledge, 1989), pp. 24–9.

9 Iain M. Banks, *Walking on Glass* (1985; rpt. London: Abacus, 1990). All quotations are from this edition; page numbers are given in the text.

10 Gray acknowledges the influence of Kurt Vonnegut on *Lanark* (Edinburgh: Canongate, 1981), by naming one of his characters after him (p. 473); Banks has acknowledged how much his own work was influenced by Gray, particularly in the fusion of realism and fantasy in *The Bridge*.

11 See Lyotard, *The Postmodern Condition*, p. 15: 'the system can and must encourage such movement [from one game to another] to the extent that it combats its own entropy'.

12 Iain Banks, *The Crow Road* (1992; rpt. London: Abacus, 1993). All quotations are from this edition; page numbers are given in the text.

13 Iain Banks, *Complicity* (1993; rpt. London: Abacus, 1994). All quotations are from this edition; page numbers are given in the text.

14 Iain Banks, *The Player of Games* (London: Orbit, 1988). All quotations are from this edition; page numbers are given in the text.

15 Iain Banks, *The Wasp Factory* (1984; rpt. London: Abacus, 1990). All quotations are from this edition; page numbers are given in the text.

16 'The Sign of History', in *A Lyotard Reader*, ed. Andrew Benjamin (Oxford: Basil Blackwell, 1989), pp. 393–411, p. 394.

17 Edmund Burke, 'A Philosophical Inquiry into the Origin of our Ideas of the Sublime and Beautiful', in *The Works of the Right Honourable Edmund Burke* (London: F. & C. Rivington, 1803), I, 133.

18 Jameson, *Postmodernism*, p. 7.

19 Ibid.

20 Ibid., p. 8.

Notes on Contributors

James Acheson is former Senior Lecturer in English at the University of Canterbury in Christchurch, New Zealand. He is author of *Samuel Beckett's Artistic Theory and Practice: Criticism, Drama, Early Fiction* (1997) and of *John Fowles* (1998); and is editor or co-editor of *Beckett's Later Fiction and Drama: Texts for Company* (1987); *The British and Irish Novel Since 1960* (1991); *British and Irish Drama Since 1960* (1993); and *Contemporary British Poetry: Essays in Theory and Criticism* (1996). A member of the editorial board of the *Journal of Beckett Studies*, he has contributed essays on Beckett and other contemporary authors to various edited collections and journals.

Daniel Bedggood lectures within the Continuing Education and English programmes at the University of Canterbury. He has recently completed his doctorate and is presently working on a book entitled *Moving Subjects: Identifying Displacements in Contemporary Postcolonial Writing*.

Cairns Craig is Head of the English Department and Director of the Centre for the History of Ideas in Scotland at the University of Edinburgh. His books include *Yeats, Eliot, Pound and the Politics of Poetry: Richest to the Richest* (1982); *Out of History: Narrative Paradigms in Scottish and English Culture* (1996); and *The Modern Scottish Novel: Narrative and the National Imagination* (1999). He was the General Editor of the four-volume *History of Scottish Literature*, and was also the General Editor of the Polygon Determinations series. He is currently a member of the editorial board of the Canongate Classics series.

David Leon Higdon is Paul Whitfield Horn Professor Emeritus at Texas Tech University, is author of *Time and English Fiction* (1977) and *Shadows of the Past in Contemporary British Fiction* (1984), and of the forthcoming *Mind the Gap: How Novels Talk to One Another*. Although his essays range from sound imagery in Geoffrey Chaucer to revenge conventions in Irvine Welsh, he has concentrated in recent years on such contemporary authors as Brian Aldiss, Julian Barnes, Margaret Drabble, John Fowles, Graham Greene, Graham Swift, Peter Ackroyd and D. M. Thomas.

Frederick M. Holmes is Professor and Chair of the English Department at Lakehead University, Thunder Bay, Canada. He is author of *The Historical Imagination: Postmodernism and the Treatment of the Past in Contemporary British Fiction* (1997), and has contributed essays on John Fowles, David Lodge, E. M. Forster, Angus Wilson, John Barth, A. S. Byatt, Graham Swift, Martin Amis, Hanif Kureishi, Salman Rushdie and Kingsley Amis, to many edited collections and journals.

Bruce King has been Professor of English at universities in the USA, New Zealand, Scotland, Canada, France, Israel and Nigeria. His recent publications include *Three Indian Poets: Ezekiel, Ramanujan and Moraes* (1991, 2nd edn 2005); *Internationalisation of English Literature, 1948–2000* (2004); *V. S. Naipaul* (1993, 2nd edn 2003); *Modern Indian Poetry in English* (1987, 2nd edn 2001); *Derek Walcott: a Caribbean Life* (2000); and *Derek Walcott and West Indian Drama* (1995). He has edited *New National and Post-Colonial Literatures: an Introduction* (1996), *West Indian Literature* (1979, 2nd edn 1995), and various other books.

Daniel Lea is Senior Lecturer in English at Oxford Brookes University. He is the author of *George Orwell: Animal Farm and Nineteen Eighty Four: a Reader's Guide to Essential Criticism* (2001); co-editor of *Posting the Male: Masculinities in Post-War and Contemporary British Literature* (2003); and General Editor of 'Contemporary British Novelists', a series of monographs published by Manchester University Press. He has contributed essays to a number of journals, and is currently writing two books: one on Graham Swift and the other on new British writing.

Hermione Lee is the Goldsmiths' Professor of English Literature and Fellow of New College, Oxford. Her books include *The Novels of Virginia Woolf* (1977); *Elizabeth Bowen* (1981, revised 1999); *Philip Roth* (1982); *Willa Cather: a Life Saved Up* (1989); *Virginia Woolf* (1996); and *Body Parts: Essays in Life-Writing* (2005). She has done numerous editions and anthologies of the work of such authors as Kipling, Trollope, Virginia Woolf, Stevie Smith, Elizabeth Bowen, Willa Cather and Eudora Welty. She was one of the co-editors of the Oxford Poets Anthologies from 1999 to 2002. She is well known for her reviews and work in the media, and from 1982 to 1986 she presented Channel Four Television's first books programme, 'Book Four'. She is currently working on a biography of Edith Wharton.

Dorothy McMillan is a Senior Lecturer in English Literature at the University of Glasgow. She has published variously in the field of Scottish and women's writing. With Douglas Gifford she edited *A History of Scottish Women's Writing*, and her anthology *The Scotswoman at Home and Abroad: Non-fiction Writing 1700–1900* (1999) covers a wide range of writers and genres. Other recent publications include *Queen of Science* (2001), an edition of *The Personal Recollections of Mary Somerville,* the nineteenth-century Scottish astronomer and mathematician, and an anthology, *Modern Scottish Women Poets* (2003).

Bart Moore-Gilbert is Professor of Postcolonial Studies and English at Goldsmiths College, University of London. He is author of *Kipling and Orientalism* (1986); *Postcolonial Theory: Contexts, Practices, Politics* (1997); and *Hanif Kureishi* (2001); editor of *Writing India: British Representations of India, 1757–1990* (1996); and co-editor of *Postcolonial Criticism: a Reader* (1998).

Laurence Nicoll teaches in the Department of English Literature and the Office of Lifelong Learning at the University of Edinburgh. He has published articles on James Kelman and also on the relationship between philosophy and the construction of identity. His doctoral thesis sought to examine the fictions of James Kelman within the context of literary and philosophical existentialism. Other research interests include Philip Roth and Samuel Beckett.

Glenda Norquay is Professor of Scottish Literary Studies at Liverpool John Moores University. Her publications include *Voices and Votes: a Literary Anthology of the Women's Suffrage Campaign* (1995); *R. L. Stevenson on Fiction* (1999); *Across the Margins: Identity and Cultural Change in the Atlantic Archipelago* (with Gerry Smyth) (2001); and *The Collected Writings of Lorna Moon* (2001). She has published a number of essays on contemporary Scottish women's writing and the Scottish novel, and is currently working on a study of R. L. Stevenson's reading practices.

Paulina Palmer is Senior Lecturer in English at the University of Warwick. She also teaches a course in Gender Studies at Birkbeck College, London University. She is author of *Contemporary Women's Fiction: Narrative Practice and Feminist Theory* (1989); *Contemporary Lesbian Writing: Dreams, Desire, Difference* (1993); and *Lesbian Gothic: Transgressive Fictions* (1999). Plans for the future include an essay on the city in lesbian fiction, and a study of lesbian narrative and the 'uncanny'. Email address: paulinapalmer@aol.com

David Punter is Professor of English and Research Director of the Faculty of Arts at the University of Bristol. His previous publications include *The Literature of Terror* (1980; revised two-volume edition 1996); *The Hidden Script: Writing and the Unconscious* (1985); *Introduction to Contemporary Cultural Studies* (ed., 1986); *The Romantic Unconscious* (1989); *Gothic Pathologies: The Text, the Body and the Law* (1998); *Spectral Readings:*

Towards a Gothic Geography (ed., with Glennis Byron, 1999); *Writing the Passions* (2000); and *Postcolonial Imaginings: Fictions of a New World Order* (2000), as well as numerous essays and articles on Romantic, Gothic and contemporary writing.

Alan Riach is Professor and Head of the Department of Scottish Literature at the University of Glasgow. He is author of *Hugh MacDiarmid's Epic Poetry* (1991), *The Poetry of Hugh MacDiarmid* (1999); and *Representing Scotland in Literature, Popular Culture and Iconography* (2004); and co-editor of MacDiarmid's *New Selected Letters* (2001) and *The Complete Poetry of Hugh MacDiarmid* (in 3 volumes, forthcoming). In addition, he is an established poet, with four volumes of poetry to his credit. His most recent volume of poems is entitled *Clearances* (2001).

Sarah C. E. Ross is Lecturer in English at Massey University, New Zealand. As an Honours student at the University of Canterbury, in Christchurch, New Zealand, she wrote a thesis on the novels of A. S. Byatt and John Fowles. In 2000, she completed her D.Phil. at St Hilda's College, Oxford, on religious verse by women in seventeenth-century English manuscript culture. She has published several articles on early modern women writers, and has worked on Nottingham Trent University's Perdita project and the University of Warwick's John Nichols project. She is currently preparing an edition of Katherine Austen's mid-seventeenth-century miscellany for Medieval and Renaissance Texts and Studies.

Sarah Sceats is Head of English Literature at Kingston University. She specialises in twentieth-century fiction and women's writing and much of her research focuses on appetites, desire and the body in a variety of late twentieth-century fiction and film. She is co-editor of *Image and Power: Women in Fiction in the Twentieth Century* (1996) and author of *Food, Consumption and the Body in Contemporary Women's Fiction* (2000). Currently she is writing a book on belonging in twentieth-century fiction.

Judith Seaboyer is Lecturer in English at the University of Queensland in Brisbane, Australia. She recently received her doctorate from the University of Toronto for a thesis on Jeanette Winterson and Ian McEwan, and has published parts of it in *Modern Fiction Studies* and *Contemporary Literature*. Currently she is rewriting her thesis for publication in book form.

Katherine Tarbox has taught modern and postmodern British literature for twenty-five years, most recently at the University of New Hampshire, which she left to devote herself to do full-time research and practise psychoanalysis. Author of *The Art of John Fowles* (1988), she has contributed articles on Fowles and other British novelists to many edited collections and journals.

Currently she is working on *The Neuromantic Novel: a Psychoanalytic Study of Postmodern British Fiction,* a book-length examination of psychological themes in the contemporary British novel. Included in the book will be interviews with ten leading British writers: Peter Ackroyd, Martin Amis, Peter Benson, Margaret Drabble, John Fowles, Penelope Lively, Iris Murdoch, Graham Swift, D. M. Thomas and Fay Weldon.

Chantal Zabus is Professor of Postcolonial and Women's Studies at the University of Paris 13. She is author of *The African Palimpsest* (1991; rpt. 2005) and *Tempests after Shakespeare* (2002), and is editor of *Le Secret: Motif et Moteur de la Littérature* (with Jacques Derrida, 1999), as well as of *Changements féminins en Afrique noire* (2000). She has published widely on postcolonialism, and her book *Between Rites and Rights: Excision in Women's Experiential Texts* is forthcoming with Stanford University Press.

Index